NOCTURNAL POETICS

Nocturnal Poetics

The Arabian Nights
in Comparative Context

Ferial J. Ghazoul

The American University in Cairo Press

Earlier versions of Chapters One through Eight first appeared as *The Arabian Nights: A Structural Analysis* (Cairo: UNESCO, 1980). Used by permission. An earlier version of Chapter Nine first appeared as "Poetic Logic in *The Panchatantra* and *The Arabian Nights*" in *Arab Studies Quarterly* 5: 1 (Winter 1983). Used by permission. An earlier version of Chapter Ten first appeared as "*The Arabian Nights* in Shakespearean Comedy: 'The Sleeper Awakened' and *The Taming of the Shrew*" in *Mundus Arabicus* 3 (1983). Used by permission.

Dar el Kutub No. 3189/95
ISBN 977 424 363 3

CONTENTS

ACKNOWLEDGMENTS

The Arabian Nights has captivated me ever since I can remember and has been a constant companion for me until today. This book has been shaped by intimate coexistence with the text as much as by studies, readings, and research undertaken over two decades during which *The Arabian Nights* was a focal point of reference and an aesthetic consolation. My professors at Columbia University, who supervised my studies and dissertation in the seventies, Michael Riffaterre, Edward W. Said, and Tzvetan Todorov—as well as Muhsin Mahdi of Harvard University, whose seminars on literature and philosophy I attended—have had a profound impact on me. I am also indebted to numerous colleagues at the American University in Cairo, where I have been teaching for the last seventeen years, as well as to friends in the Egyptian state universities with whom I have carried on a dialogue on literature. I would also like to acknowledge my students, who have— with their probing questions and indicative reactions—helped shape this study.

I have been writing this book for years, in an ongoing attempt to understand the internal structure of *The Arabian Nights,* its relationship to world literature, its significance, and its sphere of influence and correspondence. Part One of this book (the first eight chapters) is an update of my out-of-print book *The Arabian Nights: A Structural Analysis,* published in Cairo in 1980 by the National Commission of UNESCO as part of a series of awarded studies which present and illuminate Arab cultural values. This part of the book addresses the symbolic logic and inner meaning of *The Arabian Nights,* exploring the relationship between the frame story and the enframed stories and the patterns of generating stories. Having pinned down the articulations of the work, its sense and significance are then highlighted. Part Two (chapters nine through thirteen) compares *The Arabian Nights* to major literary works that relate genealogically to it, works that cover four continents—Asia, Africa, Europe, and the Americas. They span over two thousand years of world literature, from ancient India *(The Panchatantra)* and Renaissance comedy (Shakespeare's *The Taming of the Shrew)* to such postmodern New World writers as Jorge Luis Borges and John Barth, whose writings are touched by the magic of Shahrazad's narratives. Chapter Nine was published in *Arab Studies Quarterly* (1983), Chapter Ten in *Mundus Arabicus* (1983), and part of Chapter Eleven was delivered to the Eleventh Congress of the International Comparative Literature Asssociation (Paris, 1985). I have revised, updated, and linked the various chapters, and added a chapter on the newly translated novel of Nobel laureate Naguib Mahfouz, *Arabian Nights and Days* (1995), and a conclusion (Chapter Thirteen).

I am grateful to the staff of the American University in Cairo Press for the production of this book, particularly the close reading of Simon O'Rourke and the general supervision of Neil Hewison. The support of my family has been invaluable in completing this project.

PREFACE

This study is undertaken within the framework of comparative literature. Its objective is to uncover principles of construction of the literary work commonly known as *The Arabian Nights,* sometimes referred to as *The One Thousand and One Nights*—the literal translation of its Arabic title. Although it originated in the East and was given its finished and present form by the Arabs, the work has come to be part of the literary tradition of the West, if not the entire world.

The point of departure is the study of a concrete literary work whose foundations can illuminate the elusive phenomenon we call "literature." Traditional literary studies apply literary canons and criteria to a text and end invariably by passing a value judgment on the quality of the work. In this case, however, the quality of *The Arabian Nights* as a literary text is taken for granted—this study strives to extract the structural principles underlying the text. The work is analyzed and its articulations revealed in order to comprehend what Roman Jakobson has called *literaturnost,* that quality which makes a given discourse literary. After outlining the specificity of the work and revealing its inner system, I explore its relations and correspondences with literary works from other traditions.

In this context, therefore, the literary work is not treated as the final object of the inquiry, but as a particular case displaying certain processes that can be encountered in other texts and in other systems of communication. It is precisely those operations at work in a literary text that are the object of this study: operations that combine the artistic and linguistic faculties.

This approach is analytical and strives to provide a systematic presentation of a literary text based on investigation rather than speculative reasoning. My work aspires to be a step in the direction of methodological examination of the literary phenomenon. It tries to look into unfamiliar literary structures as part of the human literary production and not as deviations from given norms. Hence the importance of seeing *The Arabian Nights* as a viable literary form, within its proper cultural, traditional, and rhetorical background, before comparing it to primary literary texts from other cultures and traditions.

The focus on models in this study is a direct outcome of its analytical

intention. The meta-language—the terminology used to describe the text—
is drawn from grammar and rhetoric, on the grounds that literature is a
specific instance of language use and poetic production. I have deliberately avoided technical terminology associated with specific literary schools
and have tried to use the most accepted and accessible terms. My reason
for doing this is that I have undertaken this work in order to understand a
given text, not to support a polemical critical position. With the same attitude, I have restricted the use of diacritical marks in my transliteration of
Arabic and Persian words; Turkish words are given in their modern Turkish orthography. I transliterate according to the written form of the word,
independent of the pronunciation, using the English transliteration system
as adopted by the *International Journal of Middle East Studies.*

Chapter One ("Textual Variants and Critical Methodology") introduces
the text of *The Arabian Nights* as a phenomenon with its own peculiarity
and specificity, and then expounds the methodology underlying the study.

Chapter Two ("Narrative Dialectics") sums up the fundamental forces
and elements at work in *The Arabian Nights,* elaborating their intercon-
nections and the formation of a system. This chapter thus deals with the
organization of the text.

Chapter Three ("Discursive Significance") analyzes the narrative by
condensing it to its matrix or essential identity, and shows its diffusion in
the text through codes. This chapter describes the basic movement of the
text.

Chapters Four ("Mimesis and Meta-Mimesis"), Five ("Beastly Rhetoric"), Six ("The Spiral Metaphor"), and Seven ("The Runaway Metonym")
show the order of cohesion in the text and the rules of structuring. I explore the forms and functions of both symmetry and its violation in terms
of framed story and enframed stories. Each chapter is devoted to a configuration of stories which constitute a typological category. These four
chapters show in detail the dynamics of the "unending narrative," which is
the most salient feature of *The Arabian Nights.* Chapter Eight ("Perpetual
Narrative") concludes Part One. Here, the study of the intrinsic structure
is brought into final focus and its intelligibility is spelled out in terms of
alternatives to Aristotelian poetics.

In Part Two, chapters Nine through Twelve ("Poetic Logic in *The
Panchatantra* and *The Arabian Nights,*" "*The Arabian Nights* in
Shakespearean Comedy," "Dialectics of the Self and the Other: Arabian
Tales in American Literatures" and "Mahfouz's *Arabian Nights and Days:*
A Political Allegory") compare the poetics of *The Arabian Nights* with
earlier classics of India and later classics of the European Renaissance,
where influences have been speculated or conjectured, as well as with

narratives from the New World and from the modern Arab World where kinship with *The Arabian Nights* is in evidence. These chapters deal with contrasts as much as with affinities, with displacements as much as with correspondences. Chapter Thirteen ("Nomadic Text") concludes the book and outlines the aesthetic lessons of its migration and literary accultura- tion.

It should be perhaps pointed out that Part One is divided into two dis- tinct and complementary sections. Chapters One and Two, which consti- tute the first section, are devoted to the main narrative course in *The Ara- bian Nights* and deal essentially with the frame story. Following an order of increasing complexity, the first chapter starts with *The Arabian Nights* as a given artistic presence, the second chapter delineates the combination of its literary components, and the third chapter explores its semantic sig- nificance. Each step leads to the next and is indispensable for the develop- ment of the argument.

The second section of Part One (Chapters Four through Seven) shows how the narrative text hangs together as a whole. It deals with the enframed stories as a problem in textual homogeneity. Here, one chapter in the analy- sis does not lead to the next but simply confirms, and intersects with, the findings of the other three chapters, namely, the orders of correspondence within the text. The four chapters in this section are experiments with var- ied types of stories contained in the corpus of *The Arabian Nights,* to un- cover the relationships that govern their inclusion in the text. The arrange- ment of this section is therefore not progressive as in the first section, but repetitive. A repetition of an experiment is the only insurance one can have against the coincidental.

Part Two of the book moves out of the immediate cultural context of *The Arabian Nights* to relate the work to what has been thought of as its roots, *The Panchatantra* with its emboxed narratives and its frame story narrated to instruct the king's sons in social and political affairs. Then the study tackles Shakespeare's *The Taming of the Shrew,* which exhibits an intrigue used in one of the stories of *The Arabian Nights,* although direct borrowing cannot be documented. Then I move to the works of writers who have unquestionably adopted stories from *The Arabian Nights* for their modern and postmodern audience—Jorge Luis Borges, John Barth, and Naguib Mahfouz—and contrast their approaches to those of the mother text. The final chapter ("Nomadic Text") defines the aspects of *The Ara- bian Nights* that render it a text for all seasons and all places.

Mingling tears and laughter in the blaze of a thousand nights
with their dark corridors!

—Assia Djebar, *A Sister to Scheherazade*

The greatness of the moment of telling stayed unresolved
Until its wealth of incident, pain mixed with pleasure,
Faded in the precise moment of bursting
Into bloom, its growth a static lament.

—John Ashbery, "Scheherazade"

1
TEXTUAL VARIANTS AND CRITICAL METHODOLOGY

Text(s)

Free Text

Choosing any text for critical study invites the question of why the particular given work has been selected. With *The Arabian Nights,* this question becomes more complex, since the *why* is accompanied by the *which* as *The Arabian Nights* itself is a multiplicity of texts. Thus, an important first question is: Which *Arabian Nights,* and what version of it?

The textual history of *The Arabian Nights* is intricate and the major problems of origin and genesis remain unresolved. Our knowledge of *The Arabian Nights* stems from its numerous extant variants, and from the cursory references of Arab historians to the text.

The earliest extant fragment of *The Arabian Nights* dates from the ninth century. But to refer to it as a fragment of *The Arabian Nights* is somewhat misleading, for it is nothing more than the title page and a badly preserved first page. The manuscript is probably of Syrian origin. Its exact title is *Kitab hadith alf layla* ("Book of the Discourse of the Thousand Nights") and on the first page figures a Dinazad who asks Shirazad to relate her promised tales.[1] This much hardly allows us to conclude that this ninth-century text is identical to the version we know.

The earliest references to *The Arabian Nights* are to be found in the works of tenth-century historians. The following passage from Mas'udi in his *Golden Meadows* deals briefly with *The Arabian Nights:*

> The case with them (viz., some legendary stories) is similar to
> that of the books that have come to us from the Persian, Indian

(one MS has here *Pahlawi)* and the Greek and have been translated for us, and that originated in the way that we have described, such as, for example the book *Hazar Afsana,* which in Arabic means 'thousand tales,' for 'tale' is in Persian *afsana.* The people call this book 'Thousand Nights' (two MSS have here 'Thousand Nights and One Night'). This is the story of the king and the vizier and his daughter and her servant girl; these two are called Shirazad and Dinazad (in other MSS: 'and her nurse'; in again other MSS: 'and his two daughters').[2]

In *al-Fihrist,* written in 987 A.D., Ibn al-Nadim mentions *Hazar Afsan* and sums up the plot of the frame story.[3] However, the Persian origin of *The Arabian Nights* has been disputed by well-known Orientalists. Antoine Silvestre de Sacy (1758–1838) wrote extensively on the subject, putting forward the thesis that *The Arabian Nights* was written at a later period and without the use of Persian and Indian sources. He casts doubt on the authenticity of Mas'udi's well-known passage.[4] There are other sporadic references to *The Arabian Nights,* notably by the Egyptian historian al-Maqrizi (1346–1442), but they shed little light on the origin or the evolution of the text.

The oldest surviving version of *The Arabian Nights* is the four-volume manuscript sent to the first translator of *The Arabian Nights,* Antoine Galland (1646–1715). His translation in the early eighteenth century was only partly dependent on this manuscript. He used other unidentified manuscripts as well as oral transmission by a man from Aleppo. The last volume of Galland's manuscript is lost but the first three are in the Bibliothèque Nationale in Paris. This manuscript probably dates from the fourteenth century.

Manuscripts of *The Arabian Nights* are in libraries of major European capitals and in Cairo; their texts vary and overlap. However, there is no "complete" edition of a variant. D. B. MacDonald worked on editing the manuscript of Galland but did not finish this laborious project. Muhsin Mahdi has edited and introduced the earliest Arabic variant, based on extant manuscripts, but it stops at the 152nd night.[5]

Comparative study of these different versions and the use of internal evidence demonstrated beyond any doubt that there is no single extant text from which other variants issued—a multiplicity of texts constitute the points of departure.[6] The process of creation in *The Arabian Nights,* as in oral literature, is based on crystallization. There is neither an original text nor an individual author. *The Arabian Nights* is an artistic production of the collective mind; its specificity lies in its very emergence as a text. The typical text is often conceived as a limited and defined object—as a singular event. In contrast, *The Arabian Nights* is plural and mercurial, and herein lies its challenge. How to accommodate and grasp the complexities of this ambiguous literary phenomenon without reducing it and judging it by standards of written literature is the task I have undertaken in this study. However, the dividing line should not be between written or oral literature, for there is oral literature which has maintained the textual wording without the slightest modification, in most such cases because of its association with divine revelation or revered wisdom. Sacred texts, even when oral, tend to survive intact. So do proverbs and poems, which are generally well preserved. The real dichotomy should be between the fixed and the free text. In the fixed text the words are part of the narrative and the oral recitation resembles the written text in its adherence to wording. In free texts the lexical element varies but structural logic and thematic content remain the same. The comparison of free texts is based on the plot, characters, and setting.[7]

The various available versions of *The Arabian Nights* cannot be thought of in any hierarchical terms. There is no parent textual variant that proliferated into others, at least not that we can identify and reconstruct with any assurance. *The Arabian Nights* probably grew into what we know it to be over centuries of deposited layers of narratives. Comparison of various manuscripts reveals a similar framework story, but there are considerable variations in the nature, number, and order of enframed stories. The published "complete" editions of *The Arabian Nights* are either modifications of one manuscript, as in the first Cairo edition, commonly known as the Bulaq edition (1835), or rearrangement of a number of manuscripts, as in the second Calcutta edition (1839–1842). The translations follow the same course—they either stick faithfully to one Arabic text, as in Francesco Gabrieli's Italian translation, or translate a combination of *Arabian Nights* texts, as Edward Lane did.[8]

A diagram of the historical evolution of a "complete" text of *The Arabian Nights* from manuscript to printed form can be represented as follows:

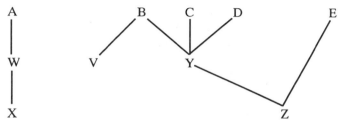

A, B, C, D, E = *identified or unidentified manuscripts*
W, X, V, Y, Z = *published editions*

It is impossible to reconstruct an accurate chart of relationships for all published editions, since some of the manuscripts which were the basis for these editions are lost.[9] However, it is important to understand that the variation in texts is not an accident due to inadequate transmission, but is rather a fundamental aspect of the narrative performance of *The Arabian Nights* and an intimate characteristic of the received texts.

Flexible Narrative

The phenomenon of a free text is not uncommon in oral tradition, but *The Arabian Nights* is not simply a manipulable substance that can be reworked and rephrased to adjust to new social and economic conditions, as can myths of preliterate peoples.[10] It seems that it was constructed in such a way as to allow and even invite radical changes in its content, yet at the same time preserve its own internal logic. *The Arabian Nights* is constructed like a game of skill (as opposed to a game of chance) such as chess. There are indefinite ways of playing the game, but it remains—despite its many variations—a chess game. Similarly, the text preserves its identity although it is performed, as it were, in more than one way.

The flexibility of the narrative is guaranteed by an enclosing structure which can contain a multiplicity of genres, conflicting styles, and divergent themes without destroying in the least the coherence of the text. We can attest to this empirically: the two French translations of Galland and Mardrus play havoc with the "original" Arabic text, and yet *The Arabian Nights* is not compromised by such "unfaithfulness." Edward Lane, the English translator, used the cut-and-paste technique rather freely, deciding to cut out whole sections and rearrange others. Adding, dropping, and reshuffling stories seems to be a temptation to any transmitter of *The Arabian Nights*. A number of writers indulged in writing sequels to *The Arabian Nights,* notably Edgar Allan Poe, who wrote a sardonic tale of the one thousand and second night. If the text has been handled frequently in this promiscuous fashion, it is indicative that the text allows itself to be "mishandled." One cannot blame a Lane or a Galland for taking liberties with the text; after all, texts get the treatment they deserve. It is true that Littmann's German translation, Haddawy's English translation, and Khawam's French translation have been praised for their consistency and accuracy, and have been considered "reliable" in relation to their Arabic source. But the fact remains that there are many editors and translators who have been tempted to revise the text. This cannot be easily dismissed—something in the text makes it subject to manipulation. It is constructed so

as to accommodate and incorporate different material, as in an anthology ˊ
or a compendium.

Though the versions and adaptations of *The Arabian Nights* vary considerably, certain structural characteristics remain constant, namely a fairly
stable enclosing story and a relatively unstable enclosed content. To establish a supreme invariant would require a delineation of the regularly oc-
curring elements. The elements that are repeated in all variants are not
necessarily worded or expressed in the same manner—they are simply the
elements that share the same function in the narrative progression. For
example, in the framework story there is a famous scene where the king's
wife is found copulating with a black slave. This incident has been rendered in variety of ways by different publishers and translators. A Jesuit
priest retold it in the following way:

> There were some windows facing his brother's palace, and while
> he was looking out, the palace door opened and out came twenty
> slave-girls and twenty black male slaves. His sister-in-law, who
> was exceptionally beautiful and lovely, was walking along with
> them until they came to a fountain and all sat at its side. Then
> they began to drink, play, sing, and recite poetry until close of
> the day.[11]

On the other hand, the well-known French translation made by Antoine
Galland lingers over this incident:

> Une porte secrète du palais du sultan s'ouvrit tout à coup, et il
> en sortit vingt femmes, au milieu desquelles marchait la sultane,
> d'un air qui la faisait aisément distinguer. Cette princesse,
> croyant que le roi de la Grand-Tartarie était aussi à la chasse,
> s'avança avec fermeté jusque sous les fenêtres de l'appartement
> de ce prince, qui, voulant par curiosité les observer, se plaçe de
> manière qu'il pouvait tout voir sans être vu. Il remarqua que les
> personnes qui accompagnaient la sultane, pour bannir toute
> contrainte, se découvrirent le visage, qu'elles avaient eu couvert
> jusqu'alors, et quittèrent de longs habits qu'elles portaient par-
> dessus d'autres plus courts. Mais il fut dans un extrême
> étonnement de voir que dans cette compagnie qui lui avait
> semblé toute composée de femmes, il y avait dix noirs, qui prirent
> chacun leur maîtresse. La sultane, de son côté, ne demeura pas
> longtemps sans amant; elle frappa des mains en criant: Masoud!
> Masoud! et aussitôt un autre noir descendit du haut d'un arbre,
> et courut à elle avec beaucoup d'empressement.
> Les plaisirs de cette troupe amoureuse durèrent jusqu'à
> minuit. Ils se baignèrent tous ensemble dans une grande pièce
> d'eau, qui faisait un des plus beaux ornements du jardin; après
> quoi, ayant repris leurs habits, ils rentrèrent par la porte secrète

dans le palais du sultan, et Masoud, qui était venu de dehors par dessus la muraille du jardin, s'en retourna par le même endroit.[12]

A Western children's version of the tale relates the incident in a radically different way:

He had a wife whom he loved dearly and many slaves to carry out his smallest wish. He should have been one of the happiest men in the world.

And so he was, until one day he found his wife plotting against him. He had her put to death at once, but still his rage was not satisfied.[13]

The most popular and one of the oldest printed Arabic editions relates the incident with a certain immediacy:

Now there were some windows in the king's palace commanding a view of his garden; and while his brother was looking out from one of these, a door of the palace was opened, and there came forth from it twenty females and twenty male black slaves, and the king's wife, who was distinguished by extraordinary beauty and elegance, accompanied them to a fountain, where they all disrobed themselves and sat down together. The king's wife then called out, O Mes'ood! and immediately a black slave came to her, and embraced her; she doing the like [and he copulated with her]. So also did the other slaves and the women; and all of them continued reveling [kissing, hugging, fucking, and so on] until the close of the day.[14]

In the most recent English translation of the earliest extant version, this episode is rendered like this:

The private gate of his brother's palace opened, and there emerged, strutting like a dark-eyed deer, the lady, his brother's wife, with twenty slave-girls, ten white and ten black. While Shahzaman looked at them, without being seen, they continued to walk until they stopped below his window, without looking in his direction, thinking that he had gone to the hunt with his brother. Then they sat down, took off their clothes, and suddenly there were ten slave-girls and ten black slaves dressed in the same clothes as the girls. Then the ten black slaves mounted the ten girls, while the lady called, "Mas'ud, Mas'ud!" and a black slave jumped from the tree to the ground, rushed to her, and, raising her legs, went between her thighs and made love to her. Mus'ud topped the lady, while the ten slaves topped the ten girls, and they carried on till noon.[15]

These five versions of this crucial incident—despite their outward differences and thematic variations—share a common trait and play the same role in the unfolding of the narrative. Whether an expurgated Jesuit variant or an obscene Cairene version, the function of the incident in the macrocontext of the plot remains constant. It is the committing of a forbidden act. The offense is no ordinary one, for the king's wife not only transgressed marital boundaries but class and ethnic ones as well. The offense approximates a violation of taboo. The nature of the offense is prescribed by the text. In all the versions cited, the act is done secretly; in the children's adaptation, the very term "plotting" implies conspiring and planning secretly. In all versions, the shock and indignation are elicited unsparingly.

The text of *The Arabian Nights* qualifies as an indeterminate text because of its plurality and flexibility. It is a text in a state of flux. However, within this insecure textual phenomenon, we can still detect patterns of repetition and modes of semantic production, which make the text more coherent and intelligible. I intend, first, to describe the overall frame, second, to relate the frame to the enframed,[16] and third, to uncover transcultural links between *The Arabian Nights* and other literary texts which parallel it and are related to it. It is unnecessary and cumbersome to compare every enframed story to the framing one. It suffices to compare configurations of diverse narrative genres of the enframed with the frame, and likewise compare samples of works related to *The Arabian Nights*.

I have decided to analyze four sample sets of stories: "Sirat 'Umar ibn al-Nu'man," the animal fables, Sindbad's voyages, and the so-called demon tales. The last two sets are considered most typical of *The Arabian Nights* and are often reproduced. "Sirat 'Umar" is considered of an alien spirit and to be a later addition. The fables are frequently left out of the collection on the grounds that they are "inferior" and "unsuitable." By analyzing the most typical and the least typical of the tales of *The Arabian Nights* and establishing their relationship to the framework story, I hope to meet the objections of selectivity among the genres.

When moving from the work itself to other works of world literature, I have chosen texts from the East and the West, from the Old World and the New World, from the South and the North, from works where the traces of *The Arabian Nights* are established and documented, and from others where they are presumed and arrived at through circumstantial evidence. I compare selections from works spanning over twenty centuries to *The Arabian Nights* in order to extract the poetic essence and power of this nocturnal discourse, with its capacity for diffusion in the world at large, penetrating different cultures and traditions.

Vulgate Classic

Though this study is based essentially on the theoretical invariant—the common denominator of the versions of *The Arabian Nights*—it seems necessary to choose one variant as the text of reference. It would not be practical to refer to several variants at every step of the analysis. When divergence or convergence of variants seems significant, I take note of it. Furthermore, one must refer to a single text when appraising its stylistic effect. Though all the variants can be thought of as expressions of the mother text, every variant is a discrete text and is experienced as such—to explore this uniqueness, one inevitably enters the domain of stylistics.[17] The stylistic differences can at times profoundly affect the fundamental structure of the work and have to be considered carefully, especially when irony is intended.

The text of reference is, therefore, simply a privileged text. I have chosen the first Cairo–Bulaq edition[18] for several reasons. First, I felt that this study should be based on an Arabic version. There are some Western scholars who have tried to argue that *The Arabian Nights* improves through translation. But such arguments have little credibility when they are advanced by people who claim no knowledge of Arabic. It is presumptuous of someone like Gerhardt, ignorant of Arabic, to suggest that it is "the non-Arabist who, with the aid of a good translation, can most fully enjoy the stories of the *Thousand and One Nights*."[19] It seems unnecessary here to defend the choice of using a work in its original language. Working from an Arabic version means using either a manuscript or a printed edition. I opted for a published version since it has the advantage of accessibility; a manuscript is available only to a minority of scholars. The principal Arabic editions are the following:

—Calcutta I (Shirwanee edition in twelve volumes), 1814–18;
—Cairo I (Bulaq edition in two volumes), 1835;
—Calcutta II (Macnaghten's edition in four volumes), 1839–42;
—Breslau (Habicht's edition in eight volumes, plus Fleischer's edition in four volumes), 1825–38, 1842–43;
—Leiden (Mahdi's edition in one volume), 1984;
—numerous other editions published in Cairo and Beirut, based on modifications of Cairo I.

Calcutta I is incomplete and covers only two hundred nights. The Leiden edition, likewise, is incomplete and covers only one hundred and fifty-two nights. Cairo I has the advantage of being the only edition based on a single manuscript, while Calcutta II and Breslau combine a number of manuscripts. Cairo I has, moreover, the distinction of being the oldest "complete" printed text. It is also probably the least modified text, published with all the "defects" and crudities of the original manscript. But the decisive factor favoring Cairo I is that it is the best known text of *The Arabian Nights* among Arab readers. A number of translations were based on Cairo I, including those of Lane, Mardrus, and Gabrieli. When quoting the text of *The Arabian Nights,* I have chosen the most adequate translation from Lane or Burton.[20]

The popularity of this classic is something of an enigma. *The Arabian Nights* has had and continues to have a strange fascination for peoples in different lands and times. It was kept alive in the Arab world for hundreds of years by oral transmission and copying. It has circulated widely, crossing cultural frontiers effortlessly. The central question that emerges is the nature of this classic which makes an entire people preserve it so fondly, and other peoples welcome it with enthusiasm. There must be in this work some textual specificity—a textual secret that fulfills a basic function and which can be elucidated. The first part of this book is an endeavor to define the textuality of *The Arabian Nights.*[21]

The secret of artistic attraction, or what turns a given discourse into a text, has never ceased to interest speculative thinkers. Even an action-oriented radical like Marx marveled at the durability of literature:

> The difficulty we are confronted with is not, however, that of understanding how Greek arts and epic poetry are associated with certain forms of social development. The difficulty is that they still give us aesthetic pleasure.[22]

This study moves from this imposing speculative question to a concrete study of the text at hand, trying all along to provide documented judgments based on observations of operations at work in *The Arabian Nights,* the operations that make of this popular collection of tales a classic.

Methodology

A text without an author, issuing from the popular imagination, and which has taken its present shape through crystallization, cannot be explained in terms of the author's personality or historical conditions. No writer can take the credit or the blame for *The Arabian Nights,* nor can we comfortably place the text in a definite historical epoch. The method I use in this book is concerned with the internal organization of the text and treats the work as an autonomous entity. The text in many ways designates its own critical methodology.

The process of critical appraisal I use includes decomposing the work into smaller units, comparing and contrasting those units, and then postulating a system in which those units function. Ultimately, the purpose of this is to construct a model with which we can comprehend the complexity of the narrative and which will contribute to our understanding of an aspect of literary activity in general. The conceptual model, or rather the networks and operations of the proposed textual system, are necessarily not final. They constitute a provisional definition of the complex phenomenon we call "the text." The result of any systematic research is a step in the dialectical progression. It is a projection of the literary text confined within the limits of the state of present knowledge or, as Foucault would say, to the *épistémè*.

The analysis of the text is a process of its decomposition into its significant units. The question of significance invites highly subjective choices and is the most controversial aspect of the research. My own analysis is based on narrative components such as characters and recurrent actions. By character I mean the fictional representation of a person or an agent, and by action, the fictional representation of an event. The crucial fact remains that when we end with units such as X and Y, what is relevant is not what X is or what Y is, but what X is to Y. That is, what is essential is the difference between X and Y. Furthermore, what is the relationship of X to Y—how do X and Y combine to generate the text? This is the methodology I propose to follow. The approach is essentially differential and integral. It aims at showing the source of difference that creates the proliferation. Some will inevitably find in such an approach something of de Saussure and Chomsky, but what they see is a function of where they stand. Someone standing in the East will see the imprints of Sibawayhi and Ibn Khaldun.

There are two main objections to the methodology I have outlined above. One accuses it of irrelevance and the other of simplification. The objection of irrelevance is based on the assumption that if the text were treated as a system of self-contained symbols, divorced from its reference, then analyzing it would be little more than a sterile game. However, the game is not sterile at all since it shows the mechanisms and the operations that trigger psychological reactions, which are the main motivation in reading fiction in the first place. Furthermore, to reveal the system underlying a given text is the first step in comparing it with systems underlying other communicative languages, such as the ritualistic or the economic. Even if such inquiries seem formal and not very practical, they remain very important as they could be applied and are potentially useful. In that sense, they are not very different from mathematical theorems, which constitute the most spectacular examples of irrelevances to everyday life until we begin to use them in scientific projects. The usefulness of formal studies depends on their application. If their conclusions are applied, they are pertinent; if not, they are irrelevant.

The second objection to this methodology centers on simplification. This is to some extent valid, but no analytic endeavor is possible without simplification and reduction, which are elemental processes in reasoning. Those who do not simplify cannot comprehend an overall structure. Furthermore, the simplification occurs only on the more accessible level of the text and such analytical simplification can reveal, paradoxically, a more subtle aspect of the text. Studying a text or any other phenomenon is essentially a process of condensation. What the text loses in volume it will gain in intelligibility. One of the best-known examples of fruitful simplification was undertaken by Claude Lévi-Strauss. Through a rigorous and dazzling set of condensations, he brought together the story of Tristan and Iseult and an American Indian myth of a brother and a sister. In this myth, the brother and sister were stuck together at birth and at the shooting of an arrow were split apart, right after which they became incestuous lovers. Lévi-Strauss shows how one story is the mirror image of the other and how both are opposite faces of the theme of unity through death for incestuous lovers. He shows, furthermore, how the European myth explains the origin of a constellation and the American myth the origin of sun-spots; hence, the inversion is completely consistent. His simplification touches the different works at their core through analogy, and relates human mental structures across time and space.[23]

The method deals with the fundamental aspects of the narrative, its synchronic organization—the set of coordinates that enter into its composition—and its diachronic movement—the transformations that occur as the narrative unfolds. One objective of this study is to show the coherence of *The Arabian Nights* not in terms of ready-made rules but by uncovering orders of unity and coherency. Clearly, the text of *The Arabian Nights*— with its ellipses, repetitions, and displacements—can hardly be explained through an organic or geometrical model. What is important in *The Arabian Nights* is neither the growth of a novel nor the precision of a poem, but the articulation of a corpus. The most crucial points in the narrative are those of connectivity. It is a series of relationships, a series of connections and disconnections, continuities and discontinuities. In many ways, the model that will account for this superb complexity should be topological. Topology is not only an abstruse branch of higher mathematics, it is the elemental way in which we grasped relationships as children before we developed a metric sense.[24]

In conventional poetry, what counts is not only connectivity but also precision and metrics. In a poem, it would be devastating to change a single word, even an inflection. This is not so in a narrative where the story can be stretched and compressed without compromising its identity; the resilience of the narrative makes its intricate atomization superfluous. What is needed is an anatomization of narrative. The geometry of narrative, if it exists at all, is a rubber geometry. If one accepts that connectivity is the main criterion, then shuffling the disconnected does not change the nature of the network.

Reading is ultimately a process of discerning differences, of separating details from outlines. To recite a text correctly is to emphasize its fundamental stresses and tensions: it is to read its "motivation." To distinguish between the motivated and the unmotivated, the ancient Egyptians developed diacritical signs by which they distinguished between hieroglyphs that could be read either as ideograms or phonograms or both. Structural reading is concerned with meaning, but at no point will it prescribe it. It underlines the basis of meaning, the very structures that carry the burden of meaning. Likewise, the task of the literary student as I see it is to provide the diacritics, to focus the text and put it in proper perspective. With some texts, one needs a lens; but with others, one needs a grid.

Transvaluation

As long as the genesis of *The Arabian Nights* remains obscure, even the most sophisticated of historical approaches is doomed for the simple reason that this text cannot be pinned down to a historical era. The only historically valid statement we can make about *The Arabian Nights* is that it was preserved and finished by the Arabs in the Middle Ages and was translated and highlighted by the Europeans from the eighteenth century onward. It should be obvious that the work must have appealed to the artistic sensibilities of medieval Arabs and modern Europeans to have gained such wide circulation. However, arguments of this kind have never deflected Orientalists from their obsessions with origins. In fact, the bulk of traditional writing on *The Arabian Nights* is primarily devoted to pointing out the country from which a certain story was exported, and if it is suspected of being Arab, then in what period it was composed. Such studies of origin are exercises in guesswork and are hardly convincing or relevant.

Antiquated approaches and arbitrary generalization must be rejected before undertaking any meaningful criticism. *TheArabian Nights* has long been held to exhibit unruly imagination and crude style; very few studies have bothered with the question of the work's coherence and even fewer with its stylistics.[25] Studies that did not try to detect the origins of individual stories tended to see *The Arabian Nights* as a kind of sociological document composed to provide posterity with ethnographic details about life in medieval Baghdad or Cairo. Such studies miss completely the transformation that occurs when "reality" is encoded in a text. What is a product *(ergon)* in reality becomes productivity *(energeia)* in the text—to borrow the terms of von Humboldt—just as in nature matter is transformed into energy. Physicists equate these two but know enough not to confuse them. Lévi-Strauss demonstrated the delicate transformations of everyday reality into textual reality, through which the events were saved from oblivion by turning them into a structure.[26] Modern Arabic and English novels illustrate the point: anyone familiar with Egypt senses instinctively in the novels of Naguib Mahfouz how the chaos of modern Egyptian life has been transformed into a magisterial structure. This structure can be appreciated even by those who know next to nothing about Egypt. By studying the correspondence and works of Joseph Conrad, Edward Said has shown how the personal experience of a man is transformed into an artistic text. The wreck of a life becomes the material for an orderly composition.[27]

Riffaterre has outspokenly and eloquently insisted on the self-sufficiency of the text. In his critical works, Riffaterre uses stylistic analyses of individual poems to show that even the most realistic of works is grasped not in reference to non-textual reality, but in terms of its internal structure.[28] The structure, then, is an intrinsic aspect of the text. A text without a structure is not a text but an event. The structure may create ambiguity and duplicity, as Derrida has eloquently shown, but even indeterminancy needs a structure to impose semantic multiplicity rather than the univocal.

Studies of Arabic literature that ignore the structural aspect of the text end up being bothered by formal repetitions which invariably are considered aesthetic defects, and the work in question is consequently declared inferior. Such assertions not only go unchecked; they are also often used as material for generalizations about "the Arab mind" and its peculiarities. The eminent scholar Gustave von Grünebaum is a master of such inference. In an article entitled "Idéologie musulmane et esthétique arabe," he argues that formalism is "la tragédie de la littérature arabe."[29] He has also written on the Greek elements in *The Arabian Nights* under the patronizing title of "Creative Borrowing." The argument implies that the Arabs are borrowers rather than creators, imitators rather than producers.[30] This is not to deny that *The Arabian Nights* has borrowed from Greek culture, but it is myopic to look upon it as one-way borrowing. The Greeks borrowed wholesale from the ancient Near East—from the Arabian phoenix *('anqa)* to the Babylonian mystique of numbers.[31] Von Grünebaum, working on the voyages of Sindbad and anxious to show the impact of the *Odyssey,* dismisses all difference between Sindbad's third voyage and Odysseus's adventure with Polyphemous as omissions.[32] He is clearly unaware of, or refuses to recognize, a work in ancient Egyptian literature, "The Shipwrecked Mariner,"[33] which has more morphological affinities with Sindbad's story than does the *Odyssey.* If one must trace borrowings, one should perhaps turn to the pharaonic classic.

The attitudes and assumptions of von Grünebaum are by no means exceptional in the study of Arabic literature. The Orientalists have, for example, convinced themselves that, first of all, there are no epics in Arabic literature, and second, this absence constitutes a defect in the heritage of the Arabs. Here is a lengthy quotation from the distinguished Arabist Charles Pellat that was deemed worthy of use in an encyclopedic work on Islam:

> The romance of Battal, the *Sirat al-Amira Dhat al-Himma,* the saga of the Banu Hilal, the romance of Sayf b. Dhi Yazan, and *Sirat 'Antar,* in particular offer features which bring them close to the great epics of universal literature, and one cannot fail to be struck by the evident resemblances between the *Sirat 'Antar* considered however, as a romance of chivalry, and the *Chanson de Roland;* but to be counted true epics, these narratives are in general lacking in the literary elaboration which is the mark of the masterpieces of epic literature. Although the *Sirat 'Antar* also contains, to a somewhat limited extent, another element of the epic, namely a feeling of the greatness of the fatherland represented by a hero who posesses all the virtues, in these narratives we are not conscious of the inspiration which animates the *Shahnama* . . .
>
> Rather than attempt to find an explanation for the Arabs' continued ignorance of a noble literary form which has contributed to the universal prestige of the great literatures of Antiquity and the Middle Ages, it is fitting simply to reflect that, while possessing all the necessary documentary, literary and technical elements for the creation of the epic, they did not achieve the final stage of the process.[34]

Charles Pellat's reasoning can be paraphrased as follows: although the Arabic language is technically rich, the Arabs, lacking inspiration, produced only *sira*s which are not epics, but an inferior genre. This is like saying that a penguin, though having wings, cannot fly and therefore is not a bird but a member of an inferior species.

Classification requires more than surface comparisons and needs a more tangible criterion than inspiration. It requires an eye for anatomical affinities. Pellat's argument is in essence not very different from that of the ninth-century Arab literary critic al-Jahiz who assumed the absence of genuine poetry in Greek, since their poems were no match for the Arabic ode *(qasida)* in its strict versification and monorhyme.[35] Inasmuch as the approach is comparative, the provinciality of both al-Jahiz and Pellat has to be rejected equally; a classificatory system that allows a measure of depth analysis and abstraction must be adopted instead.

Another ill-founded generalization concerns the poverty and crudeness of the style of *The Arabian Nights,* which traditional criticism has made use of in condemning the text. The poverty of the style is apprehended through direct comparison to the classical style. The crudeness is related to the open references to body operations and organs, which are prudishly alluded to or elegantly mentioned in the High Tradition. The supposed poverty of the style is due to nothing more than ignorance and unawareness of the multitude of figures and tropes that permeate the text, which this study will attempt to bring to the surface. As for the "obscenities" of *The Arabian Nights,* they are undeniably and obviously there, even on the most cursory reading, yet the work is not unique in this. The double standards in such value judgments are clear when we consider the fact that neither Catullus nor Chaucer are rebuked for their obscenities. And are euphemisms such as Diderot's *"bijoux indiscrets"* or Sterne's "winding clocks" more delicate? In any case, what constitutes obscenity is a very personal thing: for some it is sex, for others it is violence. Furthermore, we should allow for some metaphoric reading. After all, divine longings have been expressed in the most carnal of images. Finally, the parade of amorous vocabulary may be simply a distraction from the main thrust of the work. Only through close reading of the text can we distinguish the strategy from the maneuvers. It is important to establish what and how much is being said to test the reader. The literary text, after all, does not function like a manifesto proclaiming its point directly and forcefully, but works instead through indirection and obliqueness.

In conclusion, *The Arabian Nights* as a literary text offers some particular features that are different from the typical narrative written by an individual author, which tends to be stable, fixed, and textually secure. *The Arabian Nights* is also different from the typical folktale, which varies stylistically but retains thematic identity.

Criticism, in dealing with *The Arabian Nights,* has devalued the work partly because of ethnocentric biases and partly because traditional criticism has been unable to comprehend *The Arabian Nights* as a text.[36] The failure of Orientalists and their disciples in grasping the textual nature of *The Arabian Nights* has led them to see it as somewhat inferior or, at best, amusing and frivolous literature. Their intentions as well as their unsuitable methodologies must be rejected before we can make any critical sense of *The Arabian Nights.* What is essential and, at times, inevitable, is a fairly flexible methodology which emphasizes the internal relationships within the text.

2

NARRATIVE DIALECTICS

Segmentation

Roman Jakobson defined literature as a message centered on its mode of expression. Every literary text poses two questions to the specialist: *how* is the text generated and *what* is its final outcome? The answer to the first question, on how the text flows from its beginning to its end, throws light on the message that the text enunciates. The first step, therefore, is to try to understand the essential course of the text.

The Arabian Nights is a narrative discourse, but the narrative component does not cover the entire discourse. There are certain parts in the story which can be discarded without damaging the narrative line. This is evident enough since we know that there are many ways of telling the same story. Vladimir Propp has shown that the functions in a tale are the crucial points in the unfolding of narrative—these help us to see the story as a series of functional transformations connected in a causal relationship.[1] Tzvetan Todorov went further by demonstrating the hierarchical nature of these functions, and that some of them are more essential to the narrative line than others, thus condensing the narrative to its essential identity.[2] The analysis of *The Arabian Nights* in this chapter will follow the operations undertaken by Propp and Todorov, to observe the phenomenal changes in their essential role, and then to retain the principal transformations which will lead to the significance of the fiction.

The overall struture of *The Arabian Nights* is that of a principal preposition enclosing other prepositions connected by conjunctions, and so on. The fundamental preposition in *The Arabian Nights,* at the basic level, is the story of a king who, having found himself betrayed by his wife, vows to marry a virgin every night and behead her in the morning. After a succession of such wives, one of them—Shahrazad—manages to postpone her verdict and eventually waive it by narrating stories which captivate the

king. This is the indispensable part of the narrative; it covers but a few
pages at the beginning and the end. This is called the frame story. The
stories related by Shahrazad (as well as one related to her by her father to
dissuade her from marrying the king) can be omitted from the discourse
without infringing on the narrative thread. On the other hand, if the frame
story were omitted, the result would simply be unconnected stories. In the
first case, we have a necklace without beads; in the latter, beads without a
necklace.

The narrative line can be retold in more abstract terms as that of a rupture leading to a curse and its ultimate undoing. This invariably carries
with it overtones of Semitic sacred narratives of Creation where an initial
order and equilibrium are lost. In this sense, *The Arabian Nights* is essentially a demotic version of paradise lost and recovered. The bliss of the
original couple was ruptured when they ate the fruits of the forbidden tree,
that is, by tasting the fruits of knowledge. Similarly, taboo and knowledge
are keys to the unfolding of *The Arabian Nights*. Sin and death go hand in
hand in both. The sacred narrative in Genesis underlines the loss. *The Arabian Nights* points to recovery and redemption. Shahrazad's story echoes
and develops the myth of Origin.

Apart from the power of *The Arabian Nights* to evoke dormant mythological texts, its structure offers a model of symbolic economy. The essence of narrative is a chronological transformation, a series of changes
along a diachronic axis. Succession is as vital to narrative as seriality—
that is, paradigmatic repetition—is to poetry. The narrative is the temporal
discourse *par excellence*. There is an element of poetic justice in
Shahrazad's struggle against deadline (and it is literally a dead line) armed
with narrative: she fights time with time. In the *Odyssey,* Penelope's struggle
to gain time is based on a simple device of doing and undoing; she unrav-
els at night what she weaves in the daytime. Penelope marks time in order
to delay temporal events, but Shahrazad's art lies in annulling the very
limits of time. Penelope's struggle is against given time, while Shahrazad's
is against the notion of time itself. *The Arabian Nights* deals with one of
the most excruciatingly difficult philosophical concepts, that of abstract
time.

Technically, *The Arabian Nights* offers an example of a struggle that
has been used frequently in more modern literary works, such as *Tristram
Shandy* and *Through the Looking Glass,* where the initial binary opposition of thesis and antithesis is not resolved by a mediating synthesis, but
by the triumph of parentheses and digressions. The frame story can be
broken down into four narrative blocks. In other words, the frame story

combines four narratives which could stand independently, one from the other, although in this case they are artfully linked together.[3] The four blocks are the story of Shahrayar as a king, the story of Shahrayar as a traveler seeking knowledge, the story of Shahrazad, and the story narrated by her father.

The Story of Shahrayar

The beginning narrative block relates the story of two brothers who are monarchs; the older is called Shahrayar and the younger Shahzaman. After twenty years of happy rule, Shahrayar misses his brother and sends his vizier to fetch him. Shahzaman sets out to visit his brother. At midnight, he remembers something he had forgotten and goes back to his palace. There he finds his wife in bed with a black slave. He kills them both and goes on to visit his brother. Although Shahrayar had ordered a proper welcome for his brother upon his arrival, Shahzaman remains sullen. Sharayar assumes that his brother is homesick and Shahzaman will only refer enigmatically to an internal wound that is bothering him. One day, there is a royal hunting expedition but Shahzaman refuses to join the group and stays home. As Shahzaman is looking into the garden of his brother's palace, twenty slave girls, twenty slave men, and his sister-in-law come strolling along. They all undress and Shahrayar's wife copulates with a black slave, while the other girls do likewise. Shahzaman feels somewhat better after witnessing this orgy as it proves that his calamity is no worse than his brother's, and he soon regains his gaiety. On returning, Shahrayar is surprised by the sudden change in his brother, and he questions him about it. But Shahzaman only explains the reason for his grief by relating how his wife betrayed him, and will not explain how he got over it. Upon the insistence of his brother, Shahzaman gives in and explains how the betrayal of his sister-in-law had lessened his grief. Shahrayar then wants to check the story for himself and he arranges another royal hunting expedition, but secretly comes home and watches his wife's orgy with his own eyes.

The narrative line of this story is interrupted by introducing another narrative block, but it will be continued later.

The Voyage

Shahrayar decides with his brother to travel in order to find out if theirs is a singular case. They walk until they come to a spring next to the sea and they sit down to rest. After a while, a black column appears from the sea, and the two brothers become frightened and climb up a tree. It turns out to

be a giant demon carrying a chest on top of his head. He comes and sits
underneath their tree. The demon then proceeds to open the chest, from
which he removes a beautiful young maiden. He puts his head in her lap
and goes to sleep. The girl looks up, sees the two brothers, and asks them
to come down. They protest, to no avail, and in the end they have to come
down for fear that she will turn the demon against them. She orders them
to copulate with her and they obey. When this is over, she takes out a bag
with five hundred and seventy rings, which she has gotten from previous
lovers who made love to her while the demon slept, and she asks them for
a ring each.[4] They do as she requests. She relates to them how she had
been kidnapped on her wedding night by the demon, put into a box, placed
in a trunk with seven locks, and then put at the bottom of the sea so as to
assure her chastity. The two brothers are amazed at what has befallen such
a mighty demon and are somewhat consoled.

Here the line of the first narrative block is resumed. The two brothers
go back to Shahrayar's kingdom, and there Shahrayar puts his wife and
her slaves to death.

The Story of Shahrazad

For three years, Shahrayar marries a virgin every night and has her killed
the next morning. It becomes increasingly difficult to find brides for him.
The vizier, having failed to do so, goes home worried. The vizier has two
daughters, Shahrazad the elder, who is well read, and Dinazad the younger.
When the vizier is questioned by his elder daughter, he tells her all that has
happened. Shahrazad offers to marry the king with the hope of delivering
her fellow women. Her father warns her that she might have to face what
befell the ass and the bull with the farmer. She inquires about that, and her
father starts relating the story.

The story line of this narrative block is interrupted here and resumed later.

The Fable

There was a farmer who knew the language of animals. He owned an ass
and a bull. The bull found out that the ass was much better off and told him
how much he envied his leisurely life, as he was only occasionally used
for his master's transport. The ass advised the bull to pretend to be sick, to
lie down and not to eat, and by so doing avoid hard work. The bull did so
accordingly, but since the farmer had overheard the conversation, he gave
instructions that the ass be used to replace the bull in drawing the plough.
The ass regretted his advice and tried to get out of the new situation by

telling the bull that he had better return to work soon, as the owner intended to have him slaughtered if he continued to be sick. The next day, the bull did his best to display appetite when eating and energy at work. The farmer, who had overheard these conversations, roared with laughter. Although he knew the language of animals, he was required not to divulge what he knew, otherwise he would surely die. His wife asked him why he was laughing and he told her that it was a secret which, if revealed, would entail his death. But she insisted on knowing, even at the cost of her husband's life. The husband did not know what to do, since he loved his wife dearly. He called his relatives and neighbors and told them about his predicament. Everyone entreated the wife to abandon the matter, to no avail. So the man resigned himself to her wish and went to perform his last ablutions before telling the secret. He then overheard his dog cursing the cock and accusing him of lightheartedness when his master was about to die. The cock inquired how that had come about and the dog told him the story of their master and his wife. The cock accused his master of stupidity on the grounds that he could not manage even one wife when the cock succeeded in satisfying fifty of them, and wondered why his master did not give his wife a good beating. The farmer, having overheard this, decided to take up the cock's suggestion. He hid some branches in the closet and invited his wife in, pretending he was about to reveal the secret to her. When she came in, she got a beating and consequently asked to be pardoned.

Then the narrative takes up the story of Shahrazad, which eventually fuses with the story of Shahrayar. The vizier says to his daughter Shahrazad that her fate might very well be that of the farmer's wife. But Shahrazad insists on going ahead with her plan. Shahrazad has instructed her sister that she will ask for her on the wedding night, and that Dinazad is to ask for tales to pass the night. The vizier takes Shahrazad to Shahrayar and she requests that her sister be with her. Dinazad comes and sits under the bed. After the deflowering of Shahrazad, Dinazad asks her to relate some stories to pass the time. Shahrazad agrees to do so, if the king will permit it. He does, and is delighted with her discourse. Shahrazad continues to tell her story all night but stops at daybreak. Shahrayar, anxious to hear more, postpones her sentence night after night until one thousand nights have passed. On the thousand and first night, after finishing a story, Shahrazad asks to be granted a wish. She brings her three sons and asks Shahrayar to free her from beheading for the sake of the children. Shaharyar embraces his children and assures her that he has pardoned her. She is delighted and joy overwhelms the people. Then, Shahrayar summons his vizier and thanks him for arranging his marriage with his daughter, who has begotten him three sons. He also orders festivities for thirty days and charitable acts for the people. They live happily ever after until death separates them.

Binarism

Characters

These narrative blocks exhibit a rigorous organizational system in terms of major characters. The first block presents the reader with the most striking impulse in *The Arabian Nights,* that of binarism. The two brothers present to us in full dimension the question of duplication. They are both knights and kings and rule happily. Shahzaman's experience foreshadows Shahrayar's and is almost identical to it. He kills his wife instantly when he finds her in bed with a black slave, while Shahrayar's death order is delayed and undertaken only after his searching voyage. The striking similarity of Shahzaman's and Shahrayar's stories makes them sound like a voice and an echo. Here the text provides us with the first variant of binarism: pairing. This form of male pairing is symmetrically balanced by female pairing, represented in Shahrazad's and Dinazad's relationship in the third narrative block. However, there is a subtle difference in these two pairs. The male pair (Shahrayar and Shahzaman)—as in Flaubert's *Bouvard et Pécuchet*—is two parties in two performances of the same drama. Each reinforces the other but is completely independent in his actions. With the female pair, there is an explicit complicity between the two sisters. Dinazad is a shadow or a negative of Shahrazad, who accompanies her all along. Shahzaman is more than a negative; he is a double and a copy of Shahrayar.

The names of the dramatis personae also carry with them a phonetic duplication. Shahrazad and Dinazad share an end rhyme, Shahrayar and Shahzaman an initial rhyme. The sonorous repetition in the system of names manifests itself in the characters of the enframed stories, such as Sindbad the Porter and Sindbad the Sailor, Abdallah the Hunter and Abdallah the Mariner, and in the story of the two brothers 'Ajib and Gharib. It is a common feature of legends and mythological narratives to have two parallel characters with rhyming names, such as the two giants Gog and Magog who were believed to have been imprisoned by a great wall during the reign of Alexander the Great. Another example is that of Harut and Marut, the fallen angels who were hung by their feet in a well in Babylon, yet another is that of Qahtan and 'Adnan, the mythical ancestors of the Arabs. This phonetic parallelism in *The Arabian Nights,* a phenomenon that can be observed on the surface of the text, confirms and accentuates parallelism on the semiotic level. The significance of the correspondence between these two levels lies in the reinforcement of the impact on the reader and consequently prepares the reader for a deeper assimilation of the text and its patterns.

The protagonists in *The Arabian Nights* are Shahrayar and Shahrazad. They are the backbone of the narrative. While Shahzaman and Dinazad can be removed from the narrative, it is impossible to remove Shahrayar or Shahrazad without damaging the story. The relationship between Shahrayar and Shahrazad presents the second variant of binarism: coupling. This is how their attributes contrast:

Shahrayar	*Shahrazad*
husband	wife
sultan	subject
listener	narrator

This royal couple offers opposed and complementary polarity. The terms "husband," "sultan," and "listener" connote antinomically "wife," "subject," and "narrator" because they are parts of a split union. A husband cannot be comprehended as a term without its complementary contrast— a wife. Similarly, a king or sultan without subjects is such an incongruity that Antoine de Saint-Exupéry played on its absurdity in *Le petit prince*. In the same vein, a listener, by definition, conjures up a speaker, a narrator, or at least a voice. Shahrazad's attributes are, thus, mirror reflections of Shahrayar's, and vice versa. The interlocking of these two poles produces a totality and generates a process. They are a model of a structural couple: opposed and complementary like the yin–yang principles in Chinese cosmology. This coupling is realized on the phonetic level as well; Shahrazad and Shahrayar share both an initial and a medial "rhyme."

There is yet a third variant of binarism—ambivalence—which is presented in the character of Shahrazad on the one hand and Shahrayar on the other. On the surface, Shahrayar is a paradigm of power: an Oriental despot and virile male who consumes a woman every night, while Shahrazad embodies the very principle of female vulnerability. She is at the total mercy of Shahrayar's monstrous appetite. However, she does not try to strike at him as in the wonder tales of giants and monsters, as in "Jack and the Beanstalk" or the Biblical story of David and Goliath. She tries to appease his appetite, to tame him, as it were, and replaces his steady diet of women with tales of women. Shahrazad's genius lies in turning women from objects of sex to objects of sexual fantasy. This entry into the symbolic is the most critical step undertaken by Shahrazad. It is a crucial transformation that parallels the substitution of ritual enactment for the concrete offering of a sacrifice in religion. Once the signifier replaces the signified, language becomes possible—and once language is installed, unlimited discourses become possible.

By obtaining the privilege of narrating, Shahrazad has inverted her relationship with her master. As the narrator, she has the upper hand. Shahrazad has become a "dictator" in the etymological sense of the word—derived from the verb *dicere* (to say). The listener, by definition, is the passive party in the act of narration. Shahrazad's position is the reversal of the conventional one, where discourse is the prerogative of the sovereign. Shahrazad's narrative gift and gigantic knowledge are stressed in *The Arabian Nights*:

> The former [Shahrazad] had read various books of histories, and the lives of preceding kings, and stories of past generations: it is asserted that she had collected together a thousand books of histories, relating to preceding generations and kings, and works of the poets.[5]

Shahrazad is, therefore, an exceptional person in her own right. She is potentially powerful though technically helpless. Her status is ambivalent and so is her condition. She is—to borrow the paradox of Kierkegaard—put to death but kept alive.[6] Shahrayar, by being completely entangled in her fictional web, mesmerized by her narration, evokes the image of an enslaved titan. Both hero and heroine dramatize a case of ambivalence and are examples of *coincidentia oppositorum*.

The relationship between Shahrazad and Shahrayar becomes consequently more complex, or at least more subtle, since their opposition is further complicated by internal contradictions. Neither is a pure type. There is something of the empowerment associated with Shahrayar in Shahrazad, and something of her helplessness in him. Their struggle is not a clear-cut one of forces of light versus forces of darkness. It is by no means a Manichean struggle, but something of an unblocking of dormant potentials in the weak partner and exposing the underlying limits of the strong partner. At bottom, both Shahrayar and Shahrazad are complex and ambiguous types, combining strength with weakness.

Throughout, the text persistently displays binarism and uses the principle of duality in three logically possible ways: duplication, opposition, and ambiguity. It is perhaps worth pointing out that these three variants of binarism correspond faithfully to three orders in semantics: synonymy, antinomy, and heteronomy.

Actions

The binary scale which governs the relationships between the principal characters permeates the thematic contents of the story as well. The major themes of the narrative are the principal actions that occur. In the frame story these are unequivocally those of love and death. The relationship between these fundamental acts in the unfolding of the story falls under three dialectics—repetition, inversion, and fusion—which parallel the relationship of pairing, opposition, and ambivalence. In analyzing these three dialectics within the text, it is often important to note how stylistic craftsmanship superbly coordinates the move from love to death and from death to love.

The first dramatic incident occurs when Shahzaman finds his wife in bed with a black slave. This erotic motif recurs when Shahzaman sees his sister-in-law copulating with a black slave, and it is seen once again by Shahrayar himself. This tripling of the one single incident amplifies it. The accompanying twenty slave girls and twenty slave men copulating in the royal garden further intensify the image. The death motif is equally insistent—participants in the orgy are slain—so the first narrative block presents us with the binarism of Eros and Thanatos.

The second narrative block displays the principle of inversion, where one act changes syntactic position and becomes reversed. The force seems to change direction while maintaining its full thrust. In the voyage undertaken by the two monarchs in the second narrative block, both Shahrayar and Shahzaman have experiences which constitute a drastic change from their earlier ones in the first narrative block. The two kings have sexual intercourse with a young woman kidnapped on her wedding night and kept under many locks. Earlier, their wives had managed to have lovers despite the fenced protection of a royal palace. Shahrayar's love-making with the young woman parallels that of the black slave with his wife. The analogy is evident:

$$\text{Slave : Shahrayar} = \text{Shahrayar : Demon}$$

This neat criss-crossing process also occurs within the story related by the vizier, Shahrazad's father, about the ass and the bull. The ass who has advised the bull to feign sickness in order to have an easy life ends up replacing the bull at hard work, while the bull indulges himself in the pleasures formerly enjoyed by the ass.

The difference between the inverted dialectic of Shahrayar and the bull is that the bull's inversion represents a complete transposition in the two elements given, something akin to the rhetorical figure of antimetabole, while the inversion of Shahrayar is something of a chiasmus. Both inversions—Shahrayar's and the bull's—are crucial in the narrative context. Shahrayar learns a lesson from his experience, acknowledges that this is not a singular case, and goes back to his throne. The ass, too, realizes that he is paying dearly for his advice and sets out to regain his former prestige.

The third dialectic in the narrative text is that of fusion, where two seemingly contradictory motifs are soldered together. Both the powerful notions of blackness and defloration carry with their use in the text what Arab grammarians have called the principle of *addad,* or the fusion of two opposing meanings in one term.

The episode of Shahzaman's return to his palace shows amply the clever use the text makes of blackness:

> [He] set out towards his brother's domains. At midnight, however, he remembered that he had left in his Palace an article which he should have brought with him, and having returned to the palace to fetch it, he there beheld his wife sleeping in his bed, and attended by [in the arms of] a male negro slave. On beholding this scene, *the world became black before his eyes,* and he said within himself, if this is the case when I have not departed from the city, what will be the conduct of this vile woman while I am sojourning with my brother? He then drew his sword, and slew them both in bed.[7]

The text alone plays to the utmost on the semantic fields and associations of blackness, linking this opening and crucial incident to the stuff of the book—nocturnal narration. The text specifies that Shahzaman remembers the article he forgot in his palace at night, indeed, at the very peak of night. Night evokes darkness and midnight evokes the heart of darkness. Shahzaman, then, finds his wife in bed with a *black* slave. Blackness seems to crown this darkness. And when Shahzaman sees all this, "the world became *black* before his eyes." The final blackening of death completes the somber process. One pigment has been sufficient to describe the timing, the adulterer, and the reaction. The swift movement from one situation to the other is unified by the color scheme.[8]

The concentration on one color is a clear example of textual economy where one term functions as a conceptual transformer of the night, from being read as equivalent to erotic time to a reading of it as murder time. The darkness of the night works as a cover and is associated both with sexual love and illicit actions. In Arabic literature, the night of lovers has been glorified in the most celebrated lines in Arabic poetry (though occasionally lovers were portrayed as meeting at other times of day, such as dawn). Both Imru' al-Qays, the pre-Islamic paragon poet, and 'Umar ibn abi Rabi'a, the early Islamic playful poet, set the mode and the model. The love scene set at night builds simply on a literary cliché, but the text moves from presenting the night as a protective veil into the night as absence of vision, where it infuriates Shahzaman to the point where he kills both his wife and her lover instantly. Here, night evokes darkness and blindness. Both opposed semantic poles of the night are used in this short passage.

What turns this discourse into a text is precisely this stylistic compactness. Thematically and logically, the sequence of events in the above passage is banal enough. A man finds his wife in bed with another and commits a *crime de passion* killing both of them. It sounds rather journalistic and of only passing interest. However, the style enhancing the sequence of events turns the report of such an occurrence into a literary text. In this case, the leitmotif of blackness shows how repetitions of one vehicle can produce highly differentiated and somewhat opposing tenors, to use the terms of I. A. Richards. The fusion here can be called duality in unity.

The text offers, furthermore, a fusion in which different vehicles are united by one overriding tenor, displaying the principle of divergence in convergence. The text specifies the kind of women Shahrayar wanted every night:

> and henceforth he made it his regular custom, every time he took a virgin to his bed, to kill her at the expiration of the night. This he continued to do during a period of three years.[9]

It is clear that Shahrayar suffers from a wound and is trying to avenge himself, but what he is after is not women qua women but virginity. His own innocence, i.e., his mental "virginity," has been wounded and he is making up for it by inflicting wounds. Defloration, a symbol of the erotic act and the procreative drive, is juxtaposed and simultaneously contrasted with beheading. The antithetical nature of the defloration, which is both a synecdoche for life while being literally a bloody rupture, renders the development of the paradox possible. Shahrayar, by the very act of rendering a female procreative and life-producing by inseminating her, is condemning her to death. On the other hand, Shahrayar is doing unto his brides the same act twice over: a metaphoric death followed by a literal death. Eros and Thanatos are fused together. Deflowering and killing, opposite rites, turn out to be facets of one act, namely laceration.

Thus, the binary impulse in *The Arabian Nights* manifests itself both in characters and themes, in the nouns and in the verbs of this great preposition which constitutes the text. Binarism is used in three distinct ways which I shall call—borrowing terms from medieval Arabic rhetoric—

(1) correlation *(mumathala)* which covers pairing and repetition, (2) confrontation *(muqabala)*, which includes opposition and inversion, and (3) antithetical meaning *(addad)*, which delineates internal contradictions in characters and cleavage in actions. The effect is invariably that of amplification and hyperbole in the first place *(mumathala)*, revolution and upside-down transformations in the second place *(muqabala)*, and paradox and reversibility in the third place *(addad)*.

A dyadic organizational system such as that of *The Arabian Nights,* which cannot build a third term, is invariably committed to radical changes but not to growth. A paradox may split apart, and a force may change its position in the syntactic order, but the constituent units remain essentially the same.

If we were to think of *The Arabian Nights* as *parole,* an enunciation, then the organizational system outlined above would constitute its language *(langue)*. There is something disturbingly inorganic about this *langue*. It works through sedimentation, mutation, and explosions. The metaphors describing this text should perhaps be drawn from geology rather than biology. The mode of expression, as Jakobson points out, is profoundly linked to the message. *The Arabian Nights,* in using a binary structure, falls inevitably into repetition rather than growth.

3

DISCURSIVE SIGNIFICANCE

The Matrix

Having established the operational structure and its bipolarity, it is necessary to investigate how it functions narratively—that is, how it moves from initial to terminal situations. In order to grasp the movement in its complexity, a pivotal principle has to be extracted if we are not to be lost in this long and diversified discourse called *The Arabian Nights*. This pivotal principle, which I shall call the matricial phrase or simply the matrix, is the fundamental principle that controls and guarantees the proliferation in the text.[1]

The matrix is more than the central theme of the text, for it is both the source and the formula, the stimulus and the regulator. The symbolic systems of the text can be packed in its matricial phrase(s). The matrix is a unit of discourse around which the text is built both semantically and stylistically. It is analogous to what the Arabs have called *bayt al-qasid* in rhetorics, the line on which the *qasida* (ode) is built. Not every verse line in an ode reproduces *bayt al-qasid,* but it is the generative impetus of the poem.

The matrix, in order to qualify fully as one, should be at the center of the entire text and not simply of the plot. It has to justify the text as it stands, with its redundancies, contradictions, and digressions. In the parabolic narrative, the matrix is stated at the beginning or the end of the story so that the extended figure embodied in the parable may reach its mark. *The Arabian Nights* functions more enigmatically. The matrix is lost among the verbiage and the text does not explicitly point to it. To isolate the matrix, one need not look further than the text, which may mislead but never betrays us. Here, the composer of the work introduces a dilemma and then sets out to solve it. *The Arabian Nights* is the story of a rupture and its healing. Hence, we have a dialogical composition in the form of a crisis posed and a solution offered, a riddle and a key. *The Arabian Nights* articulates these two positions in the frame story. The first is summed up by a statement made by Shahzaman when questioned by his brother about his indisposition: "Oh brother I have an internal sore." Shahrazad sums up the solution: "And I will relate to thee a story that shall, if it be the will of God, be the means of procuring deliverance."[2]

These two statements floating on the surface of the text constitute the two complementary axes around which the text revolves. They formulate the matrix of the text. The first statement is about lost plenitude and wholeness, and the second is about mythotherapy. What we retain from this nocturnal narrative is a primal cleavage and an unrelenting verbal soldering.

The first part of the matrix—"O brother I have an internal sore"—is an example of a metaphoric statement. The internal wound is not a physical ulcer but an incision in the self and a shattering of totality. The metaphoric nature of the matrix corresponds to the intensive use of figurative language in the entire discourse of Shahrazad, where the story seems akin to a poetic narrative based on paradigmatic units, with its refrain at every dawn and its repetitions and analogies. The second part of the matrix is concerned with relating a discourse that would lead to salvation and deliverance. Here, the translation fails to give the elasticity of the Arabic term *khalas,* which denotes both "salvation" and "end."[3] The phrase implies a discourse that terminates the anguish. It is a narrative whose objective is the end of narration. It exists, as it were, in order to cease existing. The ambiguity and paradoxical nature of this statement permeates the entire discourse of Shahrazad. The entire text of *The Arabian Nights* is generated from this matrix, which works as a center for an infinite number of circles, varying in circumferences and surfaces but sharing a point of reference. Thus, the metaphor and the paradox are the governing alliance of the symbolic system of the text.

The relationship between the enframed and the enframing, the inside and the outside, needs to be elaborated. I have already noted the segmentary aspect of the enframing story made out of narrative blocks. The enframed material is equally segmentary, with the additional feature of not being sequential. One enframed story follows another, within the narration of Shahrazad, without causal relationship. In contrast, the four narrative blocks that make up the frame story—some of which are more fundamental to the plot than others—follow each other in a logical order that can neither be reversed nor shuffled.

The enframed stories vary in genre, technique, and content. They include religious exempla, magic tales, historical romances, animal fables, etc. The themes cover theological, linguistic, historical, geographical, and psychological lore. These manifold narratives seem to be lumped together in a somewhat promiscuous and random fashion. But this is justified since the mode of ordering is not any more syntagmatic and narrative, but rather paradigmatic and poetic. Every tale relates directly or indirectly to the generating tale, that is, the frame story. The orders of correspondence between the narrative units which constitute the enframed stories and the narrative units which make up the enframing story will be developed in the following chapters. It suffices here to point out that the tremendous variety is not accidental but fulfills a function which I shall call the "encyclopedic" thrust of the work. There is a preoccupation with covering the entire spectrum of narration inasmuch as it fits in the enframing cadre.

This signifies a certain obsession with totality, as if the fragmentary aspect of the tale is being substituted for by covering all or almost all samples of narration. The encyclopedic intention is to be understood as a striving toward achieving a comprehensive scope in a given field, "une sorte de corpus générale,"[4] as Foucault put it, and as Said has characterized it, a "convergence of difference and repetition."[5] The encyclopedic drive in *The Arabian Nights* does not follow an alphabetical order, or for that matter any other progressive, linear order; but this by no means diminishes the comprehensive value of the work. An encyclopedic work in medieval Islam was meant to be read in its totality for full effect.

The Arabian Nights is an attempt to bring together the dispersed by creating a model of universal narrative before our very eyes. The genesis of storytelling is accounted for in the frame story. The enframed stories present varied results. The sources of the stories of *The Arabian Nights,* whether Babylonian, Indian, Greek, Arabian, or whatever, are intentionally brought in—just as in the universal histories written in medieval Islam, chronologies of non-Arabs were included along with those of the Arabs.[6] In a more modern vein, this is what Joyce tried to do in *Finnegans Wake.* In the thirteenth and fourteenth centuries, the Arab world witnessed a movement of intellectual *rassemblement.* These efforts were triggered by the need for preservation and compilation of past and diversified knowledge.[7] *The Arabian Nights* is the popular and literary expression of this movement.

The Codes

The matrix, as I have pointed out, is the principal sentence of the text to which all other statements are subordinated. It expresses itself throughout the text by codes. A code is a combination of thematic elements that constitute a sub-language. A code is a series of consistent references and cross-references that signify a coherent message. The codes are extended translations of the matrix, which when isolated can serve to verify the matricial statement. Flaubert, for example, uses weather code words such as sunny, rainy, stormy, etc., to constitute the internal states of the hero in "La légende de Saint-Julien l'Hospitalier." The changes articulate the fluctuating matrix.

In *The Arabian Nights,* the matrix poses a dilemma and then sets out to resolve it. The codes equally pose different initial equations and offer solutions. Close reading reveals that the narrative text uses three codes intensively: the erotic, the rhetorical, and the numerical. The central thesis remains the same whether the text enunciates it in corporeal, linguistic, or mathematical idiom.

The Erotic Code

The erotic code is a chain of images and incidents relating to the sexual sphere, in both its social and natural expressions. The text of *The Arabian Nights* is articulated primarily in the erotic code.

The Arabian Nights is the story of a conjugal union ruptured by one female and restored by another. The first wife of Shahrayar was found in bed with a black slave. The implications of this relationship can be fully grasped when one understands the connotations of "black slave" in this royal household. The copulation between slave and queen represents an intercourse between two extreme poles of rank. The erotic attraction of opposite forces is evident from the connotations inherent in "slave" and "queen." The symbolic reading of this incident is facilitated by the fact that in the text the queen and the slave bear no names. Names are usually appellations to pinpoint persons, which make a character in a story seem more real. The anonymity here diminishes identity and makes a character more liable to being understood allegorically. The wife of Shahzaman and the wife of Shahrayar are nameless. So is the slave lover of Shahzaman's wife. The slave lover of Shahrayar's wife is called Mas'ud. But Mas'ud hardly functions as a personal name—an appellation that gives an individual identity to the character—since Mas'ud is the stereotypical name for a black person. In Arabic literature, and especially in oral traditions, blacks tend to have a form of "Mas'ud" as a name.[8]

Inasmuch as the name Mas'ud tends to be synonymous with blackness, there is something descriptive rather than distinctive about the name. It indicates a category rather than an individual. It is not unlike giving the king in the story the name "Sultan" or "Shah" and would parallel in Western literature calling a character who is ethnically Arab "Saracen." The name "Mas'ud" functions simply as a confirmation of group identity.

The image of black in Arabic literature is an ambivalent one, for black signifies both bad and good omens. In oral epics blacks are portrayed as sketch characters combining both an outsider status and excessive prowess that borders on supernatural heroism. The outstanding black figures in Arabic epics are 'Antar, Abu Zayd al-Hilali, and Sa'dun (in *Sayf bin dhi Yazan)*. Their color sets them apart and defines their alien quality, yet they loom as examples of physical energy and heroic valor. If anything, black connotes for the Arabic reader an uncommon vitality and irrepressible drive. The nature of the adultery committed by the respective wives of Shahzaman and Shahrayar with black slaves is perhaps made comprehensible by the appeal and attraction that is inherent in blackness, for Arab readers at least.

The adultery itself constitutes the classical triangle of husband, wife, and lover. While the relationship of husband and wife is within the confines of social culture and is considered a legitimate union, that of wife and lover is within the confines of nature and is considered unlawful. Thus, the struggle between the social and the natural forces is represented. The two men in the equation, the husband–king and the lover–slave, are extreme opposites. In the context of *The Arabian Nights,* the king is the symbol of law, order, and sovereignty, while the slave signifies anarchy, disorder, and destruction. The woman is clearly not satisfied with socialized sex and seeks a more primitive, or natural, kind of eroticism. It is a sharp image of the instincts of death intruding on the instincts of life.

In this triangular pattern, there are two kinds of relationship: a recognized one between the husband and wife and a clandestine one between wife and lover. The third party to the legal binary association is a total outsider. He is different in rank, color, and, moreover, his relationship is unilateral with the couple. He cannot relate to the king. In fact, his relationship with the king is mutually exclusive. He substitutes for the king and in some sense displaces him. The relationship has effectively a fatal end. Not only does it destroy the wife and the lover, but also a host of young maidens who are executed after their first night with the king. The relationship of lover–wife is barren. It produces death; the text is adamant about this: "He [Shahzaman] then drew his sword and slew them both in bed."[9] Furthermore,

> Shahrayar caused his wife to be beheaded, and in like manner the women and black slaves, and thenceforth he made it his regular custom, every time that he took a virgin to his bed, to kill her at the expiration of the night.[10]

The lover introduces disruption in the initial order. This disruption is seen as singular or accidental at this point of the narrative. The two shocked kings are deeply confounded and they want to know if the betrayal is a personal tragedy or a generalized phenomenon, whether it is an accident or law. The two kings undertake a voyage, during the course of which they are forced to satisfy the sexual urges of a kidnapped woman, the companion of a formidable demon. From that experience they conclude that female nature is not given to conjugal fidelity, and this convinces Shahrayar that the only way to guarantee that he is not being fooled by a woman is to have her beheaded after the first night.

So far, the erotic code reproduces the first matricial phrase. It is variation on the rupture theme. The second matricial statement is paraphrased equally in the erotic code, as analysis will show. It should be recalled that the deliverance of Shahrazad from the threat of death not only occurs after a thousand nights of storytelling, but also after bearing the king three sons. In the closing chapter of the story, the text refers three times to the three sons: first, when it is reported that Shahrazad, during this period, had borne the king three male children; second, when Shahrazad talks to Shahrayar requesting pardon she mentions the three children and asks to have her life spared for their sake; and third, when Shahrayar talks to his vizier, Shahrazad's father, he congratulates him for his daughter who had borne him three sons.[11]

The male child is in some sense the model child in a patriarchal society. He continues the lineage; posterity is only assured through a son. In the Arab world, fathers are addressed using the name of their eldest son (teknonymy). Abu Zayd, for example, would be a man whose eldest son is Zayd, though he may have half a dozen daughters older than Zayd. The Arabian Nights underlines the fertility of Shahrazad and her prolific capacity through reference to her engendering of sons. Three sons make the statement on child-bearing even more emphatic. It is as though the text is telling us, "Shahrazad bore a son! Shahrazad bore a son! Shahrazad bore a son!"

Here we have a different kind of triangle. The couple Shahrazad–Shahrayar has proliferated and added a third element, that of sons. The children are the outcome of their union and are, therefore, a native addition. While the lover as a third element in the husband–wife relationship was an intrusion, the children are an organic multiplication of the couple. In the first case the addition is obstructive, in the second it is an emanation. Shahrazad's outstanding gift is, therefore, her power for proliferation in both narrative and progeny, and the ultimate message of the story is that death can be undone by life—it is overcome through reproduction. The matrix is articulated in the erotic code in terms of episodes and imagery that point to the triumph of the life instincts over the death verdict.

This message of undoing through doing, of struggling against non-being through production of being, is a popular truth which has been embodied in proverbial sayings in Arabic. From Iraq to Morocco the by-word of *illi khallaf ma mat* (he who begets does not die) is current. Begetting and dying are clearly used in a figurative sense. Variations on this proverb are found in *mawwal*s (ballads) and a variant of the proverb was used as the opening line of an elegy by the well-known Egyptian poet Salah 'Abd al-Sabbur in memory of President Gamal 'Abd al-Nasser.

The relationship of the enframing to the enframed is that of death enclosing life, with the latter having continually to assert itself through reproduction.

The Rhetorical Code

The rhetorical code is the systematic pointing to narration and reference to language in the story. It is something of a meta-language. *The Arabian Nights* is clearly a narrative about the act of narration, and this makes it an involuted and introspective work. This feature sets it apart from other collections of narratives such as Ovid's *Metamorphoses* and Tha'alibi's *'Ara'is al-majalis.* This tendency for self-reflection is present in modern fiction, and its aesthetics was most eloquently represented in Mallarmé's "Sonnet allégorique de lui-même."[12] In Arabic literature, it is almost a national trait to point inwards. Even *Sirat 'Antar,* which is something of a historical epic, is, in the words of Heller, "a regular romance about the origin of romance."[13]

The Arabian Nights presents literature as if it were a swan-song. Shahrazad sits on her very deathbed narrating stories. She prolongs this fictional discourse, putting off the moment of death. Death, the ultimate reality, is an all-conquering and all-silencing event. It follows that the opposite of discourse is death, and consequently discourse is indispensable for life. The analogy is as follows:

Discourse : Silence = Life : Death.

Survival becomes an unrelenting struggle against silence. Life is based on the suppression of the death instinct just as discourse is the suppression of silence.

The theme of salvation through struggle against entropy is not uncommon in literature. The power of the word has been highlighted in numerous anecdotes in Arabic literature, where wit and word-play have saved the victim's life or where the hero has to pass verbal challenges. One example is when 'Antar, the epic hero, passes a test in Arabic synonyms given to him by Imru' al-Qays, the pre-Islamic poet.

The Arabian Nights seems to push the theme of reward through wit to its logical conclusion. The nocturnal cogito is: "I narrate, therefore, I am." The composers of *The Arabian Nights* seem therefore to challenge implicitly the myth of the tower of Babel, where the diversity of language caused discord, division, and chaos. Here the myth within *The Arabian Nights* uses language and narrative from different linguistic traditions as an instrument of harmony and life. It is important to note that the word in question is profane, and not the word of God which gives eternal life. The profanity of the word in *The Arabian Nights* can guarantee survival but not everlasting life. *The Arabian Nights,* then, tries to situate language in relation to men and women, indicating how the rhetorical code deals with the inaugural breach and its healing, as embodied in the matrix. Storytelling in *The Arabian Nights* is a continual crossing over a chasm. Shahrazad's discourse hovers over the brink of death. She is perpetually in a liminal state.

The introductory paragraph of *The Arabian Nights* points to the rhetorical aspect of the text. It opens up with a divine invocation (*basmala* and *hamdala*). It is well known to any one familiar with medieval Arabic texts that the *basmala* and *hamdala* are stereotyped religious formulae that signal the beginning of a formal pronouncement. On the other hand, the passages following, called the *khutba* in which God is glorified, tend to contain the seeds of the book and foreshadow its orientation.

Ibn Khaldun, writing on the philosophy of history, emphasized in his *khutba* the power and might of God, who made humankind in different nations and races and provided them with their livelihood. Time passes and their ends come about except for He who is endless and everlasting.[14] Jabir ibn Hayyan, the Sufi alchemist, on the other hand, stressed in his *khutba* that God has no archetype. He knows everything, the esoteric and the exoteric, and what is in between. He stretches without end and can comprehend everything.[15] And al-'Askari, the literary critic, starts by asserting that the most worthwhile science—after the knowledge of God— is the science of *balagha* (poetics), through which the excellence of the Qur'an can be discerned. To be ignorant of poetics is to be unaware of the brilliant construction and beautiful expression of the Divine Book.[16]

The *khutba* in *The Arabian Nights* stresses the rhetorical and allegorical nature of the discourse:

> To proceed—the lives of former generations are a lesson to posterity; that a man may review the remarkable events which have happened to others, and be admonished, and may consider the

history of people of preceding ages, and of all that hath befallen them, and be restrained. Extolled by the perfection of Him who hath ordained the history of former generations to be a lesson to those which follow.[17]

The key word in this section is *'ibra,* which Lane translates as "lesson." It has an equivocal meaning and can stand for "admonition," "monition," "warning," "example," "advice," "rule," and "precept." *'Ibra* is etymologically derived from the triliteral root *'-b-r,* which means "passing" or "crossing." This term is most appropriate as it sums up the entire enterprise: a rite of passage where an ordeal leads to an ultimate and radical transformation. The heroine spins around like a whirling dervish until the passage is accomplished.

The rhetorical code describes the fertility of Shahrazad in the discursive domain. The rhetorical and the erotic codes converge in celebrating Shahrazad's generative powers. And for Arab readers, the association of poetic gift with breeding capacity is hardly a novelty. The master poets are consistently referred to as *fuhul* (stallions).

The Numerical Code

The use of numbers is common in folk literature, where one often comes across three sons, seven voyages, forty thieves, and so on. *The Arabian Nights,* however, seems to use numbers excessively. In the frame story alone, we are faced with the following numbers: 20 years, 1/2 of the night (midnight), 2 adulterers, 20 slave girls, 20 slave men, 570 rings, 7 locks, 3 years, 1000 books, 1 day, 2 days, 3 days, 120 years, 50 hens, 50 wives, 1 wife, 3 sons, 1001 nights, 3 sons, 3 sons.

We have twenty numerical references including eleven different numbers. Nine of these numbers deal with units of time. The title of the book—which functions like a label to a commodity—is numerical: *One Thousand and One Nights.* What is the role of numbers in this story? The question imposes itself and is unavoidable. Is it simply a stylistic tick or do the numbers constitute an organized system which helps uncover certain layers of significance?

Numbers have been shown to work connotatively, just as any notional component in a sentence.[18] The example drawn from *France-Soir* of June 6, 1962, by Durand—"A Villeneuve-le-Roi, les 22222 habitants ont peur"—can be used to explain the stylistic significance of numbers in their repetitive quality (the date as well as the number of inhabitants). The number 22222 is striking by its exactness to the last digit in a context where a rounded figure would usually be given. The precision is intriguing because the number has a curious quality: the repetition of one digit five times. This suggests an exceptional coincidence. When we read of the fear of the inhabitants, we read into the number a foreboding sign. The strange number creates a fantastic mood.

Other examples demonstrating the evocative function of numbers may be cited. In a nursery rhyme from *Mother Goose*—"Four and twenty tailors went to kill a snail"—the number 24 stands for hyperbole: a great many to carry out such a small deed. Wallace Stevens' "Thirteen ways of looking at a blackbird" uses the number 20 in the same way: "Among twenty snowy mountains/The only moving thing/Was the eye of a blackbird."[19]

More than the occasional use of the symbolism of numbers, the mathematical relationship is at times the pivot of the tale. Here is an example:

> The Grand Vizier Sissa Ben Dahir was granted a boon for having invented chess for the Indian king Shirham. Since this game is played on a board with 64 squares, Sissa addressed the king: 'Majesty, give me a grain of wheat to place on the first square, and two grains of wheat to place on the second square, and four grains of wheat to place on the third, and eight grains of wheat to place on the fourth, and so, O King let me cover each of 64 squares of the board.' 'And is that all you wish, Sissa, you fool?' exclaimed the astonished king. 'O sire,' Sissa replied, 'I have asked for more wheat than you have in your kingdom, nay, for more wheat than there is in the whole world, verily, for enough to cover the whole surface of the earth to the depth of the twentieth part of a cubit.'[20]

In like manner, Shahrazad makes on the first night what seems a modest request: to narrate stories. In fact, she is asking for unlimited time, as the title suggests. *The Arabian Nights* insists on the element of one thousand and one nights in the versions we have. Earlier versions were called *The Thousand Nights (Alf layla)*,[21] but there is not, to my knowledge, any other variation on the number of nights—except for one manuscript in the National Library in Cairo (Dar al-Kutub) which has a thousand and seven nights.[22] As for *One Hundred and One Nights,* it is considered a different work and not a variant of *The Arabian Nights.*[23] Different as it may be, the significance of the number 100 in the title reflects 1000—they both stand for a very large, round figure.

The curious thing about this Egyptian manuscript in Dar al-Kutub is that it is just the same, entitled *Alf layla wa layla* ("one thousand and one nights"), and, furthermore, on the one thousand and seventh night when Shahrazad asked Shahrayar to pardon her, she refers to her one thousand and *one* nights (sic!) of storytelling:

> When it was the seventh night after the thousand ... Shahrazad
> said to him [Shahrayar], 'O King of the decade and time, your
> slave girl has been narrating for you tales of ancient times and
> stories of bygone people for one thousand and one nights; could
> your majesty allow me to make a wish?'[24]

There must be something significant about this number which has caused its retention in almost all the versions, and used even when Shahrazad has (in the Dar al-Kutub version) presumably been narrating over and above that number of nights.

The hyperbolic is often expressed in round figures, such as one hundred or one thousand. Children often use one hundred to mean the maximum, the most they can imagine. The ancient Egyptians used the hieroglyph which stood for one thousand to mean "all"; if they wanted to say "all the geese" then they would write "a thousand geese." Shahrazad herself is said to have had a thousand books. The use of one thousand signifying the maximum, the highest degree or the most conceivable, is often used in poetry, e.g., "A thousand fold moore than he kan deserve" (Chaucer, *Troilus and Criseyde*). One thousand and one can be recast as $1000 + 1$, or the maximum number imaginable, plus one. In algebra, the notion of "maximum plus one" is called infinity. So Shahrazad in fact narrates *ad infinitum*. Only in the realm of the virtual does she achieve liberation from her narration. The text here insinuates that Shahrazad went on with her narration indefinitely. The text, at this point, functions like an antiphrasis—it means the opposite of what it says. It is as if the text said, "And on the twelfth of never, Shahrazad appealed to the king and he forgave her." The paradox is clear to those who know how often the twelfth of never comes around. The book has a virtual ending which has motivated writers to compose the one thousand and second night of Shahrazad, and speculate on what went on beyond the formal ending.

The one thousand and one can stand equally for the New Era. In Islamic civilization, the millennium has a particular appeal to the masses, who feel that after the passage of each thousandth year the promised *mahdi* (redeemer) will come and a new era of justice and benevolence will begin. Shahrazad's condition is transformed on the night after the thousandth, ushering in a new regime and a new life. The significance of one thousand and one as leading to a radical metamorphosis is also exploited in some of the esoteric Islamic sects. The Truth Worshippers *(Ahl al-Haqq),* prevalent among the Kurds of Turkey, Iran, and Iraq, and of whom the first substantial account was given by de Gobineau in *Trois ans en Asie,*[25] possess a rigorous theological system based on the central belief of metempsychosis. Human beings supposedly pass through one thousand and one incarnations. Here are some quotations from their shaykh, Nur Ali-Shah Elahi:

chaque âme a un chemin à parcourir consistant à revêtir mille et un 'habits corporels.'

Nos âmes, pour nous qui appartenons au genre humain, une fois les mille et un 'vêtements' (dûn) revêtus, n'apparaissent plus sous l'habit humain.[26]

Other practices in the East confirm the auspiciousness of adding one to a round figure. In India, for example, one should not give 1000 rupees, but add one to it, making it 1001.

The number one thousand and one suggests a terminal transformation. It also suggests new life and birth in the following even more esoteric reading. So far, two features permeate *The Arabian Nights:* a binary impulse and a predilection for numbers. The numbers follow a decimal system of counting, but there is a binary or dyadic system of counting as well. The binary system was used by the Babylonians and the Chinese, among others, and is said to have been used by Russian peasants until recently. Whereas the decimal scale uses the digits zero to nine, in the binary scale only zero and one are used. This is how the first ten numbers would be written in the binary and decimal systems:

decimal	binary
1	1
2	10
3	11
4	100
5	101
6	110
7	111
8	1000
9	1001
10	1010

One thousand and one stands for nine in the decimal system. Nine is an intriguing number and was considered a magical number in medieval Islam. One of the riddles of Balqis—the Queen of Sheba—to King Solomon dealt with the significance of nine, and Solomon figured out that it dealt with the period of pregnancy. Nine is also intimately associated with the magic square—an amulet with nine boxes, each containing a number. When the numbers in the magic sqaure are added up in any way—vertically, horizontally, or diagonally—the answer is unfailingly the same: 15.

2	7	6
9	5	1
4	3	8

Such amulets were used by women in labor to facilitate delivery. They were mentioned by Jabir ibn Hayyan and by the Pure Brethren, among others.[27] Nine, then, like one thousand and one, seems to stand for a graded development. There are, for example, nine modalities for the reading and comprehension of the Qur'an, according to Imam Ja'far.[28]

The numerical code in *The Arabian Nights* starts with binarism—a split "one"—and ends up with one thousand and one. The process that starts by the breaking down of one unit is recovered through the notion of infinite counting. The initial rupture is healed by continual production, and we find the numerical code converging neatly with the erotic and the rhetorical codes. The three codes articulate and expand the matricial formula. They reinforce each other and accentuate the message: time is a function of a breach.

The Arabian Nights is a narrative whose beginning is already a repetition of past lives and stories. Its middle is indefinite and its end is virtual—we have a very mercurial and somewhat confusing text. But the solidity of its structure compensates for its fluid course; the segmentary aspect of the whole system covers a symbolic unity. And as the enframed stories, in one way or another, refer to the frame story or to a narrative block within the frame story, the structural model of the frame story proliferates through the enframed stories and provides a semblance of unity.

4

MIMESIS AND META-MIMESIS

The relationship between enframed story and frame story is indirect, for the enframed story is neither a faithful repetition of structural patterns of a given narrative block from the frame story—as it is in the case of fables discussed in Chapter Five—nor is it a development of the aesthetic orientation of the frame story as a whole. However, there are enough points of similarity in structure, and inversions in narrative components and poetic ethos, that I propose to justify bringing together the part to the whole under the formula of genre to anti-genre.[1] I will do this in this chapter by relating the enframed epic-like narrative of "'Umar ibn al-Nu'man" to the frame story in the *The Arabian Nights*.[2] The long narrative of "'Umar ibn al-Nu'man" offers the norms of an ethno-genre, and *The Arabian Nights* is an ironic manifestation of this particular genre.

Irony conveys meaning different from and often opposed to the professed one. It is essential to note that the ironic is necessarily a reduplication *(dédoublement)*.[3] The ironic always refers to something that precedes it. Irony, therefore, cannot be an original or prime form—it has to be grafted into another form. Irony is inevitably a secondary development and can only be grasped through its emulation of, and distance from, that which is being ironized.

Reading a literary text, as Edward Said points out, is necessarily a comparative activity.[4] The reader does not read in a vacuum but through reference to other works in the same or similar genre. A novel, for example, not only relates to the socioeconomic conditions that give rise to its creation and dissemination but also has strong ties with other novels. Just as one does not write from scratch, but depends heavily on the traditions of writing that the writer belongs to, a reader equally reads the text in a certain literary perspective. In other words, there are conventions for reading as well as for writing. Works such as *Les chants de Maldoror* of Lautréamont or de Sade's *Justine,* and, more markedly so, Cervantes' *Don Quixote* are only fully appreciated as a reaction to a certain literary genre and stylistic order. Lautréamont may reject Homer, but he owes as much to him as Cervantes does to medieval romances.[5] Sade's *Justine,* immoral or amoral as it may be, is rooted in the virtue novels of the eighteenth century and would have been impossible to write without that narrative background. These, of course, are instances of works that have subverted conventions, and hence they are striking as examples. Other literary works may offer more subtle variations and changes in the literary code.[6] Though *The Arabian Nights* stands without the need for crutches in any literary context, a great many of its intimate features and stylistic oddities can only be fully explained by reference to the literary background from which it emerged and developed.

It is essential to note that fiction articulates on more than one level. In narrative, we have a superimposition of one language on another. The narrator tells a story using two languages: one of events and their unfolding, and another which is the mode of presenting these events.[7] A story on the level of narration may unfold like this: A overcomes B, C, and D in order to obtain Z—a typical structure of fairy tales and adventure stories. But there is another language, that of the style in which the unrolling of events is told. A comic story may have the same narrative line as that of a tragic one, but the difference is in the choice of language and in the description of certain events. Whether it is comic or tragic depends a great deal on how the protagonist is presented. If A is of heroic stature then an adventure story with a sad ending is tragic, but if A is a ridiculous character then we are encouraged to laugh. The plight of Echo and her metamorphosis as related by Ovid is touching, while Kafka's hero in *Metamorphosis* turning into a beetle is both comic and disgusting. Clearly, if the same character were to turn into something other than a beetle—say, a butterfly—then the story would not be as horrific. The beetle has a certain stigma which comes from mythological and literary associations that are very different from those associated with the butterfly. The connotations and symbolic associations of a given sign can be fully appreciated in light of literary and aesthetic use. This is why it is essential to allow for the effect and implications of textual anomaly. And when narrative heroes are generally masculine, and suddenly we come across a hero who is a woman—as in *The Arabian Nights*—the nature of the equation changes radically.

The Arabian Nights can be classified as something akin to a mock epic, and it is read—especially by native speakers of Arabic—as an exercise in irony. It derives its canons from the widespread and popular from of narration called *sira,* the nearest Arab equivalent to the epic. *The Arabian Nights* is an *anti-sira.*

Sira as Genre

Before justifying my reasons for classifying *The Arabian Nights* as a great moment in the history of irony, it is important to review the origin and development of the *sira* from its pre-Islamic genesis to its Islamic maturity, including the influences and directions that it absorbed as it developed, in order to appreciate its transformation in *The Arabian Nights*. The *sira* offers the convergence of three literary currents: the pre-Islamic Arabian war narratives *(Ayyam al-'Arab)*, the Persian royal epics, and the Judeo-Christian hagiographies.

The original use of the literary term *sira* indicated a traditionally written biography of the prophet. By extension, the term *sira* came to mean biography of great historical figures or that of entire tribes, such as *Sirat Mu'awiya wa Bani Umayya* by 'Awana al-Kalbi.[8] The term *sira* itself occurs in the Qur'an (XX: 22): "Said He, 'Take it, and fear not; We will restore it to its first state.'"[9] Arberry in his translation of the Qur'an renders *sira* as "state." Since the subject is the transformation of Moses' staff into a sliding serpent, *sira* in this context means "form" or "manner of being." The triliteral root from which *sira* is derived *(s-y-r-)* means "betake oneself" or "to travel."[10]

With the rise of Islam, the term *sira* was frequently associated with military expeditions *(maghazi)*. The *sira* owes a great deal, in structure, to the pre-Islamic warfare narratives known as *Ayyam al-'Arab* (literally "Days of the Arabs"). The stylistic feature of these narratives is that they are constructed of episodes loosely linked within a framework that is at times not chronological. They are adorned with poetic quotations and are particularly impressive in their description of battles rather than by giving an organic survey of their connections.[11]

The Pahlavi Persian epics, with which the medieval Arabs were familiar, were something like glorified biographies, concentrating on relating the lives and deeds of kings or dynasties, and left their impact on *sira* composition. Besides the Persian influence, the *sira* showed the effects of Judaism and Christianity, whose religious narratives centered on exceptional characters, in most cases the founders of those religions. The Judeo-Christian legends dealt with the lifecycles of prophets and saints often emphasizing the supernatural. Succumbing to their influence, and to the desire to have Muhammad's life match the other founders' in glory, edifying stories of the Prophet and his perfection were narrated more and more frequently, both to venerate the Prophet and to function as religious and moral examples for the public.[12]

But the *sira* of the Prophet is not simply another narrative. It is part of the *sunna*, the tradition of the Prophet, and an important source for Islamic conduct. It maintained, at least in the beginning, a semblance of orderkeeping to the authentic records and to what actually happened. In relating the *sira* of the Prophet and in order to demonstrate its authenticity beyond any doubt, a chain of transmitters who were instrumental in communicating the incidents had to be named. This is called *isnad* and it has left its mark on all Arab narratives. It is very common in the *sira* to come across a chain such as this:

> It was narrated by Muhammad son of Ishaq on the authority of Yazid son of Abdallah son of Qasit that he [Muhammad] said he had heard from al-Hasan son of Muhammad son of Husayn saying that he [al-Hasan] heard his father saying that his grandfather said: 'I have heard Said, son of al-Masib, swearing by God and excluding none that Adam was unaware when he ate from the tree.'[13]

In the branch of *hadith* (prophetic sayings) there are systems and rules of acceptance for transmission, but inasmuch as we are dealing with the *sira* as a literary form and not as a theological or historical source, it suffices to note that the mode of presentation of the narrative is not direct, and is sometimes at many removes.

The narrators and reciters who composed and disseminated the biography of the Prophet, embellishing it all along with poetry and proverbs, were also involved in writing biographies of other prominent and religious figures of the community. Ibn al-Jawzi, for instance, wrote the biography of Hasan al-Basri, the famous early Islamic preacher from Basra. The book is basically the sermons and teachings of Hasan—very little attention is given to his life as such—so the purpose of the book is clearly moral instruction.[14]

Not all *siras* are concerned with religious topics. Some are devoted simply to entertainment. A number of them are motivated by neither history nor morality, but are simply a series of narratives dealing with adventurous and imaginative escapades, centering on an eccentric figure or a lunatic. The best example of this sub-genre is *Akhbar Sibawayh al-Masri,* written by Ibn Zulaq.

Other characters, historical or imaginary, had a series of anecdotes built around them in a biographical framework, such as al-Ash'ab, Juha, and Abu al-'Ibar.[15] *Siras* that were historical in origin were also expanded and developed, incorporating fantastic episodes and comic digressions to fill the hours of entertainment, especially in the long nights of Ramadan. Lane reports that there was public nocturnal storytelling as late as the nineteenth century: "Reciters of romances frequent the principal kahwehs (or coffee-shops) of Cairo and other towns, particularly in the evenings of religious festivals, and afford attractive and rational entertainment."[16]

The Arabian Nights as Anti-*Sira*

Genres have two aspects, which have been called by Wellek and Warren "outer form" and "inner form." The outer form consists of a series of characteristics that can be defined in specific structural terms. The inner form is more elusive and has to do with tone, aesthetic orientation, and psychological purpose.[17]

In terms of outer form, the *sira* offers salient features linked to the nature of the hero, the actions, and the development of the intrigue. Each of these components of the *sira,* as exemplified in the enframed story of "'Umar ibn al-Nu'man," is radically transformed in the frame story of *The Arabian Nights.* The genre of *sira* is negated, producing an anti-*sira.* By negation, I mean not so much the destruction of the genre, but its precise inversion—that is, a reversal of its components and function. In terms of inner form and artistic objective, the enframed *sira* is compromised to the point of parody by the frame anti-*sira.*

There is invariably in the *sira* a principal heroic figure who tends to combine wisdom, bravery, and high moral standards. He has some kind of objective or mission which he tries to fulfill against great odds and despite innumerable obstacles. He is generally a man of exceptional stature but who is not properly recognized by his group, and his greatness is only acknowledged at the end. There are exceptions to the man-hero, such as in *Sirat Dhat-al-Himma,* where the main heroic figure is a woman, but Princess Dhat-al-Himma, though female, exhibits typically male characteristics of physical valor and military planning. She is very much a masculine character in a female guise.

The heroic figure in *The Arabian Nights* by contrast is portrayed, in the context of the cultural terms of the time, as a model "feminine" woman. Shahrazad has the qualities of the idealized woman in Arab–Islamic culture. She is the attractive, educated, well-brought-up daughter of a high-ranking official. Here, the feminine heroine replaces the masculine hero of the *sira.* Instead of a traditional battlefield in which the hero proves himself, the heroine of *The Arabian Nights* carries out her struggle in a boudoir, while sitting in bed. She is not armed with weapons and an arsenal, but with narratives and discourses. While the *sira* is the story of a battle told in different ways, *The Arabian Nights* is the story of a story related in many forms. The hero of the *sira* is a person of great deeds while Shahrazad is a person of great words. She is a mock hero who does not budge from her regular posture, while 'Antar, for instance—the most celebrated heroic figure—moves East and West, covering practically the entire globe as known to medieval Arabs.

The hero of the regular *sira* re-emerges in *The Arabian Nights* as an anti-hero. The anti-hero is a protagonist who conspicuously lacks heroic stature. Shahrazad plays the leading role in *The Arabian Nights* but she is more of an anti-heroic type working against the classic norms of the *sira's* hero. Her actions are not imitations of grand events that occur in life, but reworkings of stories that are already given. While the *sira* is essentially a mimesis in the heroic mode, *The Arabian Nights* is an imitation of an already existing mimesis, which I shall call meta-mimesis. Just as metalanguage is a language speaking of language, meta-mimesis is imitation speaking of imitation. The source of mimesis is life or nature, and the source of meta-mimesis is literature or culture.

On the level of plot and fictional intrigue, the *sira* has a complex narrative machinery characterized by length, loose divisions, transmission devices, and digressive material. However, the narrative whole retains a linear integrity and persistent continuity in the history of characters. It has basically a continuous episodic structure despite the distracting sidetracks. An examination of the epical structure of "Sirat 'Umar ibn al-Nu'man" reveals the rigorous symmetry in the narrative organization and the developmental progression of events.

The narrative of 'Umar ibn al-Nu'man covers three generations: that of King 'Umar, his two sons and daughter, and his grandchildren. It is the story of the eventual triumph of Islam against its enemies. In the end, "when her companions saw what befell her, all embraced in a body the faith of Al-Islam."[18]

Though the *sira* digresses a great deal, it is always concerned with one man and his genealogical descendants. The family provides the connective thread. Eventually the sons and grandsons of King 'Umar undo the original transgression, so in a sense the circle is closed at the end. Though there are developments, one following the other, a crowding of stories and incidents, they all contribute to bringing the intrigue to an end, by canceling the original disruption or lack. In contrast, *The Arabian Nights,* with its digressions and stories, seems to lead nowhere—or rather seems to lead infinitely to more of the same thing. A synopsis of the events of "Sirat

'Umar ibn al-Nu'man" shows how the maze-like impression of the narrative reveals, on closer examination, definite patterns.

The characters in "Sirat 'Umar ibn al-Nu'man" are either believers or non-believers, and there is a struggle between them. A series of battles is related with lavish description of bloodletting, interspersed with love scenes. The quarrel is triggered by an innocent mistake. The Christian King Hardub captures a ship on which there is a beautiful maiden. He sends her—without knowing her identity—as a gift to King 'Umar ibn al-Nu'man, a Muslim who reigns in Baghdad. This maiden, Safiyya, who bears King 'Umar twins, turns out later to be none other than the daughter of another Christian king, Ifraydun (see genealogical chart, opposite page). Safiyya's father, angered by the captivity of his own daughter, consults with the villain of the story, Hardub's mother Dhat-al-Dawahi, and accordingly plans to play a trick on King 'Umar. King Ifraydun sends gifts to King 'Umar and asks to be sent military help, since a convoy destined to bring King Ifraydun three magical beads from an Arab prince has been attacked by King Hardub's soldiers. King 'Umar dispatches a force headed by his son Sharrkan and accompanied by his vizier Dandan. Sharrkan, while wandering, comes across Ibriza, the strong, handsome, and intelligent daughter of Hardub, who tells Sharrkan about the fraud and shows him that she herself possesses the magic beads. Sharrkan spends some time with Ibriza in her isolated quarters, until Dhat-al-Dawahi hears of it and arranges for Hardub's bishops to go and kill him. This starts a series of battles, fought by the three descendants of King 'Umar: Sharrkan, Daw'-al-Makan, and Kanmakan, respectively. Some of the fights are longer and more entangled than others, but they reproduce the chronological order of birth among the descendants of King 'Umar. The narrative deals first with the fortune of the eldest son, then with the twins, and last with the youngest son. The story ends with Rumzan, son of the Muslim King ('Umar) and the Christian Princess (Ibriza), recognizing who his father is, capturing his villain great-grandmother (Dhat-al-Dawahi), and putting her to death.

Though both brothers Sharrkan and Daw'-al-Makan participate in fighting against the infidels, they start in completely opposite directions. Sharrkan goes to fight the Rum in Byzantium and Daw'-al-Makan goes (with his twin sister) to Mecca for the pilgrimage. Hence, one goes north for *jihad* (holy war) and the other south for *hajj* (holy visit).

Daw'-al-Makan and his sister go to Mecca despite the refusal of their father (it is recalled that Sharrkan went in the opposite direction at the command of his father). On the way back from Mecca, Daw'-al-Makan and his sister pass by Jerusalem. There they depart unwillingly. The sister

Nuzhat-al-Zaman, while trying to raise some money for her sick brother, is kidnapped by a wicked bedouin. Her sick brother, who should be taken to a hospital in Damascus, gets dropped off by the camel-driver at the furnace of a public bath. But both are saved from their predicament, the sister by a merchant who buys her and the brother by a bath-worker who takes care of him.

Here, the problem of mistaken identity comes back. Nuzhat-al-Zaman is sold to the governor of Damascus, who happens to be her step-brother. Unknowingly they marry and beget a daughter (Qadafakan), but once the

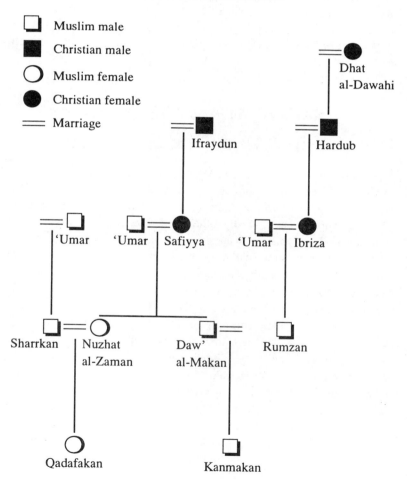

Genealogical Chart of the Main Characters
in "Sirat 'Umar Ibn al-Nu'man"

incestuous relationship is revealed through the beads (brought to King 'Umar by Ibriza who joined the Muslim camp, and given as a token to his children), the marriage is annulled and Nuzhat-al-Zaman marries the Chamberlain *(hajib)* Sasan.

The experience of the brother, Daw'-al-Makan, and the sister, Nuzhat-al-Zaman, of having one bad deed done to them by one character, balanced by a good deed done to them by another, is perfectly matched by the experience of Ibriza, the Christian princess who joined the Muslims. She gets pregnant (through rape) by King 'Umar. When nearing term, she sets out to go to her parents, accompanied by her slave girl Murjana and her black male slave Ghudban. But, having given birth to a male boy (Rumzan) while on the way, she is approached by her black slave, who wants to have sexual intercourse with her. When she refuses, he kills her and runs away. Murjana, the slave girl, takes care of the baby and, though he is brought up in the court of Christian kings, she ultimately reveals his Muslim identity to him.

Role of Minor Characters in "Sirat 'Umar Ibn al-Nu'man"

At the end of the story, the three bad types—the bedouin, the camel-driver, and the black slave—are captured by chance and, as they are relating their own stories and life histories, they are recognized as the villains and are slain for their misdeeds. On the other hand, the three good types—the merchant, the bath-worker, and the slave girl—are rewarded for their deeds. Such symmetry is also typical of the relationship between two prominent figures in the story: Chamberlain Sasan, who wants to deprive the natural heir of Nu'man's dynasty from his throne, and the vizier Dandan, who is constantly seeing to the well-being of the Nu'man clan.

The battles are innumerable and seem to dominate the narrative in the most haphazard way. Yet there are certain patterns that can be discerned. Every effective advance of the Christian armies emulates the initial trickery engineered by Dhat-al-Dawahi. Twice that old woman disguises herself as a pious Muslim and manages to infiltrate the ranks of the Muslims, the first time causing the death of King 'Umar and the second time that of his eldest son Sharrkan.

The long epic is further complicated by relating stories told while the Muslims are besieging Constantinople, and by a love affair between the two cousins, Kanmakan and Qadafakan. However, what we have, despite the sensation of being overwhelmed by events, is a tripartite composition. The first part is the introduction of the intrigue based on unrevealed identities, the second part represents a thickening and developing of the intrigue, and the third part is an end-game where the misunderstanding is revealed. In the beginning as well as in the end, bad deeds play a major role: they both trigger and resolve the problem. The end of the story coincides with the uncovering of the true ties between the various characters and each receiving his or her just dues. At this point the infidels are converted to the cause. Complete recognition coincides with the final reversal, in the best Aristotelian tradition, and the story ends.[19] In fact, this *sira* can be understood at the deep level of organization as a movement from the inaugural fight between Ibriza and Dhat-al-Dawahi to the final fight between Ibriza's son and Dhat-al-Dawahi. The first confrontation is depicted as a wrestling match between the young woman Ibriza and her grandmother Dhat-al-Dawahi. Ibriza triumphs but the match is only a game. At the end, Ibriza's son Rumzan overcomes his cunning great-grandmother and kills her. The beginning foreshadows the end, and the *sira* of 'Umar ibn al-Nu'man can be summed up as a series of intricate transformations that change the jest into the dead serious.

"Sirat 'Umar ibn al-Nu'man" offers an epic construction of many interwoven plots which modify each other and contribute to the unity of the whole. This is not to say that every element of the *sira* is functional in the development of the main plot. There are certain stories related for distraction, such as those of "Taj al-Muluk" and "'Aziz and 'Aziza," which are told by the vizier Dandan in order to divert Daw'-al-Makan while besieging Constantinople and grieving over the loss of his brother. The story told by the slave woman Bakun about the opium-eater is for diversion as well. Such stories do not in themselves change the chain of narration. They are "free" narratives, because they do not change the situation.[20] However, the three stories told toward the end of the *sira* by the bedouin, the black slave, and the camel-driver, respectively, play an important functional role in the narrative. They are biographical and reveal the past history of these three characters; they are instrumental in the restoration of order and justice. They are examples of "bound" narrative.

The Arabian Nights, in contrast, has the multiplicity of characters, actions, and plots of the *sira* but none of the *sira*'s integration of these components in a sustained and syntagmatic whole. *The Arabian Nights* lacks compositional symmetry in the arrangement of Shahrazad's tales. The intrigue in Shahrazad's discourse is ultimately circular, while in "Sirat 'Umar ibn al-Nu'man"—despite certain digressions in the unfolding of narrative—it remains linear. *The Arabian Nights* uses the techniques, devices, and monumentality of the *sira* in a parodic fashion; they are emptied of their classical literary function. Unlike the *sira,* there is no definite climax or explicit recognition in the plot of *The Arabian Nights* as a whole (though in most of the individual stories told by Shahrazad, there is a traditional narrative intrigue and its solution). *The Arabian Nights* seems to imitate the model of the *sira* while simultaneously deforming its purpose. The *raison d'être* of the *sira* is edification, while that of *The Arabian Nights* is entertainment.

The subversion of the *sira* is sensed on the deeper register of narration, as I have shown; it is also experienced by the reader on the surface register of verbal representation. The following examples demonstrate how a given situation in the enframed *sira* is imitated and subverted in the frame story.

In the *sira,* 'Umar ibn al-Nu'man is presented as a king who had a full-fledged harem which he managed rather judiciously:

> King 'Umar had four wives legally married, but Allah had vouchsafed him no son by them, save Sharrkan, whom he had begotten upon one of them, and the rest were barren. Moreover, he had three hundred and sixty concubines, after the number of days in the Coptic year, who were of all nations; and he had furnished for each and every one a private chamber within his own palace. For he had built twelve pavilions, after the number of the months, each containing thirty private chambers, which thus numbered three hundred and three score, wherein he lodged his handmaids: and he appointed accordingly to law for each one her night, when he lay with her and came not again to her for a full year and on this wise he abode for a length of time.[21]

In *The Arabian Nights,* Shahrayar, too, has a different woman every night, but unlike King 'Umar he does not make their round the next year, and their chambers and pavilions are more macabre: "and thenceforth he made it his regular custom, every time that he took a virgin to his bed, to kill her at the expiration of the night."[22] It should be noted that the language remains essentially the same, an objective presentation. Sadistic as Shahrayar's butchery is, we cannot detect lyrical despair nor revolt. The stability of the language, while the content has been inverted, gives us an uncanny sense of travesty.

There are some striking stylistic inversions in both stories, especially when it comes to scenes of war and love. While Sharrkan, for instance, in a fight with the Christian maiden, Ibriza, experiences the wrestling match as an amorous encounter, Shahrayar (and Shahzaman) experience love-making with the woman kidnapped by the demon as a defeating battle. Here is how Sharrkan's fight is presented:

> Then she called out to him, 'O Moslem, come on and let us wrestle ere the break of morning' and tucked up her sleeves from a forearm like fresh curd, which illumined the whole place with its whiteness, and Sharrkan was dazzled by it. Then he bent forwards and clapped his palms by way of challenge, she doing the like, and caught hold of her, and the two grappled and gripped and interlocked hands and arms. Presently, he shifted his hands to her slender waist, when his finger tips sank into the soft folds of the middle, breeding languishment, and he fell a-trembling like the Persian reed in the roaring gale.[23]

The act of love is presented, in Shahrayar's encounter with the kidnapped woman, as a confrontation which Shahrayar would rather decline. The incident shows a reluctant man who is obliged to perform love-making at the threat of a female. To confirm the battle-like aspect of it, the woman, using transgressive language, asks Shahrayar to "stab her violently." The scene just recounted has the effect of deflating the romanticized actions of the traditional love scenes of the *sira*. The Olympian loses its loftiness, and becomes decidedly un-Olympian.

The price or reward paid for display of form in *The Arabian Nights* is estrangement, which is experienced against the disjunctive progression of the text. *The Arabian Nights* uses the techniques present in "Sirat 'Umar ibn al-Nu'man," such as the insertion of stories and the proliferation of incidents, but without leading to a satisfactory resolution of opposition. The technique seems to be liberated from its subsidiary status in the narrative, and it seems to have a momentum of its own.

Without recognizing the ironic thrust of *The Arabian Nights,* we would be puzzled by its structure. When some critics find themselves unable to resolve problems within the text, they are likely to declare the work in question of poor quality. In *The Arabian Nights,* for example, every time one stumbles across a disjunction, it is invariably blamed by one critic or another on the ignorance of the "reciter," who had neither the benefit of their liberal education nor exquisite taste.[24] The story of 'Umar ibn al-Nu'man is illustrative; it has been considered by many critics as an intrusion into the corpus of *The Arabian Nights,* missing completely the element of self-irony.

Lane found "Sirat 'Umar ibn al-Nu'man" "objectionable" and did not include it in his translation, except for the interpolated stories within it, those of "Taj al-Muluk" and "'Aziz and 'Aziza." Burton translates it but points out that "it has its *longueurs* and at times is longsome enough, but it is interesting as a comparison between the chivalry of Islam and European knight errantry."[25]

Gerhardt, who analyzed all the stories of *The Arabian Nights* in one way or another, decided not to deal with it, saying:

> I have left out a group consisting of the two long novels of chivalry and warfare, Omar Ibn Nu'man and Ajib and Gharib, because these works which were never intended to form a part of the collection and remain alien to its spirit, represent a subject which is only on the borderline of '1001 Nights' stories, while their material requires special scholarship.[26]

But disjunctions as well as repetitions can be intentional, and irony thrives on both. The irony of *The Arabian Nights* is not a singular case in the history of Arabic literature. Ash'ab, whose stories vary from the comic to the ironic, provides us with a brilliant anecdote that parodies *isnad* (chain of transmission). Ash'ab says that he heard Ikrima (or some other well-known transmitter) report that the Prophet had said that two qualities characterized the true believer. Asked which they were, Ash'ab replied, "Ikrima had forgotten one, and I have forgotten the other."[27]

The essence of the ironic is the paradoxical. *The Arabian Nights* both mocks and preserves, ridicules and redeems the *sira*. We have in literature a number of examples where a minor plot caricaturizes the main plot. Shakespeare is a master of this construction. The specificity of *The Arabian Nights* stems from the fact that the reader recognizes the irony fully after reading the embedded *sira*. The perception of the ironic comes after one has already been a victim of a straight reading. The key to the box is within the box, as it were. The joke is basically played on the reader, and it is characteristically sadistic humor.

Irony is particularly becoming to Shahrazad's discourse, given her desperate struggle for life—as Jankélévitch puts it, "L'ironie devance toujours le désespoir."[28] It is even more becoming that she chose to ironize the *sira*. For in the *sira,* we have the transformation of a life into a narrative. In Shahrazad's story, it is the very opposite, the transformation of narrative into life.

5

BEASTLY RHETORIC

Immediately following "Sirat 'Umar ibn al-Nu'man," the reader of *The Arabian Nights* encounters a cluster of animal stories, most of which can be classified as fables. These are related by Shahrazad at Shahrayar's request for tales of "beasts and birds."[1] The story of "King Jali'ad and his son Wirdkhan" is another intensive example of the presence of the fable.[2] The use of fables in *The Arabian Nights* provides us with an example of the structural repetition of a narrative segment of the frame story into the corpus of the enframed stories. This chapter explores the fables of *The Arabian Nights* both in their figural and symbolic organizations and in their effect on the reader.[3] I will try to show the kinship between the fables in the frame story (related by the vizier to his daughter Shahrazad) and the fables related by Shahrazad. It is important, first, to examine the term "fable" and then to proceed to cover its particular manifestation in the text.

The fable is an instance of an oblique discourse. Its indirectness is instantly seized by the readers. On even a quick reading of the fables, we sense their clarity and simplicity, at least by comparison to the ambiguities and complexities of irony. The concrete aspect of the animal world in a fable leads to the abstract aphorism, almost automatically, requiring hardly any reflection on the part of the reader.

A fable is an allegory in which animals or plants speak like human beings. The first collection of Greek fables is attributed to Aesop in the sixth century B.C. They "conveyed moral or satirical lessons in the briefest and driest of verses."[4] In France, Jean de La Fontaine, who contributed a great deal to the prestige of the genre, elevated the fable to moral and philosophic planes, while Ivan Andreyevich Krylov, who popularized the genre in Russia, used it for social criticism.[5] The fable was also one of the forms which tapped the narrative productivity of the Arabs. The most famous collection of Arabic fables is that of *Kalila wa Dimna*—whose origin goes back to the Indian *Panchatantra*—which was Arabized by Ibn al-Muqaffa' from its Pahlavi translation. Other translations, adaptations, and emulations poured forth for centuries to come.[6] The function of the fable is educational; it demonstrates how to conduct oneself in life in order to achieve worldly peace, wealth, power, and privilege. It can be humanitarian or opportunistic, but its lessons are always relevant for the here and now rather than for the hereafter. As a counterpart stand the pious tales, which aim at delivering precepts that would secure eternal life.

Typology of Fables

The fable in *The Arabian Nights* occurs for the first time in the frame story, when Shahrazad's father is trying to dissuade her from marrying Shahrayar: "'Then,' said he, 'I fear for thee that the same will befall thee that happened in the case of the ass and the bull and the husbandman.'"[7]

She then asks him to clarify, and he accordingly relates the fable (see the synopsis in Chapter Two). It should be recalled that there are two fables juxtaposed in that section: "The Ass and the Bull" and "The Cock and the Dog." The fable of "The Ass and the Bull" starts with the disparity of fortune between the two animals: the Bull worked hard in the fields and the Ass was attended to and only occasionally used for transport. The initial situation is that of an imbalance where the Ass is "up," so to speak, and the Bull is "down." The Ass convinces the Bull to simulate sickness and consequently avoid work. But their master, who understands animal languages, simply takes the Ass instead of the "sick" Bull to work in the fields. Hence, the situation is reversed dramatically, with the Bull "up" and the Ass "down."

The Ass, regretting his advice, contrives to get out of his unfortunate situation by convincing the Bull that he will be slaughtered if he continues to seem sick. The Bull, believing the Ass, exhibits signs of health and agility the next morning and is taken to the field instead of the Ass. Thus, the situation reverts to its initial imbalance. The entire fable has three movements, which look graphically like a see-saw.

This animal story is quite different from that of "The Cock and the Dog," related in the same context, which is brief enough to justify quotation in full:

> Now he [the husbandman] had a cock, with fifty hens under him, and he had also a dog; and he heard the dog call to the cock, and reproach him, saying, Art thou happy when our master is going to die? The cock asked, How so? and the dog related to him the story; upon which the cock exclaimed, by Allah! Our master

has little sense: I have fifty wives; and I please this, and provoke that; while he has but one wife, and cannot manage this
affair with her. Why does he not take some twigs of the mul-
berry tree, and enter her chamber, and beat her until she dies or
repents? She would never, after that, ask him a question respect-
ing anything.[8]

This fable is very different from the previous one. First, it contains hardly
any action. It is basically a dialogue between a Dog and a Cock, in which
the latter defines his relationship to his wives, whom he manages cleverly.
Also, the effectiveness of this fable does not stem from a positional transformation, as in the case of "The Ass and the Bull," but from a radical
reappraisal of a given situation. The story told earlier from the perspective
of the farmer who finds himself in an intolerable dilemma (either he pleases
his wife and dies, or lives with a disgruntled woman) is now seen through
the eyes of a cock. By changing the narrative point of view (from the
farmer to the Cock), the perspective is changed and the reader is driven to
a new appreciation of the situation.[9] The cock is really a pretext for a
defamiliarized depiction of a given situation. The cock disregards entirely
the emotional ties that commit his master to his wife (and cousin). All he
can see is the unreasonable demands made by the wife. He contrasts his
master's clumsiness in handling his one wife with his own clever control
of fifty wives simultaneously, and questions his master's common sense.
These two fables demonstrate two distinct types of operations. I shall refer
from now on to the type of "The Ass and Bull" as the AB type and to that
of "The Cock and the Dog" as the CD type.

The AB fable requires an overall view of the internal movement intrinsic to the story, while the CD type imposes a bifocal perspective. The operations at work in these fables are those of oscillation in AB and undercutting in CD. In the AB fable, the up-and-down movements carry the
structural burden of meaning, while in the CD fable the juxtaposition of
two points of view is crucial in making the semantic point. These operations govern the animal stories as well as the pious stories in *The Arabian
Nights*. I shall concentrate on the fables.

In the first cluster of fables (covering nights 146–153), Shahrazad begins by relating the fable of "The Animals and the Carpenter." This fable
offers an excellent study of undercutting as described in type CD. It presents "man" from the viewpoint of both wild and domesticated animals.
Regarding man, to quote the duck citing a poet, "With his tongue, he will
offer thee sweet expressions, but he will elude thee like the fox."[10] The
story of this fable can be summed up as follows. The peacock and the peahen
resort to an island to live peacefully. There they encounter a frightened

duck who relates to them her fears of man, son of Adam. She, in turn, encounters a young lion who tells her of his father's advice to avoid man. Then come along the ass, the horse, and the camel, relating in their own specific terms how man abuses them. The young lion, who swears to avenge his fellow beasts, meets with a carpenter who talks him into walking into his very own cage. Having witnessed man's treachery, the duck takes refuge in the wilderness to avoid man, but is nevertheless captured later.

The process of undercutting is intensified with the description given by each of the five animals, and is further confirmed by the ingenious mode of catching the lion and the eventual capture of the duck on her far-off island.

Here is the image of man as seen by the duck in a nocturnal dream:

> And know that the son of Adam circumventeth the fish, and draweth them out from the waters, and shooteth the birds with an earthen bullet, and entrappeth the elephant by his craftiness. No one is secure from the mischief of the son of Adam, and neither bird nor wild beast can escape from him.[11]

Then the ass running away from man gives them an empirical account of man's wickedness:

> My fear is lest he employ a strategem against me, and ride me; for he hath a thing called the pad, which he placeth on my back, and a thing called the girth, which he draweth round my belly, and a thing called the crupper, which he inserteth beneath my tail, and a thing called the bit, which he putteth in my mouth, and he maketh for me a goad, and goadeth me with it, and he requireth me to exert myself beyond my ability in running. When I stumble he curseth me; and when I bray, he revileth me. Afterwards when I have grown old, and can no longer run, he putteth upon me a pack saddle of wood, and committeth me to the water-sellers *(sakkas),* who lead me with water upon my back from the river, in goatskins and in similar things, such as jars, and I cease not to suffer abasement and contempt and fatigue until I die, when they throw me upon the mounds of rubbish to the dogs.[12]

Then along comes a majestic, stout horse fleeing man and relates how he gets treated by the descendants of Adam. Finally, a huge-looking camel comes along and tells of his own oppression at the hands of man:

> He putteth in my nose a string called a nosering, and upon my head he putteth a halter: then he commiteth me to the least of his children, and the little child draweth me along by the string, not withstanding my great bulk. They load me also with the heaviest burdens, and take me with them on long journeys. They

employ me in difficult labours during the hours of the night and the day, and when I have grown old, and have become disabled, my master no longer endureth my society, but selleth me to the butcher who slaughtereth me, and selleth my skin to the tanners, and my flesh to the cooks.[13]

Then an old carpenter appears, claiming that he too is fleeing man, The lion, struck by his frailty, asks him what his business is. The carpenter claims that he is going to build a house for the lynx to protect him from the treachery of man. The lion, who considers himself the king of the beasts, sees fit to claim the priority of such a house. Once the carpenter has the lion enter into the presumed house (a cage), he then nails the plank shut and has the lion burned.

The structure of this narrative is that of repetitive and growing undercutting. The reader, necessarily man, is presented with his portrait as seen by lesser creatures. The story presents the fears of the duck, a small, weak creature, based on hearsay and vision. Then the three animals, ass, horse, and camel, who represent an ascending scale in terms of size, present their fears and exploitions. Finally, the lion, the very king of all animals, is captured and killed by man.

Duck, ass, horse, camel, and lion: this is a progression in the scale of strength. Each "point of view" deepens and furthers the undercutting process. The duck condemns in general terms. The ass, horse, and camel attest from first-hand experience how vicious man's treatment is, and the incident of the lion's capture gives the central theme of man's craftiness its finishing touch. By relating commonly shared and acknowledged facts, but presenting them from "below," as it were, the unsuspected guile of man is exposed.

The undercutting technique succeeds only when we imagine that what is said is consistent with what we know. There need not be a compatibility between the text and the reality, but an illusion of correspondence between them is indispensable. For example, the reports of the ass, horse, and camel give us the firm impression that they correspond to facts outside the text. But very few readers know whether camels have noserings, in fact. It is immaterial whether camels do or do not. The text convinces us by simulating reality, not by documenting it. Installing a nosering seems a likely thing to do to a camel. It is likely not because we can go to the Bedouin and check whether in fact a string is put into the nose of the camel, but because the very term "camel" suggests a domesticated animal and the term "nosering" is symbolic of subservient status. The nosering is emblematic of the camel's exploitation in the service of man. The "little child," as the text enunciates, drawing along "the great bulk" of the camel is an

image which is generated by a literary cliché common in fables. It is the
little leading the big by the nose; an image of mastery underlies the beastly
rhetoric of the camel. Equally, when the ass and the horse bemoan their
fortune and relate the intricate and techncial aspects of saddling them,
they are both elaborating on the commonly accepted notion of ass and
horse as beasts of burden. In a sense, their discourse is an extended definition of what they are.

Undercutting occurs again in the fable of "The Cock and the Dog,"
simultaneous with the actualization of the properties inherent in the world
"cock." The cock is not simply the adult male fowl known technically as
Gallus gallus. The word evokes a mental image of pompous masculinity
that takes itself seriously; at least it does that to the Arab reader, for whom
the image of a cock is used to stand for a slightly ridiculous male chauvin-
ist—something akin to the connotations of "rooster," "cock," and "cocky"
in English. Other male animals carry connotations of virility, but with somewhat different implications. The ram, for example, stands for sacrificial
virility, no doubt due to his association with the Qur'anic narrative of
Abraham (Sura XXXVII). The stallion, on the other hand, emphasizes the
creative aspect of virility. Not only are poets called stallions in Arabic, as
I pointed out earlier, but there are many works in medieval Arab criticism
devoted to the classification of poets according to their "stallion-ness."

The story of the cock does little more than elaborate the ready-made
imagery of "cockery." *The Arabian Nights* itself provides us with the associations inherent in a cock, within the tale of "'Aziz and 'Aziza"—which
is embedded in "Sirat 'Umar ibn al-Nu'man":

> 'All I need of thee is that thou do with me even as the cock
> doth.' I asked, 'and what doth the cock?' Upon this she laughed
> and clapped her hands and fell over on her back for excess of
> merriment: then she sat up and smiled and said 'O light of my
> eyes really dost thou not know what the cock's duty is?' 'No,
> by Allah' replied I, and she, 'The cock's duty is to eat and drink
> and tread.' I was abashed at her words and asked, 'Is that the
> cock's duty?' 'Yes,' answered she.[14]

The fable of "The Waterfowl and the Tortoise" is another one of type
CD. Here, the undermining is not comic as in "The Cock and the Dog."
nor maliciously descriptive of Man's mental superiority as in "The Ani
mals and the Carpenter," but rather it triggers feelings of awe and dread in
the reader. This fable shows us the end of a slain man as seen by a bird.
The waterfowl finds the corpse of a dead man marked with cuts of spears
and swords. The waterfowl is delighted to have his food assured for a
while. In the meantime, some ravenous birds come along and tear the corpse

into pieces. Fearing them, the waterfowl has to flee. In his exile he meets a tortoise, with whom he exchanges a conversation on the pains and sorrows of separation. When the waterfowl returns to his habitat, he finds that there is nothing left of the corpse but the bones. The danger of the birds of prey having passed, the waterfowl goes to inform the tortoise and they live happily together until the death of the waterfowl, who falls victim to a falcon. The fable seems like a pretext for showing a man's end, from the point of view of the birds that prey on his flesh. The fable disturbs in a discrete way.

The most dramatic example of tension arising from the shift of perspective is the fable of "The Sparrow and the Eagle" which is inserted into the fable of "The Fox and the Crow." The sparrow beholds an eagle who flies down and carries off a lamb. The sparrow, in imitation, flies down and lands upon the back of a sheep whose fleece has been matted with his dung. The sparrow's feet get tangled in the wool and he cannot set himself free. He is caught by a shepherd who plucks out the feathers from his wings and gives him to his children. The maxim of this fable is enunciated by the shepherd when his children ask him what it is: "This is he that aped a greater than himself and came to grief."[15] The trouble with the sparrow's perception is that he sees the action with the eye of an eagle and does not make any allowance for the change of the viewer, namely himself, and the difference between the two.

Type AB of the fable is exemplified by the fairly long story, "The Fox and the Wolf," in which the hierarchical relationships of the two protagonists are actualized through four distinct situations: the position of the wolf changes from (1) up to (2) down to (3) up to (4) down, and that of the fox follows the inverse order.

In the initial position, the fox is mistreated by the wolf who is stronger than he is. The fox's counseling of equity is reprimanded. The fox then arranges to have the wolf trapped in a snare set up in a nearby vineyard, thus reversing their hierarchical relationship. The wolf asks the fox for pardon and begs to be helped out of the pit. A repartee takes place between them, with abundant verse quotations, in which the fox compares the wolf to the falcon and begins relating the fable. However, the fox is carried away by excitement and gets so close that the wolf manages to pull him down by the tail, thus changing the balance of power once more. But the fox uses another stratagem and persuades the wolf to stand up while the fox climbs on his back and out of the pit. Another repartee takes place between the fox and the wolf, similar in tone and argument to the first one. Here again, the fox tells the wolf a fable, that of "The Snake and the Charmer." The fox leaves the wolf in the pit, where he meets his end at the hands of the vineyard owner. Two mini-fables inserted in this macro-fable are related by the fox and deal with ingratitude—the partridge trusts the falcon which eats him up, and a charmer saves a snake which then bites him. The schematization of the fable reveals that the intrigue repeats itself in almost identical terms.

The essential principle of the AB-type fable is that the protagonists are rivals and they play a zero-sum game. Any advantage to one incurs a disadvantage to the other. One's loss is the other's gain. This is also the principle of algebraic equations. In a system like this, there cannot be any room for the development of the characters. Only when the basis is organic, as in many novels, can the character grow. The AB-type fable allows only positional exchanges. Such narrative rules as seem to govern this type of fable also exist in phonetics. The linguistic phenomenon of metathesis, where two phonemes in a word are transposed, is parallel.

Two other fables, "The Mouse and the Weasel" and "The Cat and the Crow," are both of the AB type, and although they share the same structure, one is concerned with plotting against a friend and the other with plotting for a friend. In the fable of "The Mouse and the Weasel," a woman husks and spreads out sesame which has been prescribed for her sick husband. The weasel carries the grain to its hole. When the woman returns and sees that most of the grain has disappeared, she sits watching in the hope of catching the thief. The weasel sees what is going on and decides to bring back a few sesame seeds to convince the woman that he is not responsible for the loss. The weasel's plan works and the woman keeps vigilance waiting to catch the thief in action. In the meantime, the weasel goes to the mouse and fabricates a story about how everyone in the household has had his fill of sesame, and it is time for the mouse to help herself. The mouse rushes heedlessly to the sesame and starts eating it, whereupon she is struck and killed by the woman. The axis in this fable centers on innocence–guilt.

In the fable of "The Cat and the Crow," the same crafty device is used, but in order to save a comrade. Two friends, the cat and the crow, are under a tree when a leopard approaches. The crow flies up, but the cat cannot escape. He asks the crow to help him, and the latter flies to a nearby shepherd and dog. He flies very close to the face of the dog, who then follows him. The crow flies barely out of reach of the dog until he leads him to the tree. The leopard, frightened by the dog, leaves the scene; thus the cat is saved. The axis in this fable revolves around danger–security.

On this figural plane of fables, where internal relationships are explored, we find that there are basically two operations at work with an unlimited number of variations. These two operations can be called defamiliarization and positional inversion. The didactic purpose of the fable varies, but the modalities of the discourse remain the same.

The Fable as Simile

As for the symbolic organization, the fable in *The Arabian Nights* exhibits specific characteristics that can define it as an extended simile. Analysis of the story of "King Jali'ad and his son Wirdkhan" should demonstrate this amply.

The structure of the story of King Jali'ad is fairly simple, but it is complicated by the fact that almost everyone in the story utters fables instead of speaking directly. Injustice, for example, is not named in the narrative dialogue but is alluded to through a fable that signifies injustice. King Jali'ad is endowed with everything that a king's heart might desire, except a child. One night he has a puzzling dream in which he sees fire coming from a tree that he has just watered. The King calls his chief vizier Shimas and asks him to explain the dream. Shimas interprets the dream, but only partially. He says that the king is going to beget a son and refrains from continuing. The king calls upon his oneiromancers to interpret his dream, and after deliberation one of them advances an explanation. The king is going to beget a son, who will grow up to be an oppressor, and what befell "The Mouse and the Cat" will befall him. This fable is a simple narrative about the Mouse who takes pity on the Cat and lets her in. Soon after, the Cat tries to devour the Mouse. Just then, a Dog passes by and seizes the Cat, who is forced to release the Mouse.

> Then the hound brake her neck and dragging her [the Cat] forth of the hole, threw her down dead: and thus was exemplified the truth of the saying, 'Who hath compassion shall at the last be compassionated. Who so oppresseth shall presently be oppressed.'
> 'This, then, O King,' added the interpreter, 'is what befell the Mouse and the Cat and teacheth that none should break faith with those who put trust in him; for whoever doth perfidity and treason, there shall befal him the like of that which befell the Cat. As a man meteth, so shall it be meted unto him, and he who betaketh himself to good shall gain his eternal reward.'[16]

That night King Jali'ad sleeps with one of his favorite wives and she conceives. He is enthralled and gives the good tidings to his chief vizier

Shimas, who warns him about anticipating things, for he who speaks before something is accomplished is like "The Fakir and the Jar of Skimmed Milk" (a parallel version of La Fontaine's "La laitière et le pot au lait"). The king's wife gives birth to a son, and the dignitaries come to give their congratulations. The seven viziers give their ceremonial discourses, illustrating their points with appropriate fables.

The education of the young Prince Wirdkhan is attended to by distinguished professors. When he is twelve, the chief vizier Shimas tests him in the different branches of knowledge. Wirdkhan responds very well and demonstrates the exccllence of his education, illustrating fine points with fables and devout tales. When King Jali'ad dies, his son Wirdkhan takes over but is soon distracted from the affairs of his kingdom by women. Using a fable, Shimas advises him to attend to the people, but Wirdkhan's favorite woman manages to sway him, illustrating her point with a tale. For the second time, Shimas tries to give his advice, and again the woman dissuades Wirdkhan. For the third time, Shimas tries the same advice and again King Wirdkhan is turned away by the woman's talk. Every discourse is properly accompanied by fables. Wirdkhan, in order to do away with criticism, kills his chief vizier as well as the prominent and honest men of his kingdom. Soon, a neighboring king, making use of the fact that Wirdkhan has done away with his leaders, sends an ultimatum to him. Wirdkhan is baffled and his favorite woman cannot help him. He regrets what he has done and recounts the fable of "The Francolin and the Tortoises." However, a young boy, who turns out to be the son of Shimas, helps him contrive a trick to impress the neighboring king, and to discourage him from an invasion. The trick works, the boy is made heir to the throne, and the ill-advising woman is punished.

All in all, twenty fables are related within the story of King Jali'ad. One should take note of the fact that the fable, an indirect manner of communicating, becomes a story that is triggered by an enigmatic dream. The inaugural nocturnal vision expressing a message in a symbolic language leads to a story which makes consistent use of the symbolic mode.

The above fables behave as similes in the following ways. A simile is "a comparison of one thing with another, explicitly announced by the word 'like' or 'as.'"[17] In all of the fables in the story of King Jali'ad (except for one) this analogy is made, using an instrument of comparison. Shimas addresses the king after his son is born, saying: "And now Almighty Allah hath accepted of us and answered our petition and brought us speedy relief, even as He did to the fishes in the pond of the water."[18] The second vizier introduces his fable in this manner: "There hath betided thee that which betideth the Crow and the Serpent."[19] The sixth vizier phrases the analogy as follows: "And in this thou hast fared even as fared the Spider and the wind."[20]

At times, the comparsion is carried out by the verb *yashbahu,* which means "resembles" and which is rendered by Burton as "favour" (i.e., bearing resemblance to) as in the discourse of the third vizier: "And indeed he that is rebellious and seeketh other than the dole which God hath decreed unto him and for him, favoureth the Wild Ass and the Jackal."[21]

The one example where the story occurs without an instrument of comparison happens not to be, strictly speaking, a fable but a parable. It functions like a submerged simile, that is, a simile with the instrument of comparison suppressed.

> For indeed it hath reached me that many men have come to ruin through their women, and amongst others a certain man who perished through conversation with his wife at her command. The King asked, 'How was that?' and Shimas answered saying, 'Hear, O King, the tale of the Man and his Wife.'[22]

The fable is a special kind of simile—it is a proportional comparison which requires at least four terms. The fable of "The Mouse and the Cat," the first one related in the story of King Jali'ad, is about a cat who abuses a mouse and gets abused in his turn by a dog; this alludes to the end of the young prince. The comparison is not an analogy between the future king and a feline animal but between two relationships, that of cat to mouse on one hand and that of king to people on the other:

Cat : Mouse = King : People

The fate of the cat is parallel to that of the king. Since the equivalence is derived not from a correspondence between terms but between relationships, there is no reason to motivate the pair cat–king or mouse–people. In fact, the relationship between cat and king remains arbitrary. There are no ready-made symbolisms that would bring cats and kings or mice and people together. That is why it is easy to replace cat with wolf, fox, vulture, etc. The same is true of the mouse, which can be replaced at will by a pigeon, spider, or lizard, for example. But what remains essential to the equation is that the cat or its substitute should be bigger, stronger, or superior in some sense to the mouse or its substitute in order to make the relationship logical. It is obvious, then, that such a fable can be told in unlimited variations without compromising its integrity. The pheno-text, to use Barthes' terminology, changes with every variant, but the more intimate aspect of the text remains unchanged.[23]

The Function of the Fable

Fables, like similes, are used for a number of purposes: for illustration, decoration, relief, or suspense. Abu Hilal al-'Askari—the Fontanier of Arabic rhetorics—sees the prime purpose of simile as clarity and insistence on meaning.[24] Reversion to the indirect language of the simile, paradoxically enough, gets one closer to the point.

The foregoing study of the fables in the discourse of Shahrazad demonstrates that they are based on the duplication of structural patterns present in the fables of the frame story. Here, the relationship of enframing to framed is that of model to copies. In *The Arabian Nights,* the narration of stories is carried out in order to delay and eventually to overcome time. Narration serves as a liberating technique from time. However, the brief fable by itself is not particularly suited for struggling against time, so the brevity of the fable is compensated for by repetition. The intensive use of fable–similes in *The Arabian Nights* raises the question of their effect on the reader. The text, after all, is not simply a system of signification but a personal experience as well.

In *The Arabian Nights,* there are two configurations of fables and they affect the reader differently. In the first of these, fables flood the reader— they come one after the other without any syntactic order. In the other configuration, as in the story of "King Jali'ad and his Son Wirdkhan," they are rigorously placed to support different cases and causes. The effects of the two configurations are not the same. The repetition of the vacillating structural movement of the AB-type fable creates a euphoric sensation of rhythmic swaying. On the other hand, the defamiliarization of the CD-type fable disturbs the reader on a level that is perhaps not altogether conscious. The first configuration of fables, with its admixture of AB and CD types, creates a circuit combining the delightful and the painful. Perhaps this will explain why Shahrayar was lured by Shahrazad's fables—the effect of the two types of fable can be mesmerizing. Some texts do not cohere until we take the reader and the actual experience of reading into consideration. Aristotle, who was always concerned with the effect of the text on the reader, granted that good similes "have a lively effect."[25] A cluster of fables has an effect similar to that of an accumulation of similes.

In the second cluster of fables ("King Jali'ad and his Son Wirdkhan") other aspects of the fable affect the reader. The fable used as a simile is of adjunctive nature. Unlike a metaphor, one can dispense with similes. This is clear from the story of King Jali'ad, where the fables are added to reinforce an argument or enhance the meaning. Yet the size of the adjunct in the narrative seems out of proportion. It outweighs the unfolding aspect of the story. The sense of narrative narcissism is overwhelming, and a sense of competition between the adjunctive and the elemental is present throughout the entire story of King Jali'ad. The fable, which was apparently meant to be an auxiliary in the text, overshadows the textual progression, and the supplementary seems to intrude upon the basic. The instrument, which is what a fable ought to be, is not so instrumental any more. It is cultivated for its own sake.

Such deflection of the primary function of the fable is an instance of the all-too-pervasive tendency in the history of Arab aesthetics, where form seems to impose itself over content. The case of the genre of *maqama* (seance) is illustrative. It starts in the hands of Badi' al-Zaman al-Hamadhani as the adventure story of a witty, clever rogue, typical in the world of medieval Islam, and achieves at the hands of al-Hariri its culmination, where it ends up as a forum for the display of verbal punning. Such an evolution is all too common in the other arts as well. From the rug-maker to the scribe, the tendency to formalize is irresistible.

6
THE SPIRAL METAPHOR

One of the most moving figures in *The Arabian Nights*—besides that of
Shahrazad—is that of Sindbad. The shipwrecked mariner seems to be a
constant and privileged theme in world literature. The sea voyage, from
Homer to Coleridge, has had a particular hold on Western poetic imagination that cannot be adequately explained by reference to the role of seafar-
ing in the political economy of Europe. There are elements in the sea voyage which make it particularly suggestive of certain intellectual quests
and psychological operations; it is universally valid and, consequently, a
transhistoric medium of expression.

This chapter studies Sindbad's story,[1] which offers an example of the
simple form of sea voyages in order to extract the basic principles that
have contributed to its preservation and diffusion. The structure of a voyage has left its stamp on the second narrative block of the frame story,
where Shahrayar and his brother go out traveling in search of truth or,
rather, confirmation of doubts. Sindbad's voyage is a metaphoric reference to this original voyage (of Shahrayar and Shahzaman), though
Sindbad's quest is a particularly recurring one. The relationship of the
enframed to the frame is that of similarity in theme and of structural affinity, though the enframed Sindbad manages to turn the roundness of the
framing metaphor into a spiral.[2]

There are certain important elements in the story of Sindbad which somehow make it distinctive from other sea voyages. First and foremost, the
voyages are related by the traveler himself; they are autobiographical in
principle and are narrated in the first person singular. They are also quasi-
confessional in tone. The story of Sindbad's voyages is related by Sindbad
the Sailor, a wealthy Baghdadi living in a luxurious mansion, to Sindbad
the Porter, a poor and miserable worker, ostensibly to explain that riches
did not come to him effortlessly:

> He [Sindbad the Sailor] said to him, 'O Porter, know that my
> story is wonderful, and I will inform thee of all that happened to

me and befell me before I attained this prosperity and sat in this place wherein thou seest me. For I attained not this prosperity and this place save after severe fatigue and great trouble and many terrors. How often have I endured fatigue and toil in my early years! I have performed seven voyages, and connected with each voyage is a wonderful tale that would confound the mind.'[3]

The voyages of Sindbad offer a special case of embedding. It is not the usual enframed story but a case of perspectivism, similar to that used in Joseph Conrad's works. Both perspectivism and framing are compound manners of narration. The difference is that perspectivism uses composite forms of narration, the objective (the voice of the grammatical third person) and the subjective (the voice of the grammatical first person), while framing uses only one mode of presentation, and usually the objective one.[4]

Sindbad's narration of his story from the inside is in contrast to the objective representation made of him through the eyes of Sindbad the Porter. Sindbad is first introduced by an outward description by the porter, followed by the inner story told by the sailor:

And at the upper end of that chamber was a great and venerable man, in the sides of whose beard gray hairs had begun to appear. He was of handsome form, comely in countenance, with an aspect of gravity and dignity and majesty and stateliness.[5]

The specificity of Sindbad lies in the merging of the narrator with the persona. Once more we are confronted with the matricial core of *The Arabian Nights:* the interchangeability between life and fiction.

The Structure of the Voyage

How Sindbad views himself and his life can only be discerned by an analysis of the fundamental changes that he undergoes. Every voyage of Sindbad has the following schema: departure–landing(s)–return. In the seven voyages of Sindbad, the departure is always from Baghdad, Sindbad's native city, and the return is also to Baghdad via Basra. In none of the voyages does Sindbad have a precise destination—he undertakes the first voyage because he has wasted his inherited fortune and is trying to make some money. The following six voyages are motivated by a desire for the unknown. Sindbad is a strange hero, for unlike Ulysses, he leaves not because of a lack (except for the first voyage), but because of an abundance. He had everything that he desires, yet he always departs:

> When I returned from the second voyage, and was in a state of the utmost joy and happiness, rejoicing in my safety, having gained great wealth, as I related to you yesterday, God having compensated me for all that I had lost, I resided in the city of Baghdad for a length of time and in the most perfect prosperity and delight and joy and happiness. Then my soul became desirous of travel and diversion, and I longed for commerce and gain and profits; the soul being prone to evil.[6]

Here, one is struck by the singularity of Sindbad, who defies the studies so meticulously undertaken on the folktale. Dundes, inspired by Propp's work, sees the folktale as a combination of two nuclear components: lack and lack liquidated.[7] Sylvia Pavel in an interesting study[8] shows that the first grammatical rule of the tales in *The Arabian Nights* is:

TALE (récit) —> disequilibrium + equilibrium.

This is true of the voyage undertaken in block two of the framing narrative, where Shahrayar and Shahzaman leave in search of knowledge and confirmation. Having obtained knowledge through direct experience, they return home, and that is where the story of their voyage ends.

But Sindbad cannot fit here unless we consider his desire for "lack" as, in itself, a lack, which is a little too circular. Sindbad is a special case, because unlike the more reasonable heroes of folktales, he has an internal resistance to equilibrium and an unexplained drive for disequilibrium. Sindbad of course, does not cancel Dundes' law, or Pavel's rule, but he provides an exception to them. The case of Sindbad shows that there is inversion in the narrative rules of folktales. The effect of the inversion of narrative rules corresponds to that of grammatical inversions in language. It shakes us out of our complacency and heightens our perception of the message.

Inversion is an anomaly in the syntax, and Sindbad's story would have been simply an anti-folktale if it stopped there. But it does not. No sooner does the fickle Sindbad find himself in the grip of danger that he has longed for, while living as an expatriate, than he begins to want to return to his native country to rejoin his people.

The story of each voyage can be abstracted like this:

VOYAGE —> disequilibrium + equilibrium + disequilibrium.

Now, the significance of this tripartite composition lies in its instability. It can be fully grasped by comparison with the typical folktale:

FOLKTALE —> equilibrium + disequilibrium + equilibrium.

If the end of the folktale stopped at a disequilibrium we could very well count on a sequel. This is the case with Sindbad, for despite the formal and conventional return of the hero safe and sound to his native land, in his particular case to be at home does not mean the end of the tension, but rather its beginning. Sindbad exhibits a desire for uprooting. From this we can see how a spiral structure evolves. The rule is simple enough. When the end equals the beginning, it guarantees another cycle. The revolving process becomes inevitable and there is no way of ending such stories. Todorov writes in connection with *The Decameron*, "Tout récit porte en lui sa propre mort,"[9] which is true of the more linearly structured novella; with Sindbad we have a structure that assures continuity. In writing on *The Arabian Nights*, Todorov points out in his well-known essay "Les hommes-récits":

> Chaque récit semble avoir quelque chose *de trop*, un excédant, un supplément, qui reste en dehors de la forme fermée produite par le développement de l'intrigue. En même temps, et par là-même, ce quelque chose de plus, propre au récit, est aussi quelque chose de moins; le supplément est aussi un manque; pour suppléer à ce manque crée par le supplément, un autre récit est nécessaire.[10]

Though the spiral metaphor seems to have been blocked by the seventh move, it is only a simulation of an end. Seven is an emblematic number that stands for the eternal return. Its symbolism is based on a very sound mathematical principle. If we divide one by seven we get a decimal fraction that goes on indefinitely repeating a certain numerical pattern, where the seventh digit is always equivalent to the first.[11] The story of Sindbad stops more than ends. There is no release that parallels the *dénouement* in the typical folktale. In a sense, the story can stop only when the hero is liquidated either physically by death or mentally by conversion or attainment. But Sindbad suddenly gives up traveling at the end of the seventh voyage for no apparent reason. There is, however, a discrete reason why the narrative stops and the quest ceases here and not elsewhere. Since the world was seen by medieval Muslim geographers as divided into seven *kishvars* (regions), then the travelogue of Sindbad implies his covering of the entire globe. He has, so to speak, been everywhere.

Sindbad's specificity lies in the fact that he is the moving force of the action in the story. He is unlike Voltaire's Candide and Sade's Justine, who succumb to the outside world and are abused in a variety of ways and victimized. With Sindbad, the duality is internal. The real tension in Sindbad is not between Man and Nature, or the individual and society, but between the split oneness of Sindbad. He alternates between two impulses: one is the desire for the distant and the dangerous that borders on the deathly, and another is the homesickness and the desire to settle and establish roots, an impulse for life. The opposition between the fluctuating sea and the firm land, the unknown and the familiar, is a convenient way of putting Sindbad's contradiction in a narrative structure.

Sindbad is striking in the lack of change in his personality and his incapacity to develop. There are no indications that he becomes more thoughtful or more careful after so many voyages. Somehow, he does not learn any lessons from his voyages. Sindbad's story is an amoral one. The incorrigible Sindbad does not assimilate or integrate what goes on around him. His typical reaction is that of wonder and amazement. In this sense, he represents the opposite pole to Hayy ibn Yaqzan, the hero of the philosophical tale by Ibn Tufayl.[12] Hayy is constantly analyzing what he is struck with, and at times experimenting and always putting things together to make his knowledge systematic. He uses his intellect to systematize his perception, arriving eventually at knowledge of the order of the world, and even concluding that there exists a divine force behind it. True, Ibn Tufayl was writing a *roman à thèse,* an allegory to support the philosphical views of Ibn Sina (Avicenna) among others, but still the character of Hayy matures, with graded steps, throughout the narrative, in a way similar to that of Robinson Crusoe (which, some argue, was modeled or at least inspired by Hayy ibn Yaqzan).

Sindbad is really an aesthete. He wants to experience a savage sensation of life–death juxtaposition. He is not interested at all in explaining life and death or in philosophizing, lamenting, or glorifying. The world for him is neither tragic nor comic, but a place where unreconciled oppositions can be felt intensely. That is why Sindbad is both a very modern hero and a very ancient one. There is something both Lucretian and Baudelairian about his temperament—he is the most convincingly poetic figure in *The Arabian Nights.* Unlike the sedentary poet Abu Nuwas—who is presented in *The Arabian Nights* as sitting in the court of Harun al-Rashid reciting poetry at the request of the Prince of the Faithful—Sindbad, like Rimbaud, opts for the metaphors of the uncharted seas and unexplored lands. For Sindbad, the unfamiliar world is a place full of curious figures. What he reports from his voyages is a series of rhetorical experiences: hyperboles, oddities, and conceits.

The Tropes of the Voyage

Hyperbole, which is common to all literatures, is a trope that exaggerates and amplifies. Quintilian refers to it as "an elegant straining of the truth, and may be employed indifferently for exaggeration or attenuation."[13] *Al-mubalagha* (the Arabic term closest to "hyperbole"), says al-'Askari, is to reach the ultimate limits of the meaning and its furtherest borders.[14] It does not twist but it stretches the traits as far as possible. This is true of many of the wonders that Sindbad describes so vividly. They seem to be the same familiar creatures, only magnified to the maximum. Sindbad, for example, refers to the Rukh, a gigantic bird, in the second and fifth voyages. The Rukh is not a monster like the Sphinx or the Minotaur—it is not abnormal, it is supernormal, as it were. Sindbad describes the size of the Rukh, in the second voyage, by depicting the enormity of its egg, which can give us by proportional analogy an inkling of the Rukh's bulk:

> Looking, however, with a scrutinizing eye, there appeared to me on the island a white object, indistinctly seen in the distance, of enormous size: so I descended from the tree, and went towards it, and proceeded in that direction without stopping until I arrived at it; and lo, it was a huge white dome, of great height and large circumference. I drew near to it, and walked around it; but perceived no door to it, and I found that I had not strength nor activity to climb it, on account of its exceeding smoothness. I made a mark at the place where I stood, and went round the dome, measuring its circumference; and lo, it was fifty full paces; and I meditated upon some means of gaining an entrance into it.
>
> The close of the day, and the setting of the sun, had now drawn near; and, behold, the sun was hidden, and the sky became dark, and the sun was veiled from me. I therefore imagined that a cloud had come over it, but this was in the season of summer; so I wondered; and I raised my head, and, contemplating that object attentively, I saw that it was a bird, of enormous size, a bulky body, and wide wings, flying in the air; and this it was that concealed the body of the sun, and veiled it from view upon the island. At this my wonder increased, and I remembered a story which travelers and voyagers had told me long before, that there is, in certain of the islands a bird of enormous size, called the Rukh, that feedeth its young ones with elephants. I was convinced, therefore, that the dome which I had seen was one of the eggs of the Rukh.[15]

In the third voyage, Sindbad gives a description of a huge snake that was theatening him:

> And we awoke from our sleep, and lo, a serpent of enormous size, of large body and wide belly, had surrounded us. It approached one of us, and swallowed him to his shoulders: then it swallowed the rest of him, and we heard his ribs break in pieces in its belly; after which it went away.[16]

In the same voyage, Sindbad gives a portrait of a giant of a man:

> And, lo, the earth trembled beneath us, and we heard a confused noise from the upper air, and there descended upon us,

from the summit of the pavilion, a person of enormous size, in
human form, and he was of black complexion, of lofty stature,
like a great palm-tree: he had two eyes like two blazes of fire,
and tusks like the tusks of swine, and a mouth of prodigious
size, like the mouth of a well, and lips like the lips of a camel
hanging down upon his bosom, and he had ears like two mor-
tars, hanging down upon his shoulders, and the nails of his hand
were like the claws of the lion.[17]

The second figure that Sindbad makes use of is what Arab rhetoricians
call *gharib* which I render uncomfortably as "oddity." It does not have a
technical equivalent in English, but its effect is similar to that of using
archaic or far-fetched expressions. Literally, *gharib* means "strange" or
"uncommon." Technically, it is a philological term which implies a rare
and unfamililar word. It has been used in religious and literary studies.
Works were composed on the *gharib* expressions in the Qur'an and the
Tradition of the Prophet *(hadith),* and critical studies have been undertaken on the commendable and uncommendable use of *gharib* in prose
and poetry.[18]

Sindbad describes a number of oddities, animals and plants that are real
in every sense but rare and unfamiliar: "And I saw a fish whose face was
like that of the owl."[19] He goes on to say:

In that island too is a kind of wild beast called the rhinoceros,
which pastureth there like oxen and buffaloes in our country;
but the bulk of that wild beast is greater than the bulk of the
camel, and it eateth the tender leaves of trees. It is a huge beast,
with a single horn, thick, in the middle of its head, a cubit in
length, wherein is the figure of a man.[20]

Exotic trees are also described by Sindbad to impress on their strange-
ness:

And we continued to advance until we arrived at a garden in a
great and beautiful island, wherein were camphor-trees, under
each of which trees a hundred men might shade themselves.
When any one desireth to obtain some camphor from one of
these trees, he maketh a perforation in the upper part of it with
something long, and catcheth what descendeth from it. The liq-
uid camphor floweth from it, and concreteth like gum. It is the
juice of that tree, and after this operation, the tree drieth, and
becometh firewood.[21]

Another figure that permeates the Sindbadian discourse is conceit. The
conceit is a trope that was used a great deal by the French Symbolists, and
before them the Metaphysical poets, and before them Petrarch:[22]

It is an intricate and far-fetched metaphor, which functions
through arousing feelings of surprise, shock or amusement. . . .
The poet compares elements which seem to have little or nothing in common, or juxtaposes images which establish a marked
discord in mood.

The faculty of wit, the capacity for finding likenesses between the apparently unlike, is central to the conceit, and the
presence of this faculty largely determines the success of a given
conceit. For the emotion evoked by a good conceit is not simply surprise, but rather a surprised recognition of the ultimate
validity of the relationship presented in the conceit.[23]

The story of Sindbad offers two extended conceits: that of imposed
labor and that of imposed culture. In both cases, Sindbad falls unknowingly into a snare. He describes moments of intense estrangement on foreign grounds and alien cultures. The first experience gives the sensation of
repression; the second, claustrophobia.

During the fourth voyage Sindbad unsparingly describes his live burial.
He encounters the custom of live burial when his neighbor's wife dies and
his neighbor is buried with her. Sindbad, then, goes to the king and inquires about this curious custom and whether it applies to foreign residents
like him. To his dismay, he discovers that it does. Some time later, Sindbad's
wife dies and he is required to accompany her body to the grave in the
name of the alien tradition of total togetherness. He resists, to no avail:

They laid hold upon me and bound me by force, tying with me
seven cakes of bread and a jug of sweet water, according to
their custom, and let me down into the pit. And lo, it was a great
cavern beneath the mountain. They said to me, Loose thyself
from the ropes. But I would not loose myself. So they threw the
ropes down upon me, and covered the mouth of the pit with the
great stone that was upon it, and went their ways.

By Allah, my dying this death is unfortunate!! Would that I
had been drowned in the sea, or had died upon the mountains!!
It had been better for me than this evil death!![24]

The hero's sense of alienation is depicted as frantic loneliness in a background of decomposed bodies. The suppression of Sindbad's desire for
life and his confinement underground condenses beautifully his sensation
of cultural rape.

The live burial is a conceit and not a simple *gharib* for two reasons. It is
more than an isolated incident that points to a rare custom. First, it is a sign
of a personal experience and a state of mind that characterizes Sindbad's
psyche. Second, it represents the anomaly from the inside, as it is experienced—with all its horrors—and not from without, as a strange burial rite.

The account of the Arab geographer Ibn Fadlan of human sacrifice in burial
ceremonies can be characterized as *gharib*. The following is an excerpt
from Ibn Fadlan's ethnographic report that will show neatly the difference
between Sindbad's conceit and Ibn Fadlan's *gharib*. In A.D. 921 Ibn Fadlan
left Baghdad to visit the King of the Bulgars on a mission from al-Muqtadir,
then caliph. The journey was taken via Bukhara and southeastern Russia;
the peoples described are Scandinavians who had come to camp by the
Volga. The account is very well known and has been translated into many
European languages. There, according to Ibn Fadlan, a woman of the household of a dead man agrees to die with him:

> By this time, as it seemed to me, the girl had become dazed; she
> made as though she would enter the tent, and had brought her
> head forward between the tent and the ship, when the hag seized
> her by the head and dragged her in. At this moment the men
> began to beat upon their shields with staves, in order to drown
> the noise of her outcries, which might have terrified the other
> girls, and deterred them from seeking death with their masters
> in the future. . . . The old woman known as the angel of death
> now knotted a rope around her neck, and handed the ends to
> two of the men to pull. Then with a broad-bladed dagger she
> smote her between the ribs, and drew the blade forth, while the
> two men strangled her with the rope till she died.[25]

The other striking example of conceit occurs on the fifth voyage, when
Sindbad encounters the "Shaykh of the Sea." The latter is, to all appear-
ances, a harmless old man, and so when he requests Sindbad to carry him
on his shoulders to transport him across a brook, Sindbad does so. But the
old man refuses to get off, twists his legs around Sindbad, and orders him
around. Sindbad describes his captivity in these vivid terms:

> So, I was frightened at him, and desired to throw him down
> from my shoulders, but he pressed upon my neck with his feet,
> and squeezed my throat, so that the world became black before
> my face, and I was unconscious of my existence, falling upon
> the ground in a fit, like one dead. He then raised his legs, and
> beat me upon my back and my shoulders, and I suffered violent
> pain, wherefore I rose with him. He still kept his seat upon my
> shoulders, and I had become fatigued with bearing him; and he
> made a sign to me that I should go in among the trees, to the
> best of the fruits. When I disobeyed him, he inflicted upon me,
> with his feet, blows more violent than those of whips; and he
> ceased not to direct me with his hand to every place to which he
> desired to go, and to that place I went with him. If I loitered, or
> went leisurely, he beat me, and I was a captive to him. We went
> into the midst of the island, among the trees, and he descended
> not from my shoulders by night nor by day.[26]

Here the servitude is not depicted by the simple slave–master relationship, but by a two-storeyed image of beneath and above. In this construction, the upper floor controls and exploits the lower. The incongruity of the setup makes its correspondence with the alienation of the labor force all the more striking: a useless, unproductive upper echelon living on the back of an exploited, hardworking foundation.

The two conceits of the fourth and fifth voyage deal with cultural and economic alienation, respectively, and this is by no means a surprise, for the story of Sindbad is essentially a literary study in alienation in its many manifestations—from the pleasing aesthetic defamiliarization to the horrid everyday estrangement.

Nature and life in Sindbad's story seem like a series of extravagant tropes. Nature seems to be imitating art rather than the other way round. This may sound like Oscar Wilde's blaming the fog of London on impressionist painting, but the point here is not that Sindbad sees the world in a certain framework drawn by art, as much as it is an admission that classifying the world (nature and experience) can only be undertaken through mechanisms which are present and inherent in language. Codification of reality is inevitably linked to the mechanisms of codification.

Studies that try to document the borrowing of Sindbad's material from geographical and cosmographical works of medieval Islam, showing how it is a bad or confused copy of the original, miss two things in their disparaging effort. One is summed up by T. S. Eliot's dictum: "Bad poets imitate; good poets steal." Second, in their underestimation of the popular mind, such scholars see the High Tradition as creative and the Little Tradition (to use the terminology of Robert Redfield) as a poor copy, unaware that there is a continual and mutual dialectic between them, and that the erudite works owe a great deal to popular thought.

Gerhardt's literary study of Sindbad shows how far good will can take one in deforming a text.[27] Gerhardt's argument that the seven voyages constitute a lozenge cannot possibly convince anyone, perhaps not even Gerhardt. She uses a formal methodology and breaks down the voyage into the following elements:

C = Calamity
A = Adventure with subdivisions
    Ap = pleasant adventure
    Ad = dangerous adventure
W = Description of Wonder
R = Return

Then she translates each voyage into the appropriate combination of C, A, W, and R. The only pattern that can be discerned is that voyages 1 and 7 offer one item less than the package tours of 2, 3, 4, 5, and 6. The voyages between 1 and 7 offer no pattern whatsoever in their arrangement of Ap, Ad, and W. But even such an insignificant conclusion—namely, that the first and last are shorter than the rest—is obtained at the price of mishandling and mutilating the text. She cuts and pastes to suit her taste for geometry. The text she works from is nonexistent. Using a vague textual argument, she rearranges two different variants on the dubious grounds that it must have been so before some reciter or compiler messed it up.[28] She analyzes a text that is neither a given variant nor an invariant, but a collation of parts of two variants; this is doing violence to the text. Gerhardt ends up with attractive but useless results.

The voyages of Sindbad vary in length and nature of adventures, and they create no ascending, descending, or climactic pattern. They seem to fluctuate, and resist a quantitative approach. Perhaps, therefore, we should retire gracefully from finding a rigid pattern and try to relate them as a set to the frame story.

Once we abandon the desire to force the voyages into a preconceived schema, a great many things are revealed with striking consistency. The two stories of the framework and of Sindbad fit like a jigsaw puzzle. Shahrazad, the weak party, tells stories to gain pardon; Sindbad narrates to justify his eminence. Shahrazad narrates at night exclusively: "And Shahrazad perceived the dawn of day and ceased saying her permitted say."[29]

But Sindbad narrates in the daytime and the porter goes home at the end of the day:

> And as soon as day broke and the morning showed with its sheen and shone, he [Sindbad the Porter] rose and praying the dawn-prayer betook himself to Sindbad the Seaman, who returned his salute and received him with an open breast and cheerful favor and made him sit with him till the rest of the company arrived, when he caused food to be brought and they ate and drank and made merry. Then Sindbad the seaman bespake them and related to them the narrative of the fourth voyage.[30]

Furthermore, Sindbad the Sailor considers Sindbad the Porter as an equal and addresses him as brother: "Know, O my brethren, that after my return . . . "[31] while Shahrazad addresses Shahrayar as a subject does a monarch: "It hath reached me, O auspicious king, that . . . ."[32] Furthermore, the narrative of Sindbad is autobiographical while Shahrazad is relating impersonal fiction. The following table shows the opposition:

Narrator	powerful/ powerless	day/ night	personal/ impersonal
Shahrazad	—	—	—
Sindbad	+	+	+

Powerful/day/personal = +
Powerless/night/impersonal = —

Such conclusions are considered unfulfilling and gratuitous by some critics. However, they can be very useful and perhaps fulfilling if one cares to infer from them. In the case of *The Arabian Nights*—with its multi-layers, cross-genres, and shifting patterns—the difficulty of grasping the significance of the whole is staggering. But if we were to see that it is diametrically opposed to the story of Sindbad (as the table shows), then understanding the nature of Sindbad's story (which is a simpler discourse) would throw light on Shahrazad's.

Sindbad's story, as has been shown, is a quasi-confessional account of Sindbad's tumultuous life.[33] Essentially Sindbad is enacting and reliving a personal experience, and a traumatic one at that. He is publicizing his inner self and thus, in a sense, expelling the horrific visions. Sindbad the Porter simply listens to the sailor's discourse, which is at times disorderly but governed by definite repetitions, and certain obsessions of the narrator become obvious. The story and the setting of Sindbad amounts to a proto-psychoanalytic seance. If that is so, and one has not been led astray by the demon of analogy, then it follows that Shahrazad's discourse is the structural antithesis of Sindbad's discourse.

Lévi-Strauss, in a seminal article, shows that the shamanistic seance is the counterpart of psychoanalytic seance. He points out that the objective of both rites is inducing experience. Both re-enact myths that are relived. In psychoanalysis, the patient reconstructs a myth with elements from his or her own past. In shamanism, the shaman delivers a social myth which connects with the patient's past. The shaman speaks and the psychoanlyst listens.[34]

The shaman, therefore, evokes and integrates the individual experience by recalling a myth. The singularity of the experience is an individual manifestation of a more general and universal contradiction. Hence, a sense of integration is achieved by voicing the mythic narrative. In the psycho-analytic seances, the individual experience, once enunciated, begins to have the significance of a collective myth. In both cases a link has to be established between the singular and the collective. In one, by telling the singular experience, the collective aspect is uncovered; in the other, by telling a collective myth, the link between the social abstraction and the personal experience is established, and in an instant, fusion takes place until such time as the disconnection recurs.

That Shahrazad's narration parallels shamanistic practices has to be proven by the material and not simply by analogical reasoning. I. M. Lewis, who studied shamanistic ceremonies cross-culturally, describes them in terms that clearly conjure up *The Arabian Nights:*

> The atmosphere, though controlled and not as anarchic as it may seem, is essentially permissive and comforting. Everything takes on the tone and character of modern psychodrama or group therapy. Abreaction is the order of the day. Repressed urges and desires, the idiosyncratic as well as the socially conditioned, are given full public rein. No holds are barred. No interests or demands are too unseemly in this setting to receive sympathetic attention.[35]

The spectacle that Shahrazad offers in its design and conclusion is not unlike the corporal drama practiced in the possession dances of *zar* and *hadra*.[36] And Mallarmé has already noted that the dance is a poem which, if written down, would require a long text.[37]

This should help us understand the nature of the seemingly unrelated collection of tales. The haphazard clutter is meaningful in the system itself, since it airs all the contradictions, tensions, and repressions. Critics who dismiss *The Arabian Nights* as disorderly and unfit for analysis as a unit understand only one kind of structure: an organic one. *The Arabian Nights* offers something akin to what Bakhtin calls "the carnival."[38]

A number of serious studies have shown the transformation of elemental religious institutions and rituals into poetic and narrative forms. Propp wrote on the genesis of the fairy tale from initiatic ceremonies.[39] This historical work was preceded by his rigorous morphological analysis of the Russian folktale, which he considered an indispensable first step in tracing the genesis of the folktale. More studies in this vein may uncover the transformations of ancient rituals into folktales. So far there have been few studies that have documented the genesis of different genres in Middle Eastern literatures. The work of Basgöz on Turkish folk stories *(halk hikâyesi)* dealing with the traditional bard *(asik)* established the connection between such tales and magico-religious rites of the Turco-Mongols.[40] Hamori figured out the specificity of certain pre- and post-Islamic *qasidas* in terms of the ritualistic function they fulfilled.[41] Al-Bayyati has equally shown how certain Arab popular narratives are transformations of ancient Near Eastern myths.[42] As for *The Arabian Nights,* Maurice Bouisson has attempted to link Shahrazad's tales to their mythic analogues and sources.[43]

The spiral construction of Sindbad's story need not be the basis of other literary voyages in *The Arabian Nights.* Not all voyages have the same spiral pattern. The story of "The City of Brass," which follows that of Sindbad, is a different kind of journey. It has a specific destination and it is undertaken with a definite purpose in mind. When the objective is accom-plished, the return announces the end of the story. "The City of Brass" is a story about an expedition undertaken to Kerker, somewhere on the coast of Africa, in order to bring the caliph brass bottles which were reputed to be there, and in which Solomon imprisoned his demons. On its way back, the expedition comes across the legendary "City of Brass," which is in-habited by an entirely preserved dead population. Members of the expedi-tion who try to climb over the wall of the city are lured by fantastic crea-tures and jump down, killing themselves. Eventually, the leading shaykh, armed with his faith, manages to resist the enchanting invitation. He opens the gates of the city and lets the traveling company in. The theme of the ephemeral life and all-powering death is linked to Solomon's legend. The company, having gathered treasures, goes back to Damascus, from where it started.[44]

This journey, like Sindbad's, deals with life and death. Sindbad's ac-count is that of successive confrontations with death. In "The City of Brass," there is an overwhelming and powerful depiction of the dead simulating the living. Sindbad's voyages, with their death-in-life theme, echo and invert the life-in-death theme of the "The City of Brass." Thus the process of construction in *The Arabian Nights* is a continual transformation of elemental oppositions into different cases and moods.

7
THE RUNAWAY METONYM

Shahrazad's objective is to reach the infinite through a finite medium, and to create continuity through an episodic structure. In short, her aim is to annul the dictates of time through the use of temporal devices. Both in the frame story and in Sindbad's voyages, we have a structure that symbolizes the infinite. Numbers such as 1001 and 7 in this particular context signify that which goes on without end. In a number of stories, the infinite is conjured while reading through an intertextual chain, where one passage evokes another. This process produces the effect of endlessness—as in the repetitions of motifs in an arabesque—providing the readers with the illusion of the infinite. Shahrazad's task parallels that of Renaissance artists who tried to introduce the effect of depth on their canvases, thus giving the illusion of a perspective while working on a two-dimensional surface. One of her techniques can be summed up in terms of repetition of topoi that produce a radial symmetry (symmetry of rotation).

This chapter examines the cluster of demon stories that conspicuously display this tendency. These stories, which occur in the beginning of *The Arabian Nights,* resemble each other and the frame story. The peculiarity of the resemblance is that it often verges on the identical. Entire narrative sections are reproduced, giving the effect of intertextuality. While in folklore the reworking of motifs is common, *The Arabian Nights* is distinctive for its repetition more than reworking—with the result that the corpus produces the effect of a merry-go-round, where every once in a while one rider comes to the front and then soon disappears to be replaced by another. It is precisely the rotation that gives the impression of continuity. The work is something of a *bricolage,* where entire topoi are transferred from one story to another. But the phenomenon of intertext takes a disturbing aspect in *The Arabian Nights.* It is not only a question of pleasant recognition of motifs, but also the exhilarating and dangerous feeling of things being turned inside out—a sort of carnivalistic performance in which the inside leads to the outside and the outside to the inside, as in a "Mobius strip." The distinction of inside–outside or frame–enframed disintegrates, giving the impression of blissful destructuring.[1]

The devices used to create this peculiar anti-structure, not to be confused with non-structure, are a combination of interpolation and interpenetration. Here I will examine the first three complete stories narrated by Shahrazad in the Cairo-Bulaq edition,[2] with their embedded stories:

A. The story of the Merchant and the Demon
    1. The story of the first shaykh and the gazelle
    2. The story of the second shaykh and the black hounds
    3. The story of the third shaykh and the mule

B. The story of the Fisherman and the Demon
    1. The story of King Yunan and the sage Duban
        a) The story of King Sindibad
        b) The story of the disloyal vizier
        c) The story of the king and the crocodile
    2. The story of the petrified prince

C. The story of the Porter and the Three Ladies of Baghdad
    1. The story of the first mendicant
    2. The story of the second mendicant
    3. The story of the third mendicant
    4. The story of the eldest lady
    5. The story of the lady doorkeeper

The Story of "The Merchant and the Demon"

The story of the merchant is startling with its direct borrowing from the frame story. It is about a merchant who goes on a voyage and stops in the wilderness to eat his food. Just as he throws a date-pit, a terrifying demon appears and threatens to kill him. The merchant protests and learns that he has unwittingly killed the demon's invisible son with his date-pit. The merchant manages to delay his death sentence for a year, during which he settles his accounts and bids his family farewell. When the year is over, he carries his coffin under his arm and goes to the meeting-place. There, three shaykhs come along, one after the other, and the merchant tells them his story. When the demon comes to kill him, each shaykh promises to tell him a surprising story in exchange for one-third of the man's blood. The three shaykhs tell their strange stories, and the merchant is set free.

The plot of the frame story is reproduced in the story of the merchant in an obvious way. There is a breach that infuriates the demon, namely his son's death. This calls for revenge which is bought off by storytelling. What could be more reflective of Shahrazad's story than this? Still there are differences, which are mostly due to the splitting and fusion of characters. While Shahrazad combines the function of the victim and that of the narrator, in the story of the merchant the two functions are split. The victim is the merchant, and the narrators are three different shaykhs, each telling his own story. Furthermore, the wrath of Shahrayar, though caused by one specific woman, is paid for by other women, while the merchant is himself both a transgressor and object of punishment. The axis of guilt–innocence in the frame story is split and exemplified in two characters: the first wife of Shahrayar on the one hand and Shahrazad on the other. The merchant, however, fuses the two elements: he is both guilty and innocent. He has actually killed the son of the demon, although he did it unintentionally. While the plot remains essentially the same, the enframed story simply combines and splits the *dramatis personae* of the frame story, doing away entirely with secondary characters. The set of relationships remains remarkably the same.

Shahrazad : Shahrayar = Merchant : Demon
or
Woman : Man = Man : Demon

Both merchant (or to be precise, narrators on his behalf) and Shahrazad, man and woman, resort to storytelling to save themselves, but there is a crucial difference in the narration of Shahrazad and that of the shaykhs. Storytelling in the enframed story functions as a ransom: it is a contractual agreement:

> O thou Jinnee, and crown of the kings of the Jann, if I relate to thee the story of myself and this gazelle, and thou find it to be wonderful, and more so than the adventure of this merchant, wilt thou give up to me a third of thy claim to his blood? He answered, Yes, O shaykh, if thou relate to me the story, and I find it to be as thou hast said, I will give up to thee a third of my claim to his blood.[3]

The terms of the exchange are defined before the barter takes place. In this sense the story of the merchant is similar to a well-known type of folktale in which the hero is asked to fulfill a number of tasks to achieve something desired. In the Nanai folktale "Mergen and His Friends," for example, the hero has to accomplish three superhuman tasks in order to marry a girl, and he is helped by three animals in accomplishing these tasks. The motif of exchange is the pivot of *The Merchant of Venice,* for instance, though the unfolding of the story takes a radically different end.

Shahrazad's exchange with Shahrayar is more complex. There is no contract binding their relationship. She is simply awarded a privilege that can be withdrawn at any moment, and it is precisely the feeling that she may not manage to please her audience—and, therefore, the hovering possibility of her condemnation—that makes *The Arabian Nights* a suspense story throughout its course. And yet pleasing is not enough to undo her verdict. She has to continue to please as long as she wants to live. She is given the time of her narration, and therefore she has to continue to narrate. In contrast, the deal between the demon and each of the shaykhs specified that every pleasing story would be worth one third of the merchant's blood or life. Consequently, the structure of the exchange makes the story a finite one. The same structuring occurs in Boccaccio's *Decameron,* where invariably the stories told have to correspond to ten times ten. The group is made up of ten people, and each person has to preside for a day of storytelling.

What is the nature of that being exchanged? To give is necessarily to sacrifice.[4] In the case of the shaykhs, their own life histories are being given away. They are really defining narratively who they are, or as Todorov has labelled this phenomenon, they are "hommes-récits."[5] They are systematically offering themselves or an intimate part of themselves. The operation is metonymic in essence. Every shaykh, instead of offering part of his life to redeem part of the merchant's life, offers metonymically a narrative of his life. The correspondence of past life story to the present self is based on contiguity, or on a cause–effect relationship (as they are both enclosed within one social personality), thus constituting the basic principle of metonymy.

Striking in their resemblance, the stories of the three shaykhs are autobiographical pieces but by no means psychological exploration. While Sindbad's voyages constitute the prototype of the meta-psychological novel, the stories of the shaykhs do not describe how they feel but how they fit in a social context. The self is defined in terms of its relationship to others. The three stories establish the origin of kin relationships between the human narrators and the animals accompanying them, as in totemism. In the fables, animals behave like people and are allegorical, but in these demonic stories, human beings behave like animals, just as they are prone to do in myths.

The story of the first shaykh (A1) who was accompanied by a gazelle can be summarized as follows. He is married to his cousin who is barren. He then takes a concubine who bears him a son. On one of his voyages, his wife casts a spell on his concubine and his son, turning them into a cow and a calf. When the man returns home, he is told that his concubine has died and his son has run away. On the next feast day, he slaughters the cow, which is in fact his concubine. When he sets out to slaughter the calf, not suspecting that it is his own son, he is met with the calf's heartbreaking cries and moans. The man takes pity on him and instead of slaughtering him gives him away to his herdsman. When the calf is taken to the herdsman's house, his human identity is revealed by the herdsman's daughter, who is versed in the magical arts. When the merchant is informed that his own son has been enchanted, he asks the daughter of the herdsman to disenchant him, and offers her tremendous rewards, but she stipulates that she will do it only if the young man will marry her and if she will be permitted to enchant the wicked wife. The man agrees, and his son recovers his human form while his wife is turned into a gazelle.

Within this doubly enframed story of the first shaykh, the motif of exchange recurs. The herdsman's daughter demands the enchantment of the wife as a prerequisite to breaking the evil spell cast on the son. One metamorphosis in one direction requires another in the opposite direction. This exchange where one is paid in kind follows the same principle of revenge in the enframing story of "The Merchant and the Demon" (A). While in the enframed story the barter has positive results, the revenge in the enframing story has negative results, but the underlying principle is the same and there is a carry-over of the governing principle of exchange on the two levels of narration: that of enframed and that of enframing.

The stories of the second shaykh (A2) and of the third shaykh (A3) are structured in the same manner with the same implications as the story of the first shaykh just summarized. The two brothers of the second shaykh try to liquidate him with his wife, and eventually they are transformed into dogs by the Jinnee–wife. The third shaykh is transformed by his wife into a dog and then is saved by the daughter of the butcher who makes him recover his human form, and at the same time she transforms the wife into a mule.

The operations at work in the story of "The Merchant and the Demon" (A), and in the stories of the shaykhs (A1–3) are those of transgressor turned into transgressed. They are elaborations on a grammatical transformation; the subject becomes an object in the act of harming. The ransom paid to save the merchant's life is the substitute for the act of revenge. Instead of taking life, stories of three lives are offered. There is a transfer into the symbolic plane, and it is essential to note that the stories of the three shaykhs parallel the story of "The Merchant and the Demon" and echo its plot based on the notion of revenge.

The question remains as to why stories of metamorphoses are offered to the demon. The reason is simple enough. The demon or Jinn is essentially an ambiguous and multifarious form. Jinn vary considerably but they share one feature: they take different shapes at different times. Stories of metamorphoses are particularly appropriate to Jinn. It is like telling stories of thefts to robbers.

In this *mise en abyme,* as Gide called this phenomenon of intensive embedding, the element of moving from one level of discourse to another, from the enframing to the enframed, seems only to bring out the same issues over and over. The order of storytelling and the themes is as follows:

—Shahrayar wants revenge: Shahrazad is displacing the revenge by storytelling about
    —the demon who wants revenge: shaykhs are displacing the revenge by storytelling about
        —revenge.

This gives the illusion of a runaway metonym. Even when a story comes to an end, we see that the same issues are transferred to another, giving the impression of rotative symmetry. Thus the story of "The Merchant and the Demon" can be said to be an example of a transactional structure, where one direct exchange is replaced by three indirect ones.

The Story of
"The Fisherman and the Demon"

In the next story, that of "The Fisherman and the Demon" (B), the structure looks quite different. The principle is not that of action and reaction as in the revenge theme of "The Merchant and the Demon," but that of cause and effect. One action triggers another, which in turn triggers another, and so on, until we arrive at a state of equilibrium. Unlike adventure stories, the hero in this case does not remain the same. The narrative starts with the story of the fisherman followed by an expedition of the king, and then the story of the petrified prince. The story proper of the fisherman is something of a prelude to introduce the enchanted fish. The direction of the story is continually changing but the relationships are those of cause and effect.

The fisherman, while casting his net, finds on the fourth try a brass bottle which he opens and from which a demon who has been imprisoned by King Solomon appears. The demon had promised to reward whoever liberates him, in the beginning, but exasperated by the wait he decides to punish whoever lets him out. So when he is liberated he threatens to kill the fisherman. The fisherman uses a ruse to get him back in the bottle, by simulating wonder at his ability to fit in such a small bottle. The demon, fooled by the simulated disbelief, demonstrates his ability to do this, and the fisherman quickly closes the bottle. Then the demon begs the fisherman to let him out. The fisherman responds by giving him narrative examples of how doing good deeds backfires, but eventually gives in and lets the entreating demon out. The demon rewards him by taking him to a lake with magical colored fish. The fisherman catches four of these fish and sells them to the king. In the royal kitchen the fish speak and this indicate that they were enchanted beings.

The second part of the narrative is about an expedition undertaken by the king, and guided by the fisherman, to the magic lake. This leads the king to discover a palace in which he finds a prince whose lower half has been petrified. He inquires about his story, which turns out to be again one of transformation. The prince, having found his wife with her black slave lover, tries to kill the slave, but only manages to injure him. The wife casts a spell on the prince and turns his subjects into fish of four colors, each color representing a different religious sect. The king then goes and kills the black slave and takes his place; when his "mistress" comes, he pretends to be her lover. He asks her to release the prince and his subjects from the spell, and then he kills her.

Here the narrative construction is different from that of "The Merchant and the Demon," where stories of enchantment as stories resolve the dilemma. In the story of "The Fisherman and the Demon," the problems revealed through the fisherman's act are neutralized through complicated intrigue, including storytelling (i.e., "The Story of King Yunan and the Sage Duban" with its three enframed tales). But such stories do not end the narrative. They lead to the curious fish which work as a link between the two narrative blocks, namely that of the fisherman and the demon on the one hand and that of the petrified prince on the other. The fish terminate one adventure but sow the seeds for another.

When cooking the fish, demons appear and the king decides to uncover the story of these magical fish. His expedition leads him to find the petrified prince. The enigma of the talking fish is doubled by that of a prince whose lower part is petrified. The story of the prince, a man who was enchanted by his wife whom he had surprised with her black lover, is essentially the story of the third shaykh (A3). It is also, *grosso modo,* the story of Shahrayar.

In the story of "The Fisherman and the Demon," the entire narrative has the structure of two overlapping circles where the common sector or link is that of the fish episode. The story of the fisherman ends with a riddle, and the story of the prince starts with one. Both stories are brought together in a final alliance where the king and the prince and the fisherman enter into a kin relationship, finishing the story with the inevitable marriage.

The two stories of the fisherman and the petrified prince complement each other, but the stories of the three shaykhs are dominated, as it were, by their frame story. The first story related by Shahrazad, "The Merchant and the Demon," exhibits the phenomenon that we call *subordination*, where the enframed narratives are subjugated to the generative one. The second story she tells, that of "The Fisherman and the Demon," exhibits *coordination*, where different narrative blocks combine and overlap to construct a narrative whole. The third story related by Shahrazad offers yet another form of bringing narrative blocks together, namely *supraordination*. The enframed stories in "The Porter and the Three Ladies of Baghdad" offer a complete structure whose unity can be grasped only through the effort of the reader to go beyond the different narrative sets into reconstructing a meaningful whole. On the surface of it, the story of the porter seems loose and disconnected. On closer analysis, we can see that it is a series of theatrically staged tableaux whose poetic impact is derived from a skillful interplay between two limited motifs: eroticism and fiction.

The Story of "The Porter and the Three Ladies of Baghdad"

If we were to break down the story of "The Porter and the Three Ladies of Baghdad," we would end up with five movements:

1. Orgiastic banquet
2. Sadomasochistic scene
3. Threat of death
4. Storytelling
5. Reconcilation

This reproduces faithfully the schema of the frame story.[6] But there are some variations in presentation. The orgiastic banquet in the story of "The

Porter and the Three Ladies of Baghdad" is introduced through a fabulous
setting without explaining its relevance. We wonder, just like the porter—
who is hired at the beginning of the story by a fine aristocratic-looking
lady to help her buy exquisite provisions, and then remains in her mansion
in which reside two other women. The description of the lady's shopping,
and then the house and feast-like atmosphere, is meant to point to the sump-
tuousness and luxury of the setup. It evokes essentially the sensual, to
which is added the tension of an unexplained riddle.

The story starts with a porter who is asked by a veiled lady to accompany her and carry provisions, which are taken to her splendid house. There,
a feast of wine, food, music, and games (sexual and verbal) takes place.
The porter is allowed to join the three ladies in this play. References to the
five senses are made vividly so that the scene is experienced by the reader
as a total sensual event, as the following citations show.

(1) Touch is evoked through textures that are associated with wealth
and delicateness:

> there accosted him a female wrapped in an izar of the manufac-
> ture of El-Mosil, composed of gold-embroidered silk, with a
> border of gold-lace at each end, who raised her face-veil . . . [7]

(2) Taste is amply represented through reference to what amounts to
trade names of imported goods:

> She next stopped at the shop of a fruiterer and bought of him
> Syrian apples, and Othmanee quinces, and peaches of Oman,
> and jasmine of Aleppo, and water lilies of Damascus, and cu-
> cumbers of the Nile, and Egyptian limes, and Sultanee citrons,
> and sweet-scented myrtle, and sprigs of the henna-tree, and
> camomile, and anemones, and violets, and pomegranate flow-
> ers, and eglantine.[8]

(3) Smell is referred to through objects which invariably conjure up the
erotico-religious for an Arab reader:

> She bought two kinds of scented waters, rose water, and orange
> flower water, etc., together with some sugar, and a sprinkling
> bottle of rosewater infused with musk, and some frankincense,
> and aloeswood and ambergris and musk, and wax candles.[9]

(4) Sight is emphasized through showering conventional similes that
portray the object beheld:

> a damsel of tall stature, high-bosomed, fair and beautiful, and
> of elegant form, with a forehead like the bright new moon, eyes
> like those of gazelles, eyebrows like the new moon of Ramadan,
> cheeks resembling anemones, and a mouth like the seal of

Suleyman: her countenance was like the full moon in its splendour, and the forms of her bosom resembled two pome-granates of equal size.[10]

(5) Finally, the aural sense is brought in through the references to song and music:

The portress brought them a tambourine of the manufacture of El-Mosil with a lute of El-Erak, and a Persian harp; whereupon they all arose, and one took the tambourine; another, the lute; and the third, the harp; and they played upon these instruments, the ladies accompanying them with loud songs.[11]

Having presented the reader with this ceremonial setting in which three ladies and a porter, and later three dervishes and Harun al-Rashid, his vi-zier and his executioner in the guise of merchants, share in this feast, the reader expects a climactic ending. The orgiastic atmosphere is amply rep-resented in the narrative when the three ladies swim naked with the porter and exchange some obscene puns.

But the ceremony finishes, oddly enough, with a lacerating scene. Two bitches are brought in and they are whipped and caressed. Both animality and sadomasochism are intrinsic to the scene, but its importance lies mostly in the fact that it triggers the narrative-telling. When the men present see this scene, and though the ladies of the house strictly forbade them at the onset from asking any questions, they cannot contain their curiosity and inquire about the meaning of the whipping of the bitches as well as the traces of scars on one of the ladies. The narrative takes a dramatic turn then, and fierce black slaves appear to kill these curious men, when one of the dervishes offers to tell stories. The dervishes tell their own stories that explain why the three of them are one-eyed, and everyone is pardoned. The next day, Harun al-Rashid calls for the ladies and has them relate their stories, which explain the mystery of the whipped bitches and the scarred lady. The construction of the entire tale moves in time from the present to the past. At the beginning, enigmatic scenes are presented and then ex-plained through narratives.

Here, too, the narrative reproduces almost verbatim paragraphs from the story of "The Merchant and the Demon," and the story of the eldest lady resembles that of the second shaykh. The male hero is replaced by a female one. The narrative of the second shaykh in the story of the "Mer-chant and the Demon," however, exposes his relationship with his two brothers turned into hounds, and the narrative of the eldest lady in the story of the "Porter and the Three Ladies of Baghdad" presents her rela-tionship with her two sisters who are enchanted into two bitches. In almost identical terms, we are told how the two brothers insisted on traveling and wasting their money, and how they were helped by their brother, of whom they were jealous, especially as he was married; they end up by throwing him and his wife into the sea. The wife who was a Jinnee saved him and enchanted his two brothers. In the narrative of the eldest lady, the two sisters insist on marrying and are left destitute by their husbands. They are helped by their sister, but become envious when she marries the surviving Muslim of a petrified city, and so they throw the couple into the sea. Here lies the difference in the two stories. Symmetry would have required that the young man save his wife and enchant her sisters, but, I presume, since he had survived precisely through the living word of the Qur'an—a motif which was probably added later on, when the story was Islamicized—he could not very well be involved in magical arts. He is disposed of in the story, but the wife manages to survive and ends up on an island. There she sees a snake followed by a threatening serpent. The lady kills the serpent and the snake develops wings and flies away. The next day upon awakening the lady finds herself attended by a Jinnee who is in fact the snake she saved. The Jinnee returns the wife to her home and enchants her two sisters into two bitches and warns the lady that if she does not whip them three hundred times a day, she will end up like them as well.

The effect of such repetition of the same tale, in which in one version the male dominates and in the other the female, is that of déjà-vu. One remembers the narrative block borrowed from "The Merchant and the Demon," and with very slight adjustment, it is inserted into the tale of "The Porter and the Three Ladies of Baghdad." The creation of mnemonic structure is achieved by such rotative symmetrics.

In the story of "The Porter and the Three Ladies of Baghdad," the operative principles are those of heightened expectations fulfilled dramatically and inversely, and second, those of recollection. The elements of dramatic shock and reminiscence are both present. The first is based on sudden reversal and the second on recognition. The recognition, which is not organically related to what is recognized, is something akin to what Coleridge called the fancy, which he defined as "a mode of memory emancipated from the order of time and space."[12]

The relationship between the enframed and the enframing is based on borrowing entire motifs, with hardly any elaboration. The relationship can be summed up as a figure which cannot be contained and keeps slipping from one narrative to another under the auspices of contiguity. The runaway metonym is both a technique of stretching and repetition, where the reader is allowed to move both forward and backward.

8

PERPETUAL NARRATIVE

Structure

As I have tried to show, *The Arabian Nights* is generated by a binary structure. This is typical of mythical narratives, as Lévi-Strauss has adequately demonstrated on the basis of American Indian myths, in his monumental *Mythologiques*. The difference between the Arabian narratives and the American Indian ones lies in the fact that in the latter the oppositions tend to be mediated, while in the Arabian stories the oppositions remain pending, allowing the very act of narration to be generated and perpetuated by this rupture of split unity. Storytelling goes on precisely because the binary opposition is not mediated and the original rupture has not been healed. There is a virtual ending to *The Arabian Nights* where the narrative comes to a stop. In fact, it is only the illusion of an end—or rather a closing without locking—this is why the story can be opened, closed, and re-opened to add more tales. This is an example of a tentative ending.

The middle of the narrative gives the impression of vulnerability and lends itself to manipulation. It can be changed and shuffled. There is no indication that the order of the *arrangement* of stories is meaningful. They persuade through their weight and cumulative effect and not through their development. The diversity of narrative genres is not simply a disorder in the narrative organism. It plays a fundamental role: it carries weight through its coverage of narrative types, through its encyclopedic drive.

The beginning of the narrative is always compromised, whether in the frame story, where *The Arabian Nights* is supposed to be a retelling of old tales, or in the text itself, where the narration is always clouded and compounded with the effect of veiling the beginnings or encrusting them in another and previous discourse, an already given and existing discourse. The beginning of narrative remains secondary, in that it is second to something that took place before it. It is not original or primeval.

By analyzing it structurally, *The Arabian Nights* is revealed as an effort that disturbs the three syntagmatic elements in a narrative: the beginning is questioned, the middle is liberated, and the end is deferred. Binarism is further used in more than the two ways defined and practiced in traditional Western culture: repetition and difference. The *Arabian Nights* fuses the two terms, repetition and difference, in another curious combination which can be called *ambivalence*. The Arabic term *addad* (ambivalence) is the most intriguing of terms because in itself it means the thing and its opposite. It manifests its very meaning.

The frame story is— contrary to general consensus and conventional wisdom—not simply a frame that has brought together heterogeneous narrative genres. It works as a filter. It only retains stories which may vary thematically but do reproduce structurally the generative frame story, or parts of it which I have called "narrative blocks." The reproduction is not necessarily a variant, but often is sufficiently different in content that it cannot be recognized. The orders of repetition of generated narrative to generating narrative, or enframed to enframing, can be fully understood through figures drawn from poetics. This study shows that genres considered most typical and least typical, most indigenous and most foreign to the spirit of *The Arabian Nights* are related structurally to the frame story. The master figures are irony, simile, metaphor, and metonymy.

While metaphor and metonymy have been sufficiently discussed as a pair—the first relating to replacement and based on similarity, the latter based on displacement and related to contiguity—very little has been done on irony and simile by relating them to mental operations. This is not the place to explore these two figures; it suffices to suggest that in the context of this study the simile represents the most direct mode in an otherwise indirect discourse, and irony represents the farthest mode of indirectness in an indirect discourse. They represent two poles of communication, while metaphor–metonym represent two modes of substitution.

Transformation

The most striking transformation in *The Arabian Nights* is a virtual one. It is a transformation that took place on the one thousand and first night—it is the transformation of the binary impulse with its mutative tendencies into a ternary one with growing principles. It is the transformation of a couple into a family. The change from binarism to virtual ternarism is crucial in the ending of the narrative. Only the third element can guarantee an end to this endless discourse.

Another transformation that is accomplished by Shahrazad is that women are turned from sexual objects into erotic subjects. Women are used by Shahrayar as objects of consummation totally without a will or a say, to be discarded once they had fulfilled their role. Shahrazad, in contrast, modifies this principle. She has a say, and a pretty eloquent one. She becomes a partner to Shahrayar. She becomes a subject, in the sense of someone who performs an act. She also manages to transfer the openly and directly sexual act into the narrative one. The phallic pleasure is turned into a discursive pleasure, and the sexual play into verbal play. The transformation is from the concrete to the symbolic, from the direct to the indirect.

It is essential to note that the transformation of woman from an object to a subject occurs suddenly. Shahrazad appears on the scene and re-invents the rules of the game. In *The Arabian Nights,* women are of two unreconciled types: the object and the subject of a verb. There is no gradual development of the woman as object into the woman as subject, as, for example, in Nora's case in Ibsen's *A Doll's House,* where she becomes conscious of her enslaved status and rebels. In *The Arabian Nights,* women are essentially of two kinds: the active and the passive, and no change of one into the other takes place. In this sense, *The Arabian Nights* is drastically different from the novel with its characters who are, in general, constantly developing and growing with every page and every episode. Novelistic characters have an organic identity, while the characters of *The Arabian Nights* have an inorganic consistency. *The Arabian Nights* deals ultimately with the realities of the unconscious and it is structured as an endless discourse where narrative patterns conjure and cohabit each other. Without a definite destination but with a rigorous order, the narrative disseminates and proliferates. The nature of transformations in the narrative is constantly bracketed and cannot escape the confines of fictional reflexivity. *The Arabian Nights* is a pure example of the principles of *sui generis* and *demonstratio demonstrationum.* It is both self-generating and self-demonstrative. It is the best expression of a strange poetics where art does not imitate nature, but where art imitates art. It is indeed a great moment of a folding over and self-contemplation in the history of aesthetics. Culture and nature face each other in *The Arabian Nights* but they can never carry a dialogue, let alone a symbiosis as in the myths of preliterate people.

The bipolarity of Arab–Islamic culture can only be fully appreciated when one understands two of the narrative masterpieces that were produced: *The Arabian Nights,* with structures akin to the unconscious, and Ibn Tufayl's *Hayy ibn Yaqzan,* with structures reproducing the development of consciousness. Ibn Tufayl's novel is about life and conscious knowledge.

Every discovery arrived at by the hero, every page in the narrative, builds up toward the end. It offers organic unity in its purest forms. The hero moves from sensation to perception to reasoning until he discovers Truth. The transformations of *The Arabian Nights* are those based on *bricolage*, those of *Hayy ibn Yaqzan* on *planning*. It is not surprising, therefore, that with *bricolage* the play goes on infinitely, while with planning, which has a specific destination, the narrative arrives sooner or later at its end.

Humankind in *The Arabian Nights*, as represented by Shahrazad, fights destined end by continually being—by not ending—while humankind as represented by the hero in Greek tragedy tries to efface destiny once for all, and this is why the hero is a tragic figure. Humankind in *The Arabian Nights* is impotent in the face of the absolute, but master of the relative. The most fundamental victory in *The Arabian Nights* is transformation of past and future into perpetual present. The tense of Shahrazad is the present indicative.

Function

The psycho-aesthetic function of *The Arabian Nights* is a special one. There is no purgation as in the tragedy, and this is why the tension is continually maintained rather than resolved. Instead of a catharsis, we have a cathexis, a term I borrow from psychoanalytic theory. It has been pointed out that the term itself is ambiguous.[1] In my use, I enlist the etymological sense of this term, signifying "holding." The function of *The Arabian Nights* is less of purging than of possessing. It is clear that a number of repressed feelings are aired in *The Arabian Nights,* mostly those dealing with aggressive instincts and taboos, yet there is no final cleansing effect. On the contrary, the more the irrepressible is highlighted, the more it calls for more of the same. The reader or listener invests energy into the narrative, just as Shahrayar did. There is, in a sense, occupation: control without incorporation.

In *The Arabian Nights,* the diversity of the narrative is fascinating and functional. Superficially, storytelling in *The Arabian Nights* seems to be chaotic, but in reality there are recurring oppositions which embrace and let loose a variety of cultural contradictions. The most spectacular opposition is between black and white, night and day, dark and light. Storytelling in the frame story takes place strictly at night, and is done by a woman in collaboration with her sister. Different stories are narrated but they all relate to the overall frame, and the varied audiences can find in them their own favorite themes.

If we were to draw parallels between ritualistic ceremonials and narrative forms, then *The Arabian Nights* would correspond rather faithfully to the *zar,* a possession cult ceremony that is prevalent in Egypt, Sudan, and the Horn of Africa, although frowned upon by orthodox Islam. *Zar* ceremonies vary considerably, just as the texts of an oral narrative do. But the steps undertaken are the same and the main features have much in common.[2] The *shaykha* of the *zar,* or the mistress of ceremonies, starts by asking about the patient and the patient's symptoms. When the ailment is sufficiently described and the trouble diagnosed, a *zar* is held for seven days.[3] This is paralleled by Shahrazad's inquiry and her father's description of Shahrayar's story and state, followed by a ceremonial storytelling that goes on for one thousand and one nights. The *zar* is a female activity just as the unfolding of narrative in *The Arabian Nights* is essentially set up by the two women, Shahrazad and Dinazad.

The main patient in the *zar* is dressed and made up like a bride (even if the patient is a man) and, "the shaikha usually has several costumes for changes during the performance according to the personalities and the desires of various spirits."[4] The variety of stories corresponds to the different costumes worn by the master or the mistress of a *zar* ceremony, and just as in *The Arabian Nights,* the repressed—whether an erotic or a social desire—comes to the fore. In the *zar,* sexual demands, indulgence, infantile regression, and socially prohibited desires are all expressed in a way that is hardly subtle, but sanctioned within the context.

The element of sacrifice is also essential in the *zar.* A white or black cock is sacrificed and the blood is smeared on the patient. In some cases a white sheep is sacrificed first, followed by a black goat.[5] The analogy between the ritual and the narrative of Shahrazad is striking: the metaphoric use of black and white and the role of sacrifice and blood-letting are essential parts of the frame story of *The Arabian Nights* as well. Finally, in both the *zar* and *The Arabian Nights,* the ceremony ends with the patient asking for a special treat, usually from her husband. She is generally awarded what she desires.

The correspondence is not one-to-one between the *zar* and *The Arabian Nights,* but there is a carry-over of basic structures and salient features, which allows us to classify both as psychodramas. Furthermore, just as the *zar* has been frowned upon by religious orthodoxy and despised by elite organizations, so also has *The Arabian Nights* suffered rejection by the literary institutions and establishments in the Arab world. It is thought of as rather substandard literature: immoral and poor.

We can conclude that *The Arabian Nights* offers us a specific structure of what may be called the perpetual narrative. If, as Bakhtin has brilliantly shown, Dostoevsky has given us the polyphonic structure in its purest and most articulate expression, *The Arabian Nights* has equally provided the literary treasury with a many-voiced structure used not only to present the breaking down of unity to its heterogeneous elements, but also to maintain through this very structure an ever-continuing present. Time is by far the most important concern in *The Arabian Nights*. Instead of the linear presentation of time, as it occurs in the traditional European novel or as it occurs in Ibn Tufayl's narrative, *Hayy ibn Yaqzan*, here we find linear time transformed into circular time. This circularity is expressed through a series of figures that sums up the twisting back of narrative on itself and the mirroring of its components, namely irony, simile, metaphor, and metonymy. The techniques used in *The Arabian Nights* to recover and remember are not gratuitious gymnastics. As in the mystic parable, their objective is to change the listener through demonstrating and to mean through being.

It is not surprising then to find *The Arabian Nights,* in its migrations and transmigrations, adapting itself to new cultural contexts, responding to alternative literary needs, while remaining "itself." The very power of *The Arabian Nights* lies in its protean identity. Constructed like language, it allows an infinite number of discourses. Thus in its perpetual drive, *The Arabian Nights* conquers time, and in its protean drive it conquers the frontiers of place. *The Arabian Nights* has moved millions of readers and listeners, from the most sophisticated to the most vulgar, from scholars to children. The following chapters will demonstrate how this remarkable work has managed to penetrate and inspire different cultures and ethos from India to Argentina, from the New World to the Old World.

9

POETIC LOGIC
IN *THE PANCHATANTRA*
AND
THE ARABIAN NIGHTS

Poetic Logic and Narration

The paradoxical expression "poetic logic" was first used by Giambattista Vico when writing *Princìpi di scienza nuova* (1725). By "poetic" Vico meant the spontaneous, imaginative, and highly metaphoric mode of expression which he associated with folk literature and thought.[1] Logic, on the other hand, indicates a rigorous and systematic development of thinking. But the contradiction is only on the surface, since creations of collective imagination have been proven to contain within them inner systems of relations and logical coherence of an indirect nature. The poetic logic of a given work of art is, therefore, its pattern of signifying and its system of communicating.

This chapter will compare and contrast the underlying poetic logic of two world classics that have emerged from the Orient and influenced other literatures tremendously. There is probably a genetic kinship between the Indian classic *The Panchatantra* and *The Arabian Nights*,[2] and most certainly definite elements common to narrative Indian literature are present in *The Arabian Nights*.[3] However, I will not deal with the question of artistic borrowing and concentrate on structural affinities and variations in the two texts.

In a sense, both *The Panchatantra* and *The Arabian Nights* fall into the same narrative genre: a collection of tales within a frame story. Yet the function of storytelling in the two works varies considerably. In *The Panchatantra,* the purpose of telling stories is explicitly stated in the prologue as teaching "the art of practical life"or "the art of intelligent life."[4] The purpose of storytelling in *The Arabian Nights* is stated by Shahrazad secretly to her collaborator Dinazad as a strategy for survival.[5] It is interesting, therefore, to note the patterns of stories and the modes of production of meaning in the two cases.

The frame story in *The Panchatantra* is simple and undramatic when compared to the frame story in *The Arabian Nights*. The net result is that the complexity and the power of *The Arabian Nights'* prologue continues to hover over Shahrazad's discourse, while Vishnusharman, the eloquent Brahman, recedes into the background as his fables unfold. This has far-reaching implications: the reader can properly focus on the stories of *The Panchatantra* and extract their moral or lesson. In *The Arabian Nights,* the content of what Shahrazad is relating is less important as the crucial element is precisely this juxtaposition of a woman condemned to death at dawn, relating stories to postpone her fate. It is the case of Shahrazad that captivates as much as her narration. Furthermore, in *The Arabian Nights* the formulaic beginning—"Shahrazad said 'O auspicious King, it has reached me that . . . '"—and ending—"And when dawn caught up with Shahrazad, she stopped her permitted say"—of storytelling partly punctuate the narration, but mostly remind us of Shahrazad's drama.

The system of partition or division is significant too. The night is the measurement unit, as it were, in *The Arabian Nights,* but nights vary in length. In some, more than one story is told, in others, part of one. The verbal quantity also varies from one night to another, as well as from one manuscript to another. There is something arbitrary about the length and the content of each night, though all variations of *The Arabian Nights* claim one thousand and one nights. On the other hand, the units which constitute *The Panchatantra* are chapters or books, as the title "panchatantra" (five books) very clearly shows. Each "book" or chapter is a classificatory unit and the unfolding of the five parts is announced in the prologue and rigorously followed in the text. The five books—(1) The Loss of Friends, (2) The Winning of Friends, (3) Crows and Owls, (4) Loss of Gains, and (5) Ill-considered Action—are independent and tackle different aspects of socio-political relations. Each book has its own frame story which triggers the narration and develops it. Hence the five frame stories and their characters are interwoven with the inserted stories. Each inserted story, to a great extent, moves the action. For example, in the story of "The Jackal and the War-drum" in Book 1 (The Loss of Friends) of *The Panchatantra,*[6] which is told by Victor, the counseling jackal, he demonstrates to Rusty, the lion-king, that "one should not be troubled by a mere sound"[7] and hence is permitted to investigate the sound. Storytelling in the *Panchatantra* can be said to contribute to the *progression* of the plot. In contrast, inserted stories in *The Arabian Nights* often work as a *digression* from the plot. For example, the story of "'Aziz and 'Aziza"[8] is not instrumental in the un-folding of "Sirat 'Umar ibn al-Nu'man"[9] in which it is inserted, as I have mentioned. The inserted story is a distraction from the movement of the framing story.

Progression in *The Panchatantra* and digression in *The Arabian Nights* are tendencies in the line of narration rather than absolute rules. Further-more, it is wrong to assume that progression is the only manifestation of skill in narrative construction. Digression should be viewed as an alterna-tive method of fictional construction. In *The Arabian Nights,* digression is certainly functional and even rewarding, for the idea is to suspend time and to captivate. It is becoming, therefore, for Shahrazad to sidetrack, cre-ating this somewhat amusing, somewhat bewildering labyrinth in which Shahrayar as well as the reader are completely enmeshed. Since the pur-pose of *The Panchatantra* on the other hand is didactic, there is an effort to control the flow of the material and its channels. The point is not to charm, but to instruct; therefore, clarity is preferable.

When symbolization occurs in the fables of *The Panchatantra,* it is formulated in a way which makes decoding a fairly easy activity and deci-phering a simple substituting process. Not only does *The Panchatantra* use ready-made stock characters such as gullible kings (as in "The Monk Who Left His Body Behind,"[10] "The Unforgiving Monkey,"[11] and "Mer-chant Strong-Teeth"[12]) and adulterous wives (as in "The Weaver's Wife"[13] and "The Farmer's Wife"[14]), but it is also consistent in associating traits with beasts.

Hence the monkey regularly appears stupid; the lion, strong; the jackal, crafty; and so on. This helps the reader understand the situation and derive the proper moral, in the same way that masks and colors are used in Far Eastern theater to denote moral position and social status. This is hardly the case in *The Arabian Nights* where, for example, the demons *(jinn)* can be harmful (as in "The Fisherman and the Demon"[15]) or helpful (as in "'Ala' al-Din and the Magic Lamp"[16]). Women, as well, are of ambivalent disposition. There are those who are obsessed with sexual delights (the wives of Shahzaman and Shahrayar, and the kidnapped woman in the frame story,[17] and those in "The Woman and the Bear"[18] and "The Princess and the Monkey"[19]). But there are also self-sacrificing, sublimating, or pure women who function as paradigms of "proper" female behavior—as medieval Arab culture defines it—such as 'Aziza (in "'Aziz and 'Aziza"[20]) and Shahrazad (in the frame story[21]). Such vacillation prevents the stabilization of the narrative code and turns the reader away from anchoring the text into the outside social world. The emphasis is more on the transformations within the narrative sphere, hence the reading remains in its self-contained circle.

To be self-contained does not mean that the fiction does not cross into reality. In fact *The Arabian Nights,* like any text, imaginative or expository, has to use words and concepts from human language, and consequently these are necessarily pregnant with social implications. However, the specificity of *The Arabian Nights* lies in the multiplicity of stories included and points of view adopted, to the point where no coherent ideological argument can be derived from it. It is often difficult to decide under what genre to classify *The Arabian Nights* because of the richness and variety of its material. It has fantastic as well as realistic stories. It deals with erotic impulses as well as sublimated love. It has religious stories and detective stories. Some of its stories are of epic length and others are short anecdotes. But the lack of obvious unifying pattern does not mean lack of significance. For the point that the thematic complexity of *The Arabian Nights* reveals is the encyclopedic drive and the yearning for a totality—that which the mystics have called "multiplicity-in-unity."

The Panchatantra may not have a fixed ideological position, but it does bring together stories that are instructive in a realistic situation. It is not cynical, though it offers down-to-earth, unsentimental, and practical advice. It constitutes what has been called *niti-shastra,* or a manual of wise rules for social interaction.[22] It is directed thematically, while *The Arabian Nights* runs in innumerable directions. In *The Arabian Nights,* what counts is not a move in a given direction and with a foreseeable objective, but simply to move—the orientation is immaterial. In *The Panchatantra* the aim of the narrating Brahman is intelligent living, *savoir vivre*; in *The Arabian Nights,* the aim is plain living, *survivre.* It is indeed very significant that the character Vishnusharman, who is entrusted with teaching social wisdom, is a wise old man of eighty years, while Shahrazad, the symbol of struggle for life, is a young woman of childbearing age.

So, while *The Panchatantra* is characterized by a bold and çlear system of signifying, *The Arabian Nights'* message remains elusive and ambiguous. This is the distinction between formulated allegory and symbolic allegory.[23] There are many elements that contribute to the solidity of *The Panchatantra* and the liquidity of *The Arabian Nights,* as it were. Having briefly reviewed the overall construction pattern, it is now instructive to compare the use of specific construction elements in the two narratives, mainly the characters, the plots, and the formulaic expressions.

Characters, Plots, and Locutions

The characters in *The Panchatantra* are mainly animals. In Book I, the principal characters are two jackals, Victor and Cheek; the lion, Rusty; and the bull, Lively. In Book II, the characters are the crow, Swift; the mouse, Gold; the turtle, Slow; and the deer, Spot. In Book III, the action is shared by the crows and the owls. In Book IV, the exchange of stories and the intrigue is between a monkey and a crocodile; in Book V between a merchant and a monk. The talking beasts, of course, defy everyday norms— just as flying horses or gigantic demons do. Yet, somehow, the text does not fail to convey to us that the talking animal is not a wonder but an allegory. How is it done? And why is a talking monkey in *The Panchatantra* taken for granted, but not the writing monkey in *The Arabian Nights?*[24]

This is a question of narrative technique. In *The Panchatantra,* as in any fable including those that occur in *The Arabian Nights,* the act of speech by animals is presented without any indication of supernatural or fantastic event. In Book I of *The Panchatantra,* the lion is said to be the king of animals—an almost universal metaphor indicating that the lion is the most powerful and the mightiest among animals. Here, there is a poetic transfer from the human hierarchic society to the animal world. King in folk thought means the greatest or strongest. The acceptable metaphor is used here to develop an extended comparison, or what Riffaterre has called *la métaphore filée.*[25] Hence the lion has a retinue of animals and, furthermore, this retinue is divided into four sections. The comparison in one aspect, namely, the attributive, is now extended to the organizational level. Also, king lion has the given name "Rusty," which helps humanize him—especially when human sentiments of fear and concealment of fear are attributed to him.[26] Clearly, at this point the metaphor has been extended beyond the point of suspended disbelief. The lion is not simply a lion, not the kind of lion that we know—a beast of the jungle that may be able to subdue all animals but does not have in any concrete sense a court and a retinue. Here, we have a substitution that has worked progressively and inversely as follows:

1. The lion to the animals is as the king to the subjects.
2. The lion is the king of the animals.
3. The lion is the king.
4. The king is the lion.

These steps correspond to thc following mental processes:

1. Explicit analogy
2. Implicit analogy
3. Abbreviation
4. Inversion.

The analytical logic of the fables becomes clear enough. The lion now stands for the king in a four-step process of concealment. The lion simply veils the king, and it is a very thin, transparent veil. The lion refers to the king as a generic term, not a specific one. Symbolization in the fable is, then, radically different from that of a *roman à clef,* such as Diderot's *Les bijoux indiscrètes,* where narrative characters are drawn from figures that are identifiable historically and locally. The fable deals with generalities that are prevalent everywhere. In such a world, it is not surprising that the jackals who are the lion's counselors exchange pointed stories and pungent verses. The question that imposes itself is: Why the veiling? Why not call a king a king instead of a lion? Why the detour? Some may argue that it is a remnant of primitive poetic thought. But that is unlikely, for it is the deliberate translation of an already existing abstract thought. *The Panchatantra*'s fables are not pre-abstract thought, but illustrations of abstractions that are present in the text in the form of maxims and gnomic verses. The most likely explanation is that the use of fables was a mode of retaining and preserving stories in an age where writing was costly and publishing unknown. Stringing a series of rules of conduct in a plot and attributing sayings to animals is certainly more effective than memorizing a set of dry, complicated rules. Furthermore, fable-telling recovers totemism, defined in the words of Lévi-Strauss as "relations posed ideologically, between two series, one *natural,* the other *cultural.*"[27] The fables reproduce in the world of animals the behavioral code recommended by the culture.

As for *The Arabian Nights,* the animals we come across are mostly metamorphosed human beings. The animals are humanized in the presentation, just as in *The Panchatantra,* but they are by no means allegorized. In the story of "The Porter and the Three Ladies of Baghdad" we encounter two black dogs who get whipped by a lady.[28] But the whipping is so ceremonial that it includes regular sessions of torturous whipping followed by affectionate caresses, and accompanied by the crying of the dogs. All these elements contribute to make the scene enigmatic rather than allegoric. The ambivalence inherent in hurting and relieving—the ritual aspect— and finally the tears of the dogs raise the reader's curiosity and also that of Harun al-Rashid, who is posed in the narration as a puzzled spectator. Hence, this episode reveals a secret while the allegory of the fable reveals a message. In *The Arabian Nights,* we know what we see has another layer, but that layer does not provide the message. We only know that the surface of the text is a veil—but beneath the veil we cannot see clearly, if at all. What we sense lurking beneath the veil is a state of mind and a psychological disposition rather than a clear-cut social message.

The plots of individual stories in *The Panchatantra* are relatively simple and uncomplicated; they revolve around a single *discovery.* In the story of "The Wedge-pulling Monkey,"[29] the fable is about a monkey who meddles in a construction site and gets his private parts caught in a wedge. The point of this discovery is to discourage meddling into that which does not concern one. In the story of "The Jackal and the War-drum,"[30] the message centers on the deception of appearance, thus the jackal is under the impression that the skin of the drum covers rich meat, but after struggling with it, he discovers that it is empty. In the story of "Numskull and the Rabbit."[31] the point is how shrewdness can overcome force. All the animals agree to send one of them as the meal of the ferocious lion. When it is the rabbit's turn, he fabricates a story: a strong lion stopped him on the way. Having raised the lion's wrath and jealousy, he led him to a well where the lion mistook his own image for a challenging other. The lion jumped in to kill the other and in doing so met his own end. The point is made in an illustrative fashion and cannot escape the attention of the reader.

In contrast, *The Arabian Nights'* plots tend to be more complex. The story of "The Porter and the Three Ladies of Baghdad" is so rich and branches in so many directions that it is difficult to extract its significance without elaborate analytic work. Significance in the tales of *The Arabian Nights* seems to recede to fathomless depths, and it takes a certain effort of concentration and intensive penetration before one realizes the point behind it; even then the point is missed if it cannot be related to some state that one has experienced and perhaps suppressed. It is, therefore, not so much a discovery as a process of *recovery* that one encounters in the tales of *The Arabian Nights.* Whether it is the ambivalence of sadomasochism as represented in the whipping and caressing scenes, mentioned earlier, or the undressing of one's mother, as in the story of "Jawdar,"[32] the appeal is oriented to some deep psychic strata rather than surface social ones. This is not to say that *The Arabian Nights* does not have simple-structured tales or social stories, or for that matter fables. Previous chapters in this book have shown that it does, and that significance in *The Arabian Nights* as a whole lies less in the content of individual stories than in the structural relations between the various levels of narrative. But when considering individual stories in *The Panchatantra* and *The Arabian Nights* it is again a question of predominance[33]: long, complicated stories are frequent in *The Arabian Nights,* and secret underground enclosures, forbidden doors, and fulfillment of magical wishes seem to be their typical motifs.

Another indicative element in the system of signification lies in the use of locutions. *The Panchatantra* uses locutions, gnomic verses, and proverbs in a regular manner, namely, to start a tale and to end it. Hence stories are very tightly contained by the maxim or the saying, which both initiates the fable and finishes it. For example, the story of "The Mouse That Set Elephants Free"[34] is preceded by the saying:

> Make friends, make friends, however strong
> Or weak they be:
> Recall the captive elephants
> That mice set free.[35]

The fable ends with those words: "Make friends, make friends, however strong."[36]

This clearly stresses the point of the fable and makes it work as an extended illustration of the locution. The only other time that verse is inserted in this story is when the mice are having their convention and discussing the wrath of elephants:

> An elephant will kill you, if
> He touch; a serpent if he sniff;
> King's laughter has a deadly sting;
> A rascal kills by honoring;[37]

In this case, the verse highlights the power of the elephant eloquently by tying it with comparable powerful creatures such as serpents and kings. The verse in this case serves a descriptive role, but a highly hyperbolic one. The point is therefore made, or rather remade, through a shift to a metrical discourse. The verse serves to underline and to articulate eloquently the maxim of the fable.

In *The Arabian Nights,* verse as well as maxims are used, but rarely to pinpoint a moral. They are generally used at a moment of tension or emotion, as when lovers break into poetry to express their passion or their bewilderment. In "Sirat 'Umar ibn al-Nu'man," Dhaw'-al-Makan is stricken by grief and he cries, reciting a poem in which he recalls his former glory and his present predicament.[38] Verse and locutions are essentially used in an expressive way to portray that which narrative prose is incapable of doing adequately. At times, verse and proverbs are used for a descriptive purpose as when women are accused of treachery, and reference is made to Adam and Joseph[39]; however, the verses are used to demonstrate not so much the point of the story as the point of view of the imprisoned woman who was speaking.

The Arabian Nights uses locutions to dramatize a state of mind or a point of view while *The Panchatantra* uses locutions to draw a point and stress a quality. The use of stylistic locutions enhances the pitch in *The Arabian Nights* while it serves as the extraction of the lesson in *The Panchatantra*. Thus, the elements of the poetic logic of the Indian classic converge in order to *mean* while the narrative logic of the Arabian classic works in order to *be*.

10

THE ARABIAN NIGHTS IN SHAKESPEAREAN COMEDY: "THE SLEEPER AWAKENED" AND THE TAMING OF THE SHREW

Son essence est sa non-essence.
—Jacques Derrida, *La dissémination*

Literary Archaeology

Shahrazad on the 271st night begins to narrate to Shahrayar a story that lasts till the 290th night. It is a story commonly known as "The Sleeper Awakened," although the only extant Arabic text gives it a title that would literally translate as "The Sleeper and the Awakened."[1] This story bears an uncanny resemblance to the induction of Shakespeare's play *The Taming of the Shrew*. Both works employ the motif of a transportation of a man in his sleep to another distinguished man's house, after which the first man is made to believe upon awakening that he is the actual owner. This change triggers questions and doubts concerning identity and reality posed in a comic fashion. But behind the farcical tone, the philosophical issues of "Who am I?" and "What is reality?" persist. This chapter compares the two works, not simply as a study in the transformation of a source, or the affinity of literary motifs, but to try through the comparison to detect the latent answers to humankind's constant interrogation about itself and its social universe. Literature is often philosophy in disguise, and disguise seems to be the theme and the technique of these two literary works. A brief summary of the two plots will reveal, first, their similarities and second, the dominant motif of disguise in both.

The story of Abu al-Hasan the Wag opens with the death of his father who left him a sizeable inheritance. He saves half and entertains generously with the other half. When his money is spent, his companions abandon him. From then on he uses his savings but swears never to entertain anyone more than once. One night, when Harun al-Rashid arrives disguised, Abu al-Hasan entertains him and mentions his wish to get even with some troublesome neighbors. The caliph arranges to have him drugged and then brought to the royal palace where everyone is instructed to treat him as if he were the Prince of the Faithful. Disbelieving at first, Abu al-Hasan surrenders mentally in the end and, assuming the role, realizes his wish of punishing his neighbors. The next night, he is taken back to his home. Upon waking, he continues to assume the role of the caliph and consequently is taken to a mental asylum. Eventually, he renounces his claims and is taken back home by his mother. Harun al-Rashid then comes again in disguise and convinces Abu al-Hasan to receive him another time despite his resolution not to entertain anyone more than once. Again, Abu al-Hasan is drugged and brought to the palace of the caliph. This time Abu al-Hasan tries to resist the new role but, contradicted by everyone, ends up exhibiting himself like a fool. The caliph, who has been watching all along with amusement, appears laughing and rewards him by giving him a royal post as well as marrying him to a handmaid of Zubayda, his wife.

When Abu al-Hasan and his wife find themselves short of money, Abu al-Hasan designs a trick: each of them will claim that the other has died and will seek a condolence gift from the caliph and his wife. Harun al-Rashid and Zubayda discover that they have heard conflicting versions of who died, but each insists that his or her version is correct. After they receive the contraditory reports from their messengers, they decide to investigate in person, and they find both Abu al-Hasan and his wife simulating death. The caliph, still curious to know who died first, offers a thousand dinars to the one who would provide him with an answer. To this Abu al-Hasan responds, thus gaining the reward and ending the story happily.[2]

Abu al-Hasan's counterpart in *The Taming of the Shrew* is Christopher Sly, who appears in the induction and whose active presence covers only 277 lines of the drama. The play opens with a quarreling scene between Sly the drunken tinker and the hostess of a country alehouse, after which Sly falls asleep on a heath. A lord returning from his hunt finds him and decides to play a practical joke on him. The lord orders his retainers to take him to the lord's house and treat him as if he were the proprietor. When Sly awakens he is informed that he is a noble gentleman who had suffered madness for the previous fifteen years. At first, Sly resists the new role but eventually ends up believing he is a lord married to a lovely lady (who is in fact the lord's page disguised as a lord's wife). Then a troupe of players comes to entertain the lord. They perform a play that revolves around the taming of a shrew by her suitor and husband. The end of the inner play does not take us back to Sly.[3]

In raising the possibility of links between *The Arabian Nights* story and the English comedy, the first question posed is how could Shakespeare's *Taming of the Shrew,* which is dated at around 1593, be derived from *The Arabian Nights,* whose first translation into a European language did not occur until the beginning of the eighteenth century?[4]

To start with, one has to take into consideration all the oriental literature that was transmitted orally to Europe and England and whose documentary traces are absent. That oriental tales could have migrated by word of mouth to England is a question about which we can speculate but which we can never settle. However, there are sufficient indications to suggest that the impact of Arab–Islamic culture on Europe was not confined to written sources.[5] Furthermore, *The Taming of the Shrew* draws heavily on popular and folk elements that are very likely to have been intermingled with those coming from the Saracens.[6]

Besides the likely oral links, there were also written works available to Shakespeare, which reproduced, albeit in different form, the story of "The Sleeper Awakened." It has been generally accepted that Shakespeare adapted a version of *The Arabian Nights* tale for his induction:

> The plot of the Induction to Shakespeare's 'The Taming of the Shrew' is similar to the adventure of Abu al-Hasan the Wag, and is generally believed to have been adapted from a story entitled 'The Waking Man's Fortune' in Edward's collection of comic tales, 1570, which were retold somewhat differently in Goulart's 'Admirable and Memorable Histories,' 1607. Both versions are reprinted in Mr. Hazlitt's 'Shakespeare's Library,' vol. IV, part 1, pp. 403–414.[7]

Geoffrey Bullough summarizes available scholarship on the subject of this particular case of narrative migration as follows:

> The theme of the beggar transported into luxury is found in *The Arabian Nights,* where Haroun Al Raschid plays the trick on a sleeper. Philip the Good of Burgundy repeated it, according to Heuterus, *De Rebus Burgundicis,* Lib. iv, p. 150, 1584. Goulart put this version into French in his *Thrésor d'histoires admirables* . . . (1606?), translated into English in 1607 by Edward Grimeston. Burton summarized Heuterus in his *Anatomy of Melancholy,* 1621, Pt. II, Sec. ii, Mem. 4. According to Warton's *History of English Poetry* (Sect. LII) the story was printed in a jest-book 'sett forth by Master Richard Edwardes, mayster of her maiesties revels' in 1570. In Sir Richard Barckley's *A Discourse of the Felicitie of Man* (1598), pp. 24–6, the 'pretie experiment' is ascribed to the Emperor Charles the Fifth. Other versions, *The Waking Man's Dreame* and the Percy Ballad 'The Frolicsome Duke, or the Tinker's Good Fortune' are probably after Shakespeare (*cf. Boas* for the former and for other versions). The author of *A Shrew* must have used Heuterus or some version now lost.[8]

The relationship between the Arabian tale and the Shakespearean comedy has been established by critical consensus,[9] although it is impossible to assert beyond any doubt Shakespeare's exact source. Though the relationship is often described as "derivation," no one has undertaken to compare them, as if critics were content to announce the affinity or genealogy without looking into the anatomy of the two texts.

Critical Anatomy

As we begin to analyze the kindred texts constructed around Abu al-Hasan the Wag and Christopher Sly, it is immediately obvious that they are part of a whole. They are not independent texts, although they are both autonomous. The story of "The Sleeper Awakened" is embedded in the discourse of Shahrazad. The narration of the story is interrupted several times, as Shahrazad has to refrain from pursuing her story when dawn breaks. Her nocturnal discourse is a survival weapon in the face of a disillusioned monarch intending to decapitate each and every bride he takes after one night. The tyrant monarch Shahrayar postpones Shahrazad's death in order to listen to her captivating stories.

On the other hand, the "story" of Christopher Sly is not within another story, but it introduces an inner "story" of the Shrew. Christopher Sly's episode induces the inner play. This induction, an Elizabethan term and dramatic device, is not the same as framing. An induction functions as a prologue, while a framework embraces a set. While the induction triggers, the framework encloses. It is worth examining, therefore, the relationship of the part to the whole in both works. If we were to substitute for framework or induction the term "outer" and for the enframed or induced the term "inner," then we would find that the overlapping of plot in the Arabian tales and the Shakespearean comedy is accompanied by a structural inversion where the narrative inner text becomes the dramatic outer text. The following diagram shows the mirror-like inversions in the structure.

Structural Inversions

Outer	*Inner*
Shahrayar's Story (=A)	Abu al-Hasan's Story (=B)
Sly's Story (=C)	The Shrew's Story (=D)

In the four elements of the diagram, two are definitely analogous, namely B and C. In this quadruple set, it is tempting to wonder if there are other correspondences. But before we examine the relationship of A to D, let us examine the relationship of A to B and of C to D, in other words, the relationship of the outer text to the inner text in the same work. Fortunately, such relationships have already been studied and it suffices to refer to them. Superficially, of course, it may seem that there is a rupture between outer and inner stories; but first impressions can be deceptive. A number of excellent studies have shown the thematic relationship between Sly's story and the problematic of the Shrew's drama. The common denominator has been called "supposes" or role-playing or disguise, but whatever one may name the unifying factor it is undeniably there.[10]

The relationship of outer text to inner text in *The Arabian Nights* has been studied in the earlier chapters of this book, through the choice of a number of enframed tales—some of which are generally considered typical and others atypical—in comparison with the frame story. This study demonstrated the structural unity of the work. If we were to examine the story of "The Sleeper Awakened" with the story of Shahrayar as a background, we would immediately see parallelisms. Just as Shahrayar is disappointed by women and vows to spend no more than one night with each, in a similar vein Abu al-Hasan is disappointed by his fellow men and vows to entertain only strangers and never to see them again. Furthermore, points are made through narratives—such as the story of "The Larrikin and the Cook," told by Abu al-Hasan, which is a characteristic procedure in the framework.

Just as C generates D on a deep level, so does A generate B through a recombination of motifs and variation on a theme. The next question that poses itself is: What is the relationship of A to D, of Shahrayar's story to that of the Shrew? Once formulated in this way, the correspondences become apparent. Both stories are about taming a Shrew (male in *The Arabian Nights* and female in *The Taming of the Shrew*). In both cases, the taming takes place by holding a mirror up, forcing the Shrew into self-observation. In the case of Shahrazad, she tells Shahrayar stories that painfully reflect his predicament. As for Petruchio, he simulates the role of an arbitrary dictator to transform Katherina. The strategy works in both cases.

If the intricate relationships and structural inversions show something, it is the rigor and order of transformations—but to say that both works in question are a series of inversions and repetitions on the skeletal level does not mean that they are identical thematically.

The theme of being unwittingly transported from one state into another is present in both works, but is handled differently. In "The Sleeper Awakened," Harun al-Rashid arrives disguised, with his companion Masrur. When entertained by Abu al-Hasan, who offers hospitality only to strangers and then no more than once, the caliph asks him: "O youth, who art thou?" This question, though a banal one in certain contexts, carries a dimension of foreshadowing, for eventually Abu al-Hasan confuses his identity. In answer, Abu al-Hasan justifies his misanthropy by saying that there is a reason but he couches his answer in the form of an anecdote. The gist of the anecdote is that a cook, who disguises the horsemeat he sells and is then confronted by a tramp, has to accept the argument of the latter for fear of being revealed. Disguise becomes a leitmotif in the story. Later on, as Abu al-Hasan and the caliph are drinking, Harun al-Rashid decides to repay him and asks him: "O my brother, hast thou in thy heart concupiscence thou wouldst have accomplished or a contingency thou wouldst avert?"[11] To which Abu al-Hasan answers:

> By Allah, there is no regret in my heart save that I am not empowered with bidding and forbidding, so I might manage what is in my mind! . . . Would Heaven I might be Caliph for one day and avenge myself on my neighbours, for that in my vicinity is a mosque and therein four shaykhs, who hold it a grievance when there cometh a guest to me, and they trouble me with talk and worry me in words and menace me that they will complain of me to the Prince of True Believers, and indeed they oppress me exceedingly, and I crave of Allah the Most High power for one day, that I may beat each and every one of them with four hundred lashes, as well as the Imam of the mosque, and parade

them round about the city of Baghdad and bid cry before them: 'This is the reward and the least of the reward of whoso exceedeth in talk and vexeth the folk and turneth their joy to annoy.' This is what I wish, and no more.[12]

The subsequent drugging of Abu al-Hasan, and his transportation to the palace and instructing everyone to treat him as the Prince of the Believers, is a wish fulfillment engineered by the caliph. In other words, the unfolding of the story follows the dialogue of the caliph and Abu al-Hasan and can be summed up in a question—"Who are you?"—which is answered by a wish, what Abu al-Hasan would like to be: "I want to be the Caliph for a day." The identity crisis of Abu al-Hasan stems essentially from his unreasonable wish, which is fulfilled in a temporary and contrived fashion. When he returns home, Abu al-Hasan continues to assume the personality of the caliph and calls for the handmaids. His mother tries to calm him down, and he begins to waver and wonder whether his experience in the palace was not a dream. But once his mother tells him about the punishment of their neighbors and the gift she received from the caliph the day before, Abu al-Hasan has no more doubts about his earlier experience and starts beating his mother for denying him the title of the viceregent of Allah. The neighbors gather and are convinced that Abu al-Hasan is raving mad, and so they take him to a mental asylum where he is chained and beaten. The question then posed by the caliph to the Wag—"Who are you?"—thus becomes too complicated when one's wishes are fulfilled. The self as it is and as it desires to be are two distinct parts. When the two levels intermingle, confusion and madness result.

The second episode of the transportation of Abu al-Hasan to the palace of the caliph is essentially a repetition of the first episode, where the confusion about identity is re-enacted and then resolved. This time, Abu al-Hasan is less credulous about his royal appearance and tries to establish whether what he is experiencing is real or imaginary. When he cannot satisfy himself, he begins to dance naked, making a fool of himself. The bemused Harun al-Rashid reveals himself, thus resolving the contradictory state. First, Abu al-Hasan realizes that a trick has been played upon him. Second, the caliph appoints Abu al-Hasan as a companion to the caliph. This is a mediating position betwen Abu al-Hasan himself and his wished self, that of the caliph.

One expects the story to finish here, but it does not. The trick played upon Abu al-Hasan by the caliph has to be repaid, as it were. Just as the caliph carried out disguised visits to Abu al-Hasan and amused himself by his confusion, Abu al-Hasan in turn disguises himself and is amused by the caliph's confusion.

Abu al-Hasan instructs his wife—the handmaid of the caliph's wife, Zubayda—to go to her mistress and claim that her spouse had died, thus receiving a gift in compensation, while he intends to tell the caliph his spouse had died. When Harun al-Rashid and Zubayda exchange condolences, the confusion sets in. Who died, Abu al-Hasan or his wife Nuzhat al-Fu'ad? The heated argument is extended in the narrative by sending messengers, one from the entourage of the caliph (Masrur) and later one from the entourage of Zubayda. Abu al-Hasan and his wife guess what is coming and pretend, alternately, that the other has died, in such a way that Masrur will confirm Harun's version and the old duenna will confirm Zubayda's version. Ultimately the caliph and his wife decided to go to see for themselves only to find that both Abu al-Hasan and his wife are lying there "dead." The caliph is still puzzled as to who died first and therefore whose account is correct, and so he offers a thousand dinars as a prize for the one who solves the puzzle. At this, Abu al-Hasan answers, thus revealing that death was a pretense.[13] The narrative in all its details and conjugal arguments between the caliph and his wife is comic. However, beneath the comedy, a question persists, perhaps not stated but suggested. As the states of reality and dream, sanity and insanity are confused, so now also the states between life and death. The question is how do we know what we know? The issue here is epistomological, while in the frame story where Shahrazad strives for survival, the issue is ontological.

As for Christopher Sly in the induction of *The Taming of the Shrew,* the question is not "who are you?" but "what are you?" and the transportation fulfills not a future wish but a past claim: his noble ancestry. In the opening scene of the induction, a quarrel takes place between the hostess of the tavern and the drunken Sly. The hostess accuses Sly of being a rogue, to which Sly retorts in a confused but nevertheless telling fashion by saying what he is and what ancestors he has:

> Y' are a baggage, the Slys are no rogues. Look at the Chronicles,
> we came in with Richard Conqueror. Therefore *paucas pallabris,*
> let the world slide. Sessa![14]

In Sly's statement there is a confusion between Richard Coeur-de-Lion and William the Conqueror. But notwithstanding the historical confusion, the statement reveals a pride in, and a claim of, aristocratic descent which foreshadows the lordly role which will be assumed by Sly.

The transportation of Sly the tinker from the heath to the lordly mansion does not follow an articulated wish but fulfills a claim. What motivates the lord to carry out this experiment is jest: to see if Sly would renounce his actual identity, that of a tinker. The element of testing is also present in Harun al-Rashid's plan, but is secondary to the element of rewarding Abu al-Hasan. The lord proposes his experiment on the drunken, sleeping Sly in these words:

> O monstrous beast, how like a swine he lies!
> Grim death, how foul and loathsome is thine image!
> Sirs, I will practise on this drunken man.
> What think you, if he were conveyed to bed,
> Wrapped in sweet clothes, rings put upon his fingers,
> A most delicious banquet by his bed,
> And brave attendants near him when he wakes,
> Would not the beggar then forget himself?[15]

When the transportion of the beggar into lordly surroundings occurs and Sly wonders why he is being addressed as "your honour," the lord tries to remind him of his descent, having concocted a story about Sly's lunacy for the last fifteen years that causes him to forget that he was actually a lord. The element of descent fits into the fabricated story but also touches on Sly's claim or subconscious wish:

> Heaven cease this idle humour in your honour!
> O, that a mighty man of such descent,
> Of such possessions, and so high esteem.
> Should be infused with so foul a spirit![16]

The transformation of Sly from a tinker to the assumption of a lordly role, encouraged by the lord and his retainers, takes two steps. As he is told that he is a lord and finds himself in such lordly context, he asks himself first, "Am I not Sly the tinker?" and second, "Am I not a lord?" We see from the shift in the question the gradual giving in to the new identity. Furthermore, the very way of posing the first question presupposes yet another transmutation in the identity of Sly:

> What, would you make me mad? Am I not Christopher Sly, old Sly's son of Burton-heath, by birth a pedlar, by education a cardmaker, by transmutation a bear-herd, and now by present profession a tinker?[17]

After being served and attended and told about his strange lunacy, Sly begins to wonder:

> Am I a lord and have I such a lady?
> Or do I dream? Or have I dreamed till now?
> I do not sleep. I see, I hear, I speak.
> I smell sweet savours and I feel soft things.
> Upon my life, I am a lord indeed,
> And not a tinker nor Christopher Sly.[18]

Clearly the change in the nature of the question is followed by "yes" to the second and "no" to the first. It is also accompanied by a change from spoken language to rhythmic verse, an indication perhaps of an entry into the realm of imagination.

Then a troupe of players is announced to entertain his lordship with mirth and merriment. Sly welcomes the occasion and shows his receptivity by saying, "Let the world slip," just as he said to the alehouse hostess, "let the world slide." The latter statement ushers in Sly's drunken sleep, the former ushers in the play's performance. In both cases an entry into a dream world is induced. What we have is a series of embedded pretenses or supposes. The lord and his entertainers are pretending that Sly is the lord—they are acting. The inner play, as well as the outer play, is of course staged. The motifs in the inner play revolve around acting and role-playing: Lucentio, the son of a wealthy Pisan merchant, pretends to be a tutor to gain admittance as the teacher of Bianca, with whom he has fallen in love. His servant Tranio is to take his place as Lucentio. Hortensio, another suitor of Bianca, pretends to be a music teacher in order to enter Bianca's house. Petruchio, who proposes to Bianca's sister, Katherina the Shrew, plays the role of a tyrant in order to reform her.

The theme of the induction is, therefore, a pre-text as well as a pre-taste of the themes of the inner play. The inner play's theme of disguise is also a metatext, a commentary on the nature of performance. Thus, in *The Taming of the Shrew* the pretext, the text, and the metatext overlap and interweave in a way that reproduces the problematic of the play and the essence of the drama. The symbolic economy of *The Taming of the Shrew* is based on telescoping, while that of "The Sleeper Awakened" is based on mirroring. But the issue in both cases remains a fundamental one in the history of literary theory: reflection.

A closer look at the leading characters, Abu al-Hasan the Wag and Christopher Sly, reveals some instructive differences. Clearly they are both victims. Abu al-Hasan can be characterized from the very beginning of the story as a disillusioned man, deserted by the very friends he entertained. One cannot, of course, be disillusioned without having entertained illusions first. His disenchantment is summed up in an epigram:

> An wane my wealth, no man will succour me
> When my wealth waxeth all men friendly show:
> How many a friend, for wealth showed friendliness
> Who, when my wealth departed, turned to foe![19]

The disappointment of Abu al-Hasan is fully described when he wakes up at home after having spent a day as the caliph, only to find his old mother instead of the beautiful handmaids. Later on he has to confront the asylum's cruel nurses instead of the gentle damsels. Furthermore, Abu al-Hasan is later disappointed by the neglect of his patron, the caliph Harun al-Rashid.

As for Sly, he defines himself in terms of his professional metamorphoses: peddler, cardmaker, bear-herd, and tinker. When the lord offers Sly paintings to decorate his surroundings, they are scenes of Ovidian metamorphoses:

> SECOND SERVINGMAN:
> Dost thou love pictures? We will fetch thee straight
> Adonis painted by a running brook,
> And Cytherea all in sedges hid,
> Which seem to move and wanton with her breath,
> Even as the waving sedges play wi' th' wind.
>
> LORD:
> We' ll show thee Io as she was a maid,
> And how she was beguiled and surprised,
> As lively painted as the deed was done.
>
> THIRD SERVINGMAN:
> Or Daphne roaming through a thorny wood,
> Scratching her legs that one shall swear she bleeds,
> And at that sight shall sad Apollo weep,
> So workmanly the blood and tears are drawn.[20]

Both characters share a certain lack of *savoir faire* in the new surroundings. Their disbelief and bewilderment are eventually changed into self-indulgence. The subtle contrast in their characterization between the "disillusioned" Abu al-Hasan and the "metamorphosed" Sly intimates the unfolding narrative; Abu al-Hasan is essentially fulfilled after his many disillusionments, and thus the story closes. As for Sly, the metamorphoses seem to be left in a final *media res*. What happens to Sly can be assumed or imagined but it is not stated in the play. It is as if the game of "supposes" triggered by the play should continue indefinitely.

Poetic Philosophy

We can see from the comparison that there is kinship between these two texts. Both works raise the same pressing questions. But do they answer them in the same way?

We know that human beings pose to themselves fundamental questions that seem to vary little from one epoch to another. What varies, and what distinguishes epochs, is how the answers to these basic questions vary. The fields of knowledge are different modes of answering these questions and of favoring some and dropping others. The question that has preoccupied human thought from the dawn of civilizations has to do with self-definition and human identity.

If Socrates' famous statement was "Know thyself," then the stories of both Abu al-Hasan and Christopher Sly seem to ask: "How do I know myself?" Identity seems to be in both of them a mercurial entity, vulnerable to suggestions, to conscious and unconscious wishes, to surroundings, and to the discourse of others. In other words, the essence of one's identity seems to be its non-essence. Identity can be eroded, displaced, and transformed at will and by manipulation.

The self in both works is seen as something lacking constancy. Like a fluid, it takes the forms of the container, but unlike fluid it offers resistance before it yields. The method of adjusting to the new context is role-playing—some characters seem to play their new roles consciously and others play them unwittingly. Some resist them obstinately and others slip into them easily. In both works there is a correlation between identity and role-playing. However, there is a difference in how the correlation is perceived.

The story of Abu al-Hasan shows two kinds of role-playing: conscious and unconscious. In the first half of the story, Abu al-Hasan plays the role of the caliph without realizing the nature of the game. Consequently, he is the victim and does not know how to handle the situation. On the other hand, when he plays the role of the mourning widower knowingly and cunningly, he is fully rewarded. The agonizing confusion now falls upon the puzzled caliph. The self-conscious role-playing, therefore, leads to self-integration and fulfillment. This point can hardly be escaped.

In *The Taming of the Shrew,* there is also conscious and unconscious role-playing. The first is manifested in Petruchio, Lucentio, Tranio, Hortensio, the lord, the retainers, and the players. The unconscious role-playing is Sly's. The point in the Shakespearean comedy is hardly how unconscious role-playing is self-destructive. It is true that Sly's lack of consiousness makes him a clumsy lord and an awkward performer of an aristocratic role—but Sly is too-soon dropped from the drama to make such a message primary. The point is, rather, how the role-playing, forced consistently on Kate the Shrew, leads to the development of self-consciousness and an awareness of her own image toward the end of the play—which in turn helps her play the required conjugal role in the comedy, as an obedient wife in this case.[21]

To sum up, in the medieval Arabic tale the emphasis is on consciousness that leads to self-integrating play, while in the Elizabethan English comedy the emphasis is on self-integrating play that leads to consciousness. The differcnce is a matter of precedence, but in the history of ideas precedence is not a negligible matter.

11

DIALECTICS OF
THE SELF AND THE OTHER:
ARABIAN TALES IN
AMERICAN LITERATURES

I have loved since childhood The Book of the Thousand and
One Nights . . .

—Jorge Luis Borges[1]

Scheherazade's my *avant-gardiste* . . .

—John Barth[2]

That Arabian tales had penetrated Western literature can hardly be debated
today. Scholars have seen the imprint of Arabian folktales in major European narrative texts, including Boccaccio's *Decameron* and Chaucer's
Canterbury Tales. While the Arabian impact on medieval Western literature has been a matter of conjecture and guessing, as it was mostly transmitted orally, such Arabian influence on modern Western literature can be
documented. As long ago as 1704, when Antoine Galland's publication of
the first volume of *Les mille et une nuits* appeared, *The Arabian Nights*
has been recognized as a major text influencing not only Western literature and giving rise to what has been called the "Oriental tale," but it has
also been an important factor in shaping critical theory from the eighteenth century up to the writing of French structuralists and
poststructuralists: Tzvetan Todorov,[3] Michel Foucault,[4] and Jacques Lacan.[5]

Jorge Luis Borges, the contemporary Argentine writer (1899–1986), referred to the translation of *The Thousand and One Nights* as a major literary event that transformed literary and critical norms:

> We are in 1704, in France. It is the France of the Grand Siècle; it is the France where literature is legislated by Boileau, who dies in 1711 and never suspects that all of his rhetoric is threatened by that splendid Oriental invasion.[6]

Borges goes on to attribute the genesis of the Romantic revolution to *The Arabian Nights*:

> Galland publishes his first volume in 1704. It produces a sort of scandal, but at the same time it enchants the rational France of Louis XIV. When we think of the Romantic movement, we usually think of dates that are much later. But it might be said that the Romantic movement begins at the moment when someone, in Normandy or in Paris, reads *The Thousand and One Nights*. He leaves the world legislated by Boileau and enters the world of Romantic freedom.[7]

As for the contemporary American writer John Barth (1930–), he admires *The Arabian Nights* so much that he recommends it as a mentor for young writers.[8] In an article published in 1967, Barth admitted that he would have liked to have been the author of *The Thousand and One Nights*.[9]

But to admire a work of literature does not necessarily mean incorporating it in the same way. A writer may choose to engage in a dialogue or in a struggle with the precursor. Both the dialogue and the struggle are faces of dialectics; the creative writer has to establish that delicate balance between originality and imitation in his intertextual creations. Such dialectic becomes further dramatized when the model is drawn from another culture or tradition. Therefore, the way *The Arabian Nights* has been acculturated in the Americas throws light on the typology of literary assimilation.

I have chosen to examine the direct influence and inspiration that *The Arabian Nights* provided for Borges and Barth for a number of reasons. Each of them is a major writer in his own continent. Both share literary affinities. Barth has declared his admiration for Borges;[10] and they have been connected in a number of comparative studies.[11] They have both consistently confessed their love for Shahrazad's discourse. In studying the use of the Arabian tales by Borges and Barth and their modes of acculturating from Arab patrimony, insights may be gained into the collective cultural unconscious, so to speak, and the modes of literary intercourse.

Let me state my conclusion, which I shall demonstrate step by step in this chapter, at the beginning so as the reader may follow the nuanced differences between two types of acculturation. Barth *appropriates* the work of the Other and uses their structures, plots, and themes to present the Self. Borges *joins* the works of the Other, seeing the concerns of the Self in them. Barth annexes the Other while Borges unites with the Other. There is a kind of violent possession in Barth's treatment of *The Arabian Nights* while Borges submits almost mystically to its matrix. This is by no means intended to be a moral judgment on either of them, but it is an analytical judgment passed on both. They both treat the Arabian tales with love—but the love of Barth is *possessive* while that of Borges is *possessed*. Other examples from the two American continents seem to confirm the contrast. Edgar Allan Poe, in his story "The Thousand-and-Second Tale of Sheherazade," alludes constantly to the American scene.[12] He appropriates it, as it were, while the Mexican writer Carlos Fuentes, a leading Third World novelist, says in a tone reminiscent of Borges, "Now, at 54, I write not to die. Like Sheherazade in *The Arabian Nights*, I'll live as long as I have another story to tell."[13]

Both Borges and Fuentes find themselves engaged in endeavors parallel to Shahrazad, while both Barth and Poe have tried to domesticate *The Arabian Nights*—that is, to Americanize it. Analogies drawn from myths and sacred narratives may illustrate the point. The North American culture behaves like Oedipus, killing the father unwittingly and appropriating the mother and the throne. The South American culture behaves like the son (Isma'il in the Islamic tradition, and Isaac in the Biblical tradition) obeying the father Abraham and submitting to him because the order is ultimately that of the Divine Being. As Borges once said on writing in an interview, "Besides, you might think there is no author, after all. There is only the muse or the Holy Ghost."[14]

To substantiate the contrast, I shall start with two contemporary works directly and intertextually linked to *The Arabian Nights;* one is a 1946 short story by Borges entitled "The Two Kings and their Two Labyrinths"[15]; the other is a novella by Barth entitled "Dunyazadiad," which is one of three novellas that constitute his book *Chimera*, which won the National Book Award in 1972.[16]

Let us start with the revealing titles. Barth calls his novella "Dunyazadiad" because it is narrated by Dinazad/Dunyazade, Shahrazad's sister. The suffix *-iad* at the end of the name of the heroine is done "in keeping with Barth's . . . habit as in 'Menelaiad' and 'Anonymiad' of imitating ancient titles like the *Iliad* and *Aeneid*."[17] It should be noted that, in the title, the Eastern has been turned morphologically into something Classical; i.e., Greek and Latin. In contrast Borges demonstrates a rare sensitivity to the syntactical nature of the Arabic title and its significance:

In the title *The Thousand and One Nights* there is something
very important: the suggestion of an infinite book. It practically
is. The Arabs say that no one can read *The Thousand and One
Nights* to the end. Not for reasons of boredom: one feels the
book is infinite.[18]

Borges comes back to the haunting title in another context:

I know there's a book known as 'The Thousand and One Nights.'
Now when Jean Antoine Galland did that into French, he translated it as *Les mille et une nuits.* But when Captain Burton attempted his famous translation, he translated the title literally.
Following the original Arabic order, he called his book *The Book
of the Thousand Nights and One Night.* Now there he created
something not to be found in the original since to anyone who
knows Arabic the phrase isn't at all strange; it is the normal way
of saying it. But in English it sounds very strange, and there is a
certain beauty attained, in this case, through literal translation.[19]

It is clear that the title of Borges' story "The Two Kings and their Two
Labyrinths" with the repetition of "two" simply reproduces the dual form
(al-muthanna) typical of Arabic grammar. Di Giovanni, who translated
the work (in collaboration with the author), said:

We deliberately gave an archaic flavor to the little tale called
'The Two Kings and Their Two Labyrinths.' We wanted to make
that sound as Borges later described it, as 'a page—overlooked
by Lane or Burton—out of *The Arabian Nights.*' I steeped myself in Burton while working on the story. 'O king of time and
crown of the century!' —I think I lifted that straight out of Burton, which is exactly what Borges did in the first place.[20]

This story by Borges about the two kings and the two labyrinths does
not exist in the extant versions of *The Arabian Nights* nor in any of its
translations, though Borges attributes it to *The Arabian Nights,* another of
his authorial deceptions which have come to be considered the hallmark
of Borges. The story pretends to be an overlooked page from *The Arabian
Nights.*[22] What he borrows from *The Arabian Nights* is not the text of a
narrative, but its spirit. Borges in this story does not lift a theme, but an
attitude and a vision. In that vision based on the opposition between the
labyrinthical and the infinite, he sees echoes of his own national history,
thus he does not need to Latin-Americanize *The Arabian Nights.* He only
creates along its lines, which embodies both the Middle Eastern and the
South American dichotomies.

He writes in a footnote to his story:

Several elements or personal whims may be found in this
unpresuming fable. Firstly, its Eastern setting, its deliberate aim

to be a page—overlooked by Lane or Burton out of *The Arabian Nights*. Secondly, that obvious symbol of perplexity, the maze, given in the story two forms—that of the traditional labyrinth, and, even more sinister, that of the unbounded desert. After some twenty-five years, I am beginning to suspect that the king of Babylon, with his lust for winding ways and devious complexity, stands for civilization, while the Arabian king stands for unrelieved barbarism. For all I know, the first may be a *porteño* and his antagonist a gaucho.[21]

The story itself is pithy. It opens with a note pointing to another story written by Borges in 1949, entitled "Ibn Hakkan al-Bokhari, Dead in his Labyrinth"[22] in what amounts to both intertextuality and foreshadowing. This parabolic story is said to be told by Reverend Allaby from the pulpit at the end of the story of Ibn Hakan al-Bokhari. This technique of textual and temporal overlapping is typical of *The Arabian Nights,* thus we find Borges embodying the narrative strategies of the Arabian classic rather than its narrative characters or episodes.

The story of "The Two Kings and their Two Labyrinths" is essentially a one-page narrative about a Babylonian king who tries to match God's enigmatic universe by creating a confusing labyrinth. One day when the Arabian king calls on him, the Babylonian king invites his guest to visit the labyrinth in order to make a fool of him. Indeed, the Arabian king is bewildered, but he calls upon God and finds the right exit. Humiliated and suffering, but not complaining, the Arabian king invites his host to his country and promises to show him an Arabian labyrinth. Upon returning to his country, he avenges himself by conquering the realm of the Babylonian king. The captured Babylonian king is let loose in the Arabian desert and told,

> O king of time and crown of the country! In Babylon you lured me into a labyrinth of brass cluttered with many stairways, doors, and walls; now the Almighty has brought it to pass that I show you mine, which has no stairways to climb, no doors to force, no unending galleries to wear one down, nor walls to block one's way.[23]

The point of the story is that the maze is Janus-faced: intricacy and void are masks of the same enigma.

Barth, on the other hand, does not see his history and institutions in terms of the Other as Borges does. He sees the contrast between the Western tradition and the Eastern tradition. Thus he says in the last part of "Dunyazadiad," which is a metafictional epilogue:

> They [the Arab Storytellers] ended their stories not 'happily ever after,' but specifically 'until there took them the Destroyer of Delights and Desolator of Dwelling-places, and they were

translated to the truth of Almighty Allah, and their houses fell waste and their palaces lay in ruins and the Kings inherited their riches.'[24]

This difference in norms as seen by Barth is often bridged by Americanizing his heroines, complete with their nicknames; hence, Shahrazad becomes Sherry and Dinazad/Dunyazade, Doony. Barth projects them as modern-day American feminists rather than Eastern princesses:

> My sister was an undergraduate arts-and-sciences major at Banu Sasan University. Besides being Homecoming Queen, valedictorian-elect, and a four-letter varsity athlete, she had a private library of a thousand volumes and the highest average in the history of the campus. Every graduate department in the East was after her with fellowships—but she was so appalled at the state of the nation that she dropped out of school in her last semester to do full-time research on a way to stop Shahrayar from killing all our sisters and wrecking the country.[25]

Barth brings together the 'Eastern' and 'Western' elements in order to juxtapose the two, unlike Borges who does it to fuse and harmonize them. Barth is deliberately incongruous in order to provoke his reader into rethinking the American cultural scene. Borges blends the Buenos Aires setting with English ones, medieval Oriental concerns with those of Spanish Renaissance, and the Argentine twentieth-century Borges with the twelfth-century Andalusian Averroës[26] because he sees all these manifestations as variations on a single axis or metaphors of a central core. Barth, in contrast, is oxymoronic, bringing together what he sees as opposed elements and creating monsters, that is, beings made out of mixing different parts of different animals, or—to say it in yet another way—creating chimeras.

Barth mentioned in a conversation with David Morrell in 1975 that having written "Perseid" and "Bellerophoniad" (the other two novellas of *Chimera)* he felt "Dunyazadiad" would be an appropriate addition:

> Aside from the pleasure he would have in working at last with Sheherazade, there was as well the felicity he noted that this Persian-based material would jar somewhat with the Greek nature of the other stories and thus reinforce the monstrous, mixed-metaphor notion that the book's title, *Chimera*, represented.[27]

Last but not least, one should point to the manipulation by both writers of the narrative technique called *mise en abyme* (Gide's expression) or, more technically, complex embedding which is characteristic of *The Arabian Nights*. Borges uses this technique to efface himself; he achieves a kind of self-obliteration to allow the Other to shine in all its splendor.

Barth uses the same technique to emphasize his own presence in the text and to draw attention to the Self and away from the Other.

The story of Borges is introduced by a note between brackets that informs the reader of the following: "[This is the story the Reverend Allaby tells from the pulpit in 'Ibn Hakkan al-Bokhari, Dead in His Labyrinth']."[28] In other words, the story is attributed to another who takes it from Eastern chronicles, thus Borges is distancing—fictionally at least—himself as an author. The following shows the use of dicursive layering to conceal the author:

—*Narrator 1:* Borges (author) narrating the story of "The Two Kings . . ." to his anonymous readers.

—*Narrator 2:* Dunraven (poet) narrating the story of "Ibn Hakkan . . . " to his friend Unwin (mathematician).

—*Narrator 3:* Allaby (rector) delivers a sermon to his parishioners.

—*Narrator 4:* Chronicler's record of the story of "The Two Kings . . . "

With Barth's novella "Dunyazadiad" we have the same construction but not the same effect. Barth the author keeps popping up into the narrative, either directly using the first person singular or indirectly alluding to autobiographical details that can hardly escape readers.[29] The following shows the constant intrusion of Barth on the different layers of the narrative:

—*Narrator l:* Barth (author) narrating "Dunyazadiad" to his anonymous readers.

—*Narrator 2:* Dinazad/Dunyazade narrating Shahrazad's story to Shahzaman.

—*Narrator 3a:* Shahrazad narrating stories to Shahrayar.

—*Narrator 3b:* The Genie (Barth) transmits Shahrazad's stories to her by dictation.

—*Narrator 4:* Shahzaman narrates his story to Dinazad/ Dunyazade.

—*Narrator 5:* Barth (critic) commenting on *The Arabian Nights.*

Barth of course speaks with many voices. He is the author of the story, but he is also the one who inspires Shahrazad and makes her wear a Barthian face. He dictates to her, as a new Shahrazad, the stories of old Shahrazad. There is no doubt that the Genie described as a balding, forty-year-old man is Barth. Barth, also, has the Genie make an autobiographical reference to Barth's undergraduate years at The Johns Hopkins University:

Years ago, he said, when he'd been a penniless student pushing book-carts through the library stacks to help pay for his educa-

tion, he contracted a passion for Scheherazade upon first reading the tales she beguiled King Shahrayar with.[30]

Finally, Barth interferes in the narrative and comments on it, on the very
story he is narrating: "If I could invent a story as beautiful, it should be
about little Dunyazade and her bridegroom."[31]

What is the story that the author John Barth contrives? It is the story of
Dunyazade/Doony avenging her gender, rather than appeasing the opposite gender by captivating narratives in the style of Shahrazad/Sherry. The
story becomes that of contemporary patriarchy and the feminist retalia-
tion. In other words, the story weaves on the patterns of *The Arabian Nights*,
but clearly presents modern issues. Even names are modified to suit personal actuality, thus not only are the women protagonists given American
nicknames, but the third child and offspring from the union between
Shahrazad and Shahrayar is not a boy as in *The Arabian Nights,* but a girl
so as to be named after the girlfriend of the author/Genie. Her name is
Jamilah-Melissa; her second name was chosen, as the mother says "in
honor of our friend's [Genie's/Barth's] still beloved mistress, whom he
had announced his intentions to marry."[32] This Pirandello-like gesture,
whether it actually refers to Barth's personal life or not, does give the
illusion of the real, as if we have moved from the level of the text to that of
life.[33] This conversion of *dramatis personae* to accommodate the American scene is matched by engendering a plot that reverses the original setup.
Here Dunyazade has the upper hand and is about to castrate Shahzaman
with a razor in hand, while he tells stories to gain time, but also to com-
ment on fiction. His stories revolve around a colony of breastless women
instead of a cemetery of decapitated women. These Amazonians have been
spared but mutilated due to Shahzaman's wrath on women. The principle
of analogy and reversal are obvious. Threatened by woman's mutilation,
he narrates stories about mutilated women.

The kinds of ruptures, juxtapositions, and confrontations that Barth attempts create the effect of irony and intellectual comedy. They are there to
entertain and distract. Borges, on the other hand, with his analogies, parallelisms, and harmonies, triggers contemplation. His story instructs and il-
luminates. Perhaps we can say that the relationship of Borges to Barth, as
revealed in their use of *The Arabian Nights,* is like the relationship of
parable to parody. Both are intertextual creations, but one reconstructs and
the other deconstructs.

The Arabian Nights has penetrated the imagination of Borges and Barth
in somewhat different ways. While Barth attempts to retell the stories of
this fabulous book by rendering them relevant to the here and now, seen

from his persepective—America in the twentieth century, the novel in its wane, the author as a middle-aged man—Borges does not so much try to retailor the stories of Shahrazad to suit his actual and concrete circumstances, as to find in *The Arabian Nights* the enigmas of existence and being everywhere and at all times. Borges glimpses eternity in *The Arabian Nights*, and it is that vision which he foregrounds when he creatively manipulates the work. Barth on the other hand anchors the work in his own harbor and invest it with his predelictions and anxieties.

In the corpus of Borges, *The Arabian Nights* appears as a pretext for critical discourse and philosophical speculation on language, as in "The Thousand and One Nights" in his *Siete noches*, a collection of reflective essays; and as in "The Translators of the *Thousand and One Nights*" in his *Historia de la eternidad*, as well as in his long poem entitled "Metaforas de las mil y una noches."[34] There are also references and allusions to *The Arabian Nights* in many of his narratives, as well as references to specific nights, motifs, stylistic formulae, and underlying themes and issues. The implicit and explicit presence of *The Arabian Nights* in the writings of Borges makes us suspect that every utterance of his refers in some way or another to Shahrazad's discourse, or at least wonder if it does. The distinction between the Borgesian corpus and the Arabian classic—between the Self and the Other—is rendered problematic. Borgesian textuality becomes in itself an extension and rearticulation of the content or significance of *The Arabian Nights*.

With Barth, the presence of *The Arabian Nights* is less pervasive though quite important. It is flaunted in such obvious works as "Dunyazadiad" in *Chimera* and in *The Last Voyage of Somebody the Sailor* but also suggested in *The Tidewater Tales: A Novel* and in *Once Upon a Time,* and directly tackled in his *Don't Count on It: A Note on the Number of the 1001 Nights*. If in "Dunyazadiad" the frame story is refashioned to suit the ethos of America of the late sixties with its sexual and gender revolution, *The Last Voyage of Somebody the Sailor* uses the Sindbad voyages of *The Arabian Nights* to tell, or rather to confess with giggles, an American mood of the *fin-de-siècle,* and the position of an author brushing with death and reminiscing over life. Again in this work of Barth, the American Self and the Arabian Other remain distinct, often contrasted, and occasionally made to illuminate each other. Nowhere does the reader feel, as in the works of Borges, that the boundaries between Self and Other are erased. In fact, the Self is often pitted against the Other in a hilarious fashion in Barth's novel. The digital watch characteristic of every American is considered as a magical amulet in medieval Baghdad; Julie Moore, the beloved of the protagonist Simon William Behler, is taken in Sindbad's entourage as Jew Moor, and thus the surprise that she is blond. Perhaps it is in this indulgence in facile humor that Barth's poetics has gained the dubious epithet of "aesthetic of the cute."[35] In fact, he has been accused of perpetuating an Orientalist vision of the Other:

> Time after time he [Barth] tries to score points by depicting the Arabs as dim provincials. In doing so, he indulges what is most provincial in himself and his readers: their ugly and worn stereotypes of a foreign culture. . . . His Arab men are lusty, greasy misogynists, always prattling about *zabbs* and *wahats*. The women are sultry, sexy, belly-dancer types. *The Last Voyage* is squarely within the tradition of cultural perception and misperception that has been called Orientalism.[36]

Another scholar displeased with this lack of sensitivity and understanding of the Other writes:

> *The Last Voyage* presents difficulties in its comic treatment of Islamic characters. In this day of the 'postcolonial' critic and intellectual, in the wake of the critique of Orientalism, we would do well to ponder the practical effects of Barth's comic representation of his Arab characters.[37]

Critics with eyes on political correctness, however, do not perceive that Barth is essentially a satirist. His fiction builds on all kinds of ready-made cultural imagery, only to make readers glimpse the contemporary East Coast in the medieval East. One of the commentators on the book has pointed out that there is a caricatural representation of "obsessive Arabic proccupation with the virginity of brides and the value—monetary or otherwise—assigned to it."[38] But what makes this trivialization of the Other less damning is the equal trivialization of the Self. What this novel presents is a wasteland with rare moments of grandeur. The world is seen as an island on which we are all stranded, and in which we are trying to survive. Physical survival of Sindbad the Sailor is turned into the metaphorical survival of Behler the Failer, and his efforts to find meaning in an otherwise trashy existence.

The Last Voyage of Somebody the Sailor, like "Dunyazadiad," reverses situations. Instead of Shahrazad, a young woman narrating stories to survive as in *The Arabian Nights,* she is here a grandmother, old and decrepit, looking forward to death to save her from the agonies of old age. But death is not forthcoming, and so a deal is struck: if she tells a virgin tale, she will be delivered. Delivery here is the opposite of the perpetual narrative: it is the end of narratives. Does Barth's Shahrazad succeed in telling a virgin tale? The virginity of her tale is analogous to the "virginity" of

Yasmin, the bride of Behler who simulates a hymen rupture, or as the narrator says in the novel, she gets redeflowered. This may be read by a hyper-sensitive critic as poking fun at the Arabs and their honor values, but in fact it refers essentially to the state of fiction-writing in America—the loss of innocence and the effort to capture it, and the state of artistic exhaustion—rather than nuptial practices in present-day Arab culture. A virgin tale, a fresh tale, can only be feigned and simulated in today's Barthian world. American innocence is lost, and it can only be reintroduced through masquarading.

What triggers this story of the deal between Shahrazad and death is a rather moving epilogue. The narrator-protagonist in *The Last Voyage of Somebody the Sailor* is in the hospital attended by a young woman doctor who sums up—as in Campbell's *The Hero with a Thousand Faces*—the many women to whom the narrator-protagonist had been attached: his twin sister who died at birth (BeeGee, Bijou, Baby Girl Behler), his first girl friend who initiated him into sex (Crazy Daisy) who ends up in a mental institution, his wife Jane who divorces him, his daughter Julia who has an affair with an Omani student (a substitute figure for Sindbad, who in turn substitutes for the new Sindbad/Behler), and his love of mature years Juliet Moore whom he lost. Thus the liminal situation between life and death, albeit in a clinical setting, brings forth Shaharazad's predicament in an inverted form.

The analogy between the narrator–protagonist and John Simmons Barth, from name to date of birth to background, is too obvious to warrant more than mention. What is interesting though is Barth's use of Sindbad's voyages to tell autobiographical fiction. Each voyage stands for a decade in twentith-century American history, and in each voyage/decade there are as many wonders as Sindbad encountered. But Barth/Behler is adamant about not confusing himself with the Sailor from Baghdad. He alternates with Sindbad in telling their voyages, in order to contrast them and occasionally to find analogical situations in both. Barth is most convincing and moving when he turns the everyday object into an abstract issue. Thus the watch becomes a synecdoche of Time, the bracelet with its missing links and empty name-plate a substitute for contemporary narrative. Both watch and bracelet function as leitmotifs linking the dispersed episodes and anecdotes in the novel. Less touching is the evocation of the Arabian links through such conventional labels as Camel cigarettes and Sheik condoms.

> Dad took a cigarette from the pack with its desert scene like our illustrated lessons, tamped its end against the torn button, and pressed his thumb against the cigarette lighter on the dash.[39]

When Behler's first girlfriend Daisy opens her hand, he sees

a small flat packet with a picture on it of a handsome Arab chief-
tain. . . . The packet said in smaller letters: *3 prophylactic sheaths.
For prevention of disease only.* There were two white Sheiks
inside, tightly rolled but not otherwise sealed. I pinched one
out—it looked like a model of those inflatable life rafts that
downed flyers sometimes drifted in for days and weeks—and
Daisy tossed the packet over.[40]

Rafts, islands, tubs, and drowning recur in the novel. They relate to
Sindbad's voyages and to Behler's sailing in the Carribean, South Asia,
and the Persian Gulf. The reported loss of his brother during World War II,
when Behler was celebrating his fourteenth birthday, mixes the adventurous, playful, and fantastic with the tragic.

The structure of the novel juxtaposes Sindbad's narration of one of his
voyages to the narration of a voyage by Behler, to be followed by discussion, evaluation and criticism, as if Behler's voyage is a new book being
reviewed by critics. Sindbad's voyages rewritten by Barth in this novel
stick to the incidents as they occur in *The Arabian Nights,* and they are
used to remind the reader of the Arabian text, in order to compare the
fantastic of Sindbad with the reality of Behler. Thus the first voyage of
Sindbad is paralleled by child Behler's first airplane ride offered to him as
a birthday present on his seventh year. The wonders encountered by
Sindbad, the mature man, are compared implicitly to the ones the child
glimpsed. The point suggested is that the real itself is wonderous:

I had a long view out toward the hazy great mouth of the
Chaptico, miles wide where it joined Chesapeake Bay at what
remained of Piney Island; and to southward now stretched the
endless marshes of the lower country: a maze of ready necks,
meandering tidal creeks, and spattered low islets, like the pattern on scorched French toast.[41]

The sense of deathly danger sensed by Sindbad is introduced in Behler's
first voyage by a furtive view of the cemetry where Bijou, his twin sister,
lies buried. The child is invaded by a sense of distress and the feeling that
this is her birthday as well—had she not been entangled by the umbilical
cord, she would have been with him; or alternately, he could have been in
her place had he been the first of the twins to come out of his mother's
womb. He insists, therefore, on visiting his little sister's tomb on his birthday, thus juxtaposing the motif of death anniversery with that of birth an-
niversary—a juxtaposition that marks the very nature of *The Arabian
Nights'* frame story.

In the second voyage of Behler, known as Somebody, there is another birthday in which he indulges in sex on Bijou's tomb, again bringing together Eros and Thanatos. *The Arabian Nights* is again evoked in this adolescent affair as the sixteen-year-old Daisy is imagined by Behler narrating to her younger sister, Julia, what happened, and "it was exciting to imagine her telling her rapt sister *everything*."[42] It is precisely this younger sister who will become the love of Behler in his mature years.

In light of the aesthetic logic of the work, we understand the ambivalent need of the narrator to both fuse with the Other and to keep the Other at a distance. Behler wears the mask of Sindbad, but also contrast himself to the Iraqi sailor. This twin discourse with all its tensions and dramas colors the novel. The Moore girls, Daisy and Julia, overlap in the life of the narrator–protagonist and play similar if not identical roles: the first initiating him into the physical dimension of love-making and the second into the partnership of love and fulfillment. This dualistic tendency pointing to split oneness in the novel leads to momentary fusion at times and to contrasts at others. It is an aesthetic device that has its counterpart in psychoanalysis and philosophy. At bottom, this "schizophrenic" desire implies the need to be and not to be, to live and to cease living, to love and to die. No narrative text is more fitting for such a forked human condition than *The Arabian Nights,* and no biological context is more appropriate than the birth of twins, one of whom lives and the other who dies instantly.

When Barth adapts *The Arabian Nights* to his narrative purposes, we sense a boundary, an iron wall, which he constructs between the Self and the Other, and simultaneously moments when the author is engaged in trying to break down the separating wall. The failure to do so is part of the inner hermeneutic drama of the novel. Borges, on the other hand, dazzles us by erasing the very notion of cultural boundaries. Does the difference of approach to the Other come from the fact that for Borges the Other— the Arabian literary tradition—is part of his own patrimony as a Latin American whose roots go back to Spain, with its Arab chapter of history? Or is it the fact that Borges belongs to the Third World and does not have the distant cultural stance of an author from the First World? Or have the modes chosen for integrating the Other led to such a contrast between Borges and Barth—the first opting for a parable and the second for a mock-epic? Or is it simply the difference between two authors, one of whom (Barth) admits his debt to the other (Borges) and names his fictional ship *Zahir* after Borges' story, and yet intends to reorient himself and displace the father figure in his anxiety about influence? The answer may be any, some, all, or none of the above.

12

NAGUIB MAHFOUZ'S
ARABIAN NIGHTS AND DAYS:
A POLITICAL ALLEGORY

He who's too decent goes hungry in this city.
—Naguib Mahfouz, *Arabian Nights and Days*

The Arabian Nights has long been a favorite of Arab audiences and a subaltern classic, to judge by the many versions, manuscripts, editions, discussions, and controversies over the book. In 1985–86, a popular edition of *The Arabian Nights* and its publisher were tried and condemned (by banning the text and fining the publisher), but eventually the judgment was reversed and the text liberated in an appeal in a Cairo court.[1] The traditional Arab literary establishment, however, had steered away from *The Arabian Nights* for a millenium, expressing its contempt partly by dismissing it as lowly and mostly by ignoring it. Important as it may have been in the landscape of imagination, the critical discourse around it amounted to practically nil.

However, this ignored classic has been allowed to surface only in twentieth-century Arab criticism. And probably no one should receive more credit for highlighting the significance of this work than the Egyptian intellectual and educator Taha Hussein (1889–1973). He wrote works inspired by *The Arabian Nights,* adapting its outline to air his positions and views. Taking on *The Arabian Nights,* he wrote a slim novella entitled *Ahlam Shahrazad (The Dreams of Scheherazade)* in 1942–43, after having co-authored with Tawfiq al-Hakim another fiction drawing on *The*

Arabian Nights' material entitled *al-Qasr al-mashur* ("The Enchanted Palace") in 1936.[2] But above all, he supervised in the forties a Ph.D dissertation on *The Arabian Nights* by one of his brilliant students, Suhayr al-Qalamawi, and when the dissertation was published as a book (dedicated to him), he wrote an introduction to it.[3] This was a provocative project for academia, and the study proved to be a pioneering step in unleashing the critical faculties and creative powers of many writers. It ushered a new outlook on *The Arabian Nights* and opened it up for serious research and contemplation, as if al-Qalamawi's study was a key unlocking this hidden literary treasure.

Since then studies have continued to pour forth on this rediscovered item in Arab heritage; this trend was recently crowned by devoting to it four volumes of *Fusul*, the Cairo-based academic quarterly of literary criticism. Along with the modern critical interest in *The Arabian Nights*, and overlapping with it, went creative explorations, renditions, and adaptations of *The Arabian Nights* in fiction and drama.[4] In modern Arabic poetry allusions to *The Arabian Nights* became common; in contrast, I could find none in classical poetry.[5] Modern Arab readings and adaptations of *The Arabian Nights* have generally emphasized the political component inherent in the narrative. Poets, dramatists, and novelists used it to speak allusively of ideological issues and most strikingly of the abuses of absolute power. *The Arabian Nights* itself invites such an interpretation since the frame story revolves around a despotic Oriental king and the strategy to resist him and liberate the citizens. What could be more pertinent to present-day Arab regimes than such a story? Notions of philosophical mazes, castration complexes, and existential predicaments may be extracted from *The Arabian Nights* by a Borges, a Barth, or an Ashbery, but Arab writers have predominantly seen the political implications in the work— that of ruler versus citizens.

This is hardly surprising, given the roots of *The Arabian Nights* in *The Panchatantra,* which is essentially a political manual handed down in the form of a narrative work. The precepts taught in the Indian classic deal with modes of behavior appropriate for social and political interaction which rulers ought to know. There is also a long-standing tradition in Arab culture of writing allegorically and allusively about political issues,[6] and it is against and within this coded discourse that we can understand why *The Arabian Nights* has been interpreted as a veiled political treatise.[7] This political dimension of the work and its discursive background, combined with the volatile political situation of the contemporary Arab world, have contributed to the primacy of the ideological message in readers' reception.

The Fiction of Politics

The best-known symbolic narrative in Arabic literature that falls under the rubric of political allegory is that of *Hayy ibn Yaqzan,* written by the medieval philospher, physician, and statesman Ibn Tufayl (d. 1185). In this allegorical narrative, Ibn Tufayl discusses in a coded fashion, among other things, the relationship between the King and the Philosopher, or power and knowledge, and comes to the conclusion that they cannot be joint (or have not been joint). Hayy, the self-taught philosopher, at the end of the narrative is unable to reconcile himself to the stupidities and superficialities of civil society and opts to return to his isolated island and live as a loner in order to mystically contemplate the divine. The relationship of philosophy to kingship, or wisdom to power, was a prominent concern in medieval Islamic thought, and the issue of a philosopher king as advocated by Plato in his *Republic* received constant commentaries and interpretations.

In this vein of political theory Taha Hussein approached the relation of the ruler to the ruled and the responsibilities of power in his transparently veiled narrative *The Dreams of Scheherazade,* written with the atrocities of WWII as a backdrop. In this novella, magic and supernatural incidents are contrived, not so much in an artistic spirit, but in a heavy-handed allegory presenting an argument against war-mongering rulers whose focus on power rather than intellect leads them to play havoc with innocent and guiltless citizens. This view is put forward in a narrative which Shahrazad enunciates in her sleep between the 1009th to the 1015th nights, and to which Shahrayar captively listens. In these articulated dreams, the protagonist Fatina—a woman who parallels Shahrazad in intelligence and wisdom—tells her father's generals: "Armies are a means of preventing war, not waging it, of forestalling evil and not invoking it. . . . Let those of you who would risk their lives do so without involving the lives of innocent soldiers!"[8]

Shahrayar is so enchanted, in this fictional work of Taha Hussein, by Shahrazad and her dream narratives and by the knowledge she imparts to him through them, that he begins to think of her as his spiritual guide to mysticism, Sufi truth, and gnosis.[9] In Fatina's discourse, kings are referred to as tyrants, and in the story she forces those kings who have tried to possess her, and having failed waged war against her, to admit that they are despots who have denied their people their rights, and therefore these rulers deserve to be handed to their people for just retribution.[10] Fatina, using the power of the jinn, achieves victory and her despotic adverseries are punished. At the end of *The Dreams of Scheherazade*, Shahrazad herself addresses Shahrayar and reminds him that his time should belong to his people and that any indulgence in individual pursuits is a betrayal of the political trust and royal responsibilities.

The message of Fatina's story is re-enforced by Shahrazad's advice in what seems like a starkly transparent allegory. The fantastic episodes, simplistic plot, and flat characters are there not to captivate the senses but to make analogic sense. There is no doubt or ambiguity about what is being indicated and stressed: the ruler should be not the master but the servant of the people, and power should be used to avoid hostilities, not score victories. The fantastic element is brought in as *deus ex machina,* solving the problems of the heroine. This novella of Taha Hussein incorporates the problematic of *Hayy ibn Yaqzan* into the broad narrative structure of *The Arabian Nights'* frame story. The ruler is here admonished by Shahrazad's direct and indirect (Fatina's) discourse.

In the same vein writes Naguib Mahfouz his *Layali alf layla (Arabian Nights and Days),* which comprises—like *The Dreams of Scheherazade*— the ruler, the ruled, and the mystic guide, albeit with considerable sophistication.[11] The aesthetic complexity of Mahfouz may distract from its kinship to the simple-minded narrative of Taha Hussein, but both works exhibit the same touchstones and are concerned with issues that have been dominant in political theory and Islamic philosophy.

The political thrust of Mahfouz's *Arabian Nights and Days*—written in 1979 against the backdrop of Anwar Sadat's Open-Door Policy and the rise of militant Islam in Egypt—has been acknowledged by the author himself in an interview with Hussein Hammouda:

> I think that in this novel *[Arabian Nights and Days]* I expressed my fundamental concerns, and that I produced a blend of what can be called 'political realism' and 'metaphysical speculation,' which may be labelled as 'Sufi speculation.' I found in *The Thousand and One Nights* a space which allowed me to express such an admixture of widely separate components.[12]

This stands in contrast to Mahfouz's earlier use of *The Arabian Nights* in his short story, "Shahrazad," published in a collection entitled *Khammarat al-qitt al-aswad* (The black cat bar), published in 1969, in which he calls upon Shahrazad's tactic of regularly interrupted speech to tell the listener in the story—a journalist at the end of the telephone line—the miseries of a woman.[13] The several telephone calls made by the woman, who gives herself the pseudonym of Shahrazad, serve to create suspense and anticipation at the other end with the male listener. But upon meeting the woman, the element of imagination that excited the listener and eroticized the image of the speaker dissipates and the man ends up simply suggesting that she depend on God, as a way of not involving himself. Here gender relations and the interplay of desire and status are crucial.

Modalities of Encoding

That Mahfouz's *Arabian Nights and Days* is a political allegory very few can doubt, but the content of its political message is more debatable, given the complexity and ambiguity of the allegory. The work combines allegorical strategies akin to the Platonic "allegory of the cave" or Gilgamesh's quest for the flower of immortality, as well as strategies used in the *roman à clef* genre such as Voltaire's *Candide*. It is precisely this double-decked or forked allegory in which the key alternates between the world of Ideas and the world of Reality that makes this work so enigmatic and so resistant to instant deciphering. Mahfouz manages to bring together the lofty ideals of kingship with the *faits divers* and daily scandals one finds in Third World tabloids. His characters stand for abstract notions (Shahrayar, Shahrazad, Sahloul, and Sheikh Balkhi) as well as human types ((Ma'rouf the Cobbler, Aladdin, Anees al-Galees, and Qut al-Quloub).

Mahfouz uses enframed stories and characters from *The Arabian Nights* to depict reality with all its stock characters and contradictions in the Egypt of the seventies, where the new economic policy of privatization and primacy of profit ruptured the social fabric and toppled the ethical codes of the poeple. Sexual violations, harlotry, kin murders for money, thefts, and sudden emergence of fabulous wealth were reported in the media. Touched and dramatized by popular imagination, such events are echoed in the stories narrated by Mahfouz, with the leitmotif of the struggle between the government—with its pious pretensions—against the more "fundamentalist" Islamic opposition, dubbed in the novel as "Shiites" and "Kharijites," in allusion to the sectarian anti-establishment movements in medieval Islam.

In a nudging reference to President Sadat (assassinated by militant Islamicists in 1981) who called himself "al-ra'is al-mu'min" (the believing president), a character says: "What an extraordinary sultanate this is, with its people and its genies! It raises aloft the badge of God and yet plunges itself in dirt."[14] What makes such an allusion globally, not just locally, subversive is that it is pertinent to so many countries whose heads claim piety and pretend to have God on their side, while indulging in less-than-pious behavior. But such a statement is equally relevant to secular governments, which make claims of equality and human rights while the facts on the ground belie them.

In yet another place in the narrative, Mahfouz reproduces a widely circulating joke about Sadat and his minister of interior who extracted several confessions from citizens concerning their theft of Mrs. Sadat's golden pen. When the first lady calls and says that she has found her misplaced pen, the chief of police asks what should he do with the confessions! Similarly, Ali al-Salouli, the governor of the quarter in the chapter entitled "Sanaan al-Gamali," responds laughingly to Sanaan's question, "Have you discovered who the culprit is?" by saying, "Those confessing to the crime number over fifty."[15]

Mahfouz combines these oral narratives, news items, jokes, and scandals of a decade and weaves them into the stories of *The Arabian Nights,* modifying as he goes along the stories of Shahrazad and embellishing the collective gossip. Unlike Sonallah Ibrahim, another novelist who uses the corruption of the seventies to depict the changing value system in his novel *Dhat* (1992), Mahfouz avoids Ibrahim's documentary approach, where actual news and editorals are reproduced verbatim in the body of the novel,[16] and opts for winks at the informed reader, counting on author–reader complicity in the face of ticklish subjects and official censorship.

The twelve enframed stories narrated in *Arabian Nights and Days* invariably evoke deteriorating values, ruling repression, corruption, hypocrisy, and opportunism. The mode of encoding depends on orienting the fantastic incidents—drawn from the repertoire of *The Arabian Nights*—to point to actual events and scandals, commonly circulating among the people but banned from press mention. It is Mahfouz's talent for charging the fabulous and fantastic with the familiar and the actual that turns the marvelous dimension on its head.

The gist of the political position of Mahfouz's novel—as can be extracted from the enframed stories—is that social disorders are symptoms of an unhealthy political rule and rampant injustice. The unjust ruler lies behind civil disobedience and inspires violent reaction and delinquency. In an indicative episode, Shahrayar, pretending to be a merchant, hears one of his subjects say: "It is for the ruler to dispense justice from the beginning so that genies don't intrude on our lives."[17]

Another modality of encoding can be observed in Mahfouz's frame story, which overlaps with that of *The Arabian Nights* but is not a replica of it. Each of the three main characters to whom a chapter is dedicated in the opening of the novel, namely, "Shahrayar," "Shahrazad," and "The Sheikh," stand for three allegorized notions: political power, creative power, and mystic power, respectively. Shahrayar is the opposite of the Sheikh, for the first stands for worldy power and violence, while the Sheikh stands for spiritual power and love. Shahrazad, a disciple of the Sheikh and a conjugal partner to Shahrayar, functions as a mediator. Her creative powers are not indifferent to the worldy as the Sheikh's mystic powers are. What she seeks is a measure of justice in this world. She manages to tame Shahrayar in Mahfouz's novel, but not to change his nature once and for all. Regression is possible at any moment, as different comments in the fiction indicate.[18]

The fourth chapter, entitled "The Café of the Emirs," provides the setting. It is a microcosm of the City/Egypt/the World; it is a cafe where all classes—upper and lower—meet, although they are distinguished by the seats they sit on, which vary from comfortable sofas to pads on the floor. This chapter presents the hierarchical stratificaton in the male-dominated society and identifies the principal characters mostly in terms of their profession, as customary also in *The Arabian Nights* and in folktales in general:

> Along its [the cafe's] sides were couches for the higher-class customers, while in a circle in the middle were ranged mattresses for the common people to sit on. A variety of things to drink were served, both hot and cold according to the season; also available were the finest sorts of hashish and electuaries. At night many were the high-class customers to be found there, the likes of Sanaan al-Gamali and his son Fadil, Hamdan Tuneisha and Karam al-Aseel, Sahloul and Ibrahim al-Attar the druggist and his son Hasan, Galil al-Bazzaz the draper, Nur al-Din, and Shamloul the hunchback.
> There was also ordinary folk like Ragab the porter and his crony Sindbad, Ugr the barber and his son Aladdin, Ibrahim the water-carrier and Ma'rouf the cobbler. There was general merriment on this happy night, and soon the doctor Abdul Qadir al-Maheeni had joined the group that included Ibrahim al-Attar, Karam al-Aseel the millionnaire, and Sahloul the bric-a-brac merchant and furnisher.[19]

The framework then allegorizes by narrating the trials and tribulations of opposing forces—power, spirituality, art, and knowledge—while the enframed stories allegorize the state of political affairs in a specific context. These two modes of allegorizing and encoding cross and reinforce each other. The enframed stories are narrated in an interlocking mode that is intended to create through their varied narratives a panoramic view of the society and its contradictions. Sexual pleasure, wealth, and power seem to be dynamic forces, even to those who stand in opposition to the system.

This point comes into focus when contrasted with the mystic position ex-emplified by Sheikh al-Balkhi who seems indifferent to the ups and downs of life around him and is able to transcend daily dramas, including the cruel beheading of his son-in-law Aladdin. His story about the man who was saved from death by death is a Sufi parable demonstrating sacred irony and the pointlessness of human desires:

> I fell into a hole and after three days there passed by a caravan of travelers. I told myself that I should call out to them. Then I went back on my decision, saying that no, it was not proper that I should seek help other than from Almighty God. When they approached the hole they found that it was in the middle of the road and they said, 'Let's fill this hole lest someone fall into it.' I was so exceedingly perturbed that I lost all hope. After they had filled it in and gone on their way, I prayed to Almighty God and gave myself over to death, relinquishing all hope in human beings. When night fell I heard a movement at the surface of the hole. As I listened to it the mouth of the hole was opened and I saw a large animal like a dragon. It let down its tail to me and I knew that God had sent it to rescue me. I clung on to its tail and it drew me up. Then a voice from the heaveans called out to me, 'We have saved you from death with death.'[20]

One of the characters remains, throughout the novel, an anthropomor-phic presentation of death and thus remains without a story, apart from his sinister appearance in graveyards and his enigmatic comments—this is Sahloul, the bric-a-brac merchant and furnisher. Sahloul, like the weird "man" personifying Death who engages Antonius Blok, the medieval knight, in Ingmar Bergman's film *Det Sjunde Insegelet* ("The Seventh Seal") has no story of his own, but has an important function that throws light on the ephemeral nature of existence, and replaces Shahrazad's for-mulaic ending of each story in *The Arabian Nights*: "....lived happily until visited by the Destroyer of all earthly pleasures, the Annihilator of men."

In twelve chapters, each devoted to a principal character, stories based on tales or characters of *The Arabian Nights* mix the mundane with the supernatural, the real with the magical.[21] This combination functions as a veil both hiding and revealing contemporary life with its plights and plea-sures, with its dramas and trivialities. In these stories the supernatural char-acters entice, torment, and test humans. The demons Singam, Qumqam, Sakhrabout, and Zarmabaha represent two pairs and stand for good and evil respectively, or possibly pangs of conscience and drives of desires.

The final chapter, "The Grievers," concludes the frame story of *Ara-bian Nights and Days* and provides the key to comprehending the allegory in the book.[22] It reveals that these enframed stories in the garb of *The Arabian Nights*, yet pointing to everyday situations, are in fact episodes in a cosmic journey through infernal reality. This glimpse of the quotidian hell will eventually bring at the end of the novel a momentary vision of paradise. If Dante and before him Homer and Virgil have sent their protagonists to the Underworld, so has Mahfouz, though the Mahfouzian underworld, is in this very real life. It is the underview, as it were, of everyday life stripped of the claims of official propaganda. In this sense, the underworld of Mahfouz is closer to that of Italo Calvino. To both this world is infernal, and while Mahfouz appeals to the mystic dimension to pacify its horrors and randomness, Calvino seeks it in perpetuating the humane and the beautiful.[23]

To familiarize himself (and indirectly the reader) with what goes on in the city, the sultan—as in *The Arabian Nights*—dresses like a merchant, visits his subjects, and learns of their agonies and delights; but instead of Harun al-Rashid of *The Arabian Nights,* we have in Mahfouz's work Shahrayar playing this role, after he has pardoned Shahrazad but while he is still not completely reformed and is suspected of reverting to his old way: "There is still a side of him that is unreliable and his hands are still stained with the blood of innocent people."[24]

Shahrayar partakes in the lechery of his high officials and is equally humiliated. He visits a married woman, Anees al-Galees, in the hope of seducing her, but she contrives a trick and manages to allow him as well as the other dignitaries to go as far as taking off their clothes and then pretends that her husband is knocking at the door. In this way, she manages to rush each of her lovers stark naked, into a cupboard. She locks them in and threatens to sell the cupboards in the marketplace. Only the madman manages to save them, yet he throws their clothes away to oblige them to experience shame. They go home in the darkness of the night:

> The men warily crept out of the cupboards, staggering with exhaustion. With feelings of subjection and shame not one of them opened his mouth; naked in body and in self-esteem, they stumbled about in the darkness.[25]

Though political power is derided, Mahfouz by no means reserves corruption for the ruling elite. The immorality of the oligarchy is only matched by the moral degradation of the merchant class. One of the first murders encountered in the novel is that of Sanaan al-Gamali, the rich businessman, who rapes and smothers a girl of ten. Nor are the lower classes spared: when Fadil al-Gamali (now a poor peddler of sweets after the decapitation of his father and his family's fall into disgrace) gets hold of the cap of invisibility, he begins to use it in thefts and to get even with his enemies.We get the impression that the whole social fabric is collapsing.

Within this social order, however, there is a voice of integrity raised by the sayings of the madman. In a complicated plot where chance plays a crucial part in revealing a murdered woman's stolen necklace, Ugr the Barber is led to be interrogated. Thanks to the madman's information, the truth becomes known, namely, that the actual murderer of the young woman is her older sister who had set up a brothel, murdered her younger sister out of jealousy, and silenced her brother—a high-ranking official—with money.

In the story of Nur al-Din and Dunyazad of *Arabian Nights and Days,* an example is offered of medieval infatuation that parallels that of the story of "Budour and Nur al-Din" in *The Arabian Nights.*[26] Dunyazad, however, replaces Budour in Mahfouz's novel in order to create drama in the royal household itself and complicate the intrigue. Everyone fears Shahrayar's wrath if he were to know about the amorous relation between his sister-in-law and a stranger, especially since he had promised Dunyazad to the ugly millionnaire Karam al-Aseel in order to get him to replenish the coffers of the kingdom after a costly war. On the other hand, when Shahrayar goes roaming in his kingdom incognito, he comes across the forlorn lover Nur al-Din, and promises that he will marry him to the woman of his "dream"—the one with whom he spent a night thanks to the intervention of the jinn. And yet this Mahfouzian rendering of the story turns it into a domestic drama. It ends up happily, however: Shahrayar who was torn between two promises made, but leaning toward the lover rather than the official suitor, learns of the latter's death.[27] The plot is fantastic, but the concern of Shahrazad and her mother about the sudden infatuation of Dunyazad with a man who turns to be real—and their strategy in handling the crisis—is all too realistic. They pretend that Dunyazad is sick and thus cannot marry; however, the response of her suitor, the millionnaire, blocks their scheme for he agrees that the wedding may be delayed but the marriage contract should be signed. After a dialogue between Shahrazad and her mother in which women's worries and their conniving resistance to patriarchal authority are sketched, Shahrazad's concerns about Shahrayar are articulated to echo the impossibility of trust in despots even when they claim repentance:

> 'I am frightened,' said Shahrazad, distraught, 'for Dunyazad and for myself too. There is no trusting the blood-shedder. The worst affliction a man can suffer is to be under the delusion he is a god.'[28]

These domestic scenes capture feminine apprehensions and schemes, and anchor the narrative in the déjà-vu, while a political point is made about those despots who take themselves for gods. The fantastic and supernatural camouflage the worldly, the political, and the familiar. The reader naturally hesitates between trying to find actual referents and contemporary equivalents on one hand, and between dismissing actuality on the other hand, and indulging in the magical ambiance where jinn bring lovers together—not withstanding palace guards and fortifications. The medical doctor, Abdul Qadir al-Maheeni, for example, says to his friend the Sheikh:

> Noble and God-fearing people have been martyred. How sorry I am for you, O my city, which today is controlled solely by hypocrites! Why, master, are only the worst cattle left in the stalls?[29]

Other examples of implanted political common sense with its subversive overtones are encountered through the novel. The madman says, "If the head was sound, the whole body was sound, for soundness and corruptness come down from above."[30]

Saying obliquely what cannot be said directly, and attributing the unspeakable to the insane, is a device commonly used not only in this novel but in literary discourse in general. The "madman" roams around the people, speaking in aphorisms and making subversive statements. He seems to constitute a counterpoint to Shahrayar, as Sabry Hafez has demonstrated in his extensive analysis of this novel.[31] Eventually, after six governors and their chiefs of police are murdered, Shahrayar assigns, surprisingly enough, the humble, honest, and kind Ma'rouf the cobbler as the seventh governor. It should be remembered that Ma'rouf the cobbler had refused to obey the order of the wicked genie to kill the Sheikh and the madman. The people side with the cobbler, who had bestowed his wealth on the poor, and go out in a demonstration of support for him. Shahrayar gives in to popular demands and assigns him as a governor entrusted to mend the society and the affairs of the people. Ma'rouf in turn assigns the lover Nur al-Din, husband of Dunyazad, as his personal secretary and the madman as chief of police, who ends up being called "Abdullah the sane." The circle seems to be closed and the good guys take over on the seventh round. The symbolism of seven has already been explained in this book when discussing the voyages of Sindbad—it stands for the eternal return and indicates the move to a different level. Shahrayar expresses this point when he says to his vizier, who was worried about the lack of competence of such governing team, by saying "Let us venture upon a new experience."[32]

The full cycle having come to a head, we encounter in the Café of the Emirs Sindbad himself, who interprets to us the significance of his voyages. Here the inner meaning is not smuggled in, as in the twelve enframed narratives of *Arabian Nights and Days*—where the carnivalistic setup helps cover up the intended significance, and where the ending is the triumph of the will of the people. Meaning here is is not concealed, but packaged, the way a gift is wrapped to enhance the present. Sindbad tells the stories of his voyages after Ma'rouf the cobbler has told his story. Sindbad interprets the hidden significance of his adventures, while Ma'rouf's remain uninterpreted, as if inviting the reader to do so having learned from Sindbad's clearly enunciated decoding. The discourse of Sindbad starts after he tells Ma'rouf the cobbler (now governing the neighborhood) that he deserves to be the governor, and Ma'rouf responds, "I am the servant of the poor under God's care"[33]—a statement that sums up a position we already encountered in the finale of Taha Hussein's novella, *The Dreams of Scheherazade.*

Sindbad explains the lesson he extracted from the voyage in which he mistook a sleeping whale for an island as the need to distinguish truth from an illusion resembling truth. In other words, one has to understand the nature of things and not their superficial appearance; human senses and reason are to be used to tell the difference.[34] Missing the ship because he fell asleep, Sindbad learns that one should not sleep or be unconscious when wakefulness and awareness are required. He ties himself to the mighty Rukh and thus escapes to another place, proving that when there is life there is always hope and one should use one's wits rather than despair.[35] When he is stranded on an island and the giant king offers the shipwrecked men food, Sindbad eats in moderation, as his Sheikh had instructed him. And it is precisely this moderation that keeps him lean-looking, which in turn helps him survive. His mates eat immoderately and end up plump and appetizing for the cannibalistic king. This shows the importance of moderation in carnal appetites.[36] In another of his voyages, Sindbad finds himself in an alien country and marries a woman from there, only to discover that their customs impose the burial of spouse upon the death of the partner. He escapes this fate and learns "that to continue with worn-out traditions is foolishly dangerous."[37] His experience with the domineering old man, whom he carried as a kind act and who refused to let go of him until Sindbad made a wine potion and drugged him with it, shows that freedom is most precious.[38] Finally, his voyages lead him to a land where everything seems beautiful and he could even fly using feathers. He realizes though, thanks to a piece of advice, that if he does not mention God he will be burned up. Recognizing the diabolic nature of the powers and wicked practices of this land, he decides to go back home. He learns from this adventure that whatever marvel one is granted, "it is not sufficient that he should use it and appropriate it; he must also approach it with guidance from the light of God that shines in his heart."[39]

Hearing all this, Shahrayar loses interest in power and sees the vanity of his wealth. He sees the analogy between Sindbad's stories and Shahrazad's; in other words he sees the inner meaning of her stories, having now learned how to decode tales. He refuses to go on his nightly entertainment excursions and admits his lack of knowledge, saying: "it [wisdom] is not inherited as a throne is."[40] He gives up the throne to go on his own voyage seeking wisdom, truth, and salvation, saying against the protestations of Shahrazad that the "sultan must depart once he has lost competence."[41]

In the meantime, Sindbad has a dream of a Rukh and gets an irresistable urge to travel again. On visiting Sheikh Abdullah al-Balkhi for consultation, he is given advice on how to attain spiritual excellence:

> Know that you will not attain the rank of the devout until you pass through six obstacles. The first of these is that you should close the door of comfort and open that of hardship. The second is that you should close the door of renown and open that of insignificance. The third is that you should close the door of rest and open that of exertion. The fourth is that you should close the door of sleep and open that of wakefulness. The fifth is that you should close the door of riches and open that of poverty. The sixth is that you should close the door of hope and open the door of readiness for death.[42]

In the last chapter of the book, entitled "Grievers," Shahrayar, having abandoned power and family, strays into "the green tongue of land"—a place where the magical and the alternative seem to occur. It was there that Abdullah the porter was submerged into the water by Abdullah of the Sea, in a kind of baptismal rite, to emerge as a different persona and acquire the name "Abdullah of the Land." It is also the place where people set up their alternative kingdom and where Shahrayar found a plebeian impersonating him to administer justice that was denied in real life. There is clearly a play on the notion of a green strip of land and Khidr—the supernatural character—associated with Gilgamesh in Babylonian legends, with Alexander the Great in medieval epics, and with the quest of Bulukiyya in *The Arabian Nights*. Khidr is also evident in Islamic legends, where he is associated with the water of life and immortality. Greenness is a common symbol for organic, natural life, and water is necessarily associated with verdure. In one of the stories narrated by the Sheikh, the protagonist says:

> I wrote a book about Sufism which only the perfect could aspire to, and my brother the Khidr asked it of me, and God ordered that the waters should take it to him.[43]

The play on words is more obvious in Arabic since the name Khidr is the same as greenness. Immortality, rejuvenation, and eternal youth are synonymous with defeating death, and legends around the spring of water that grants such a wish are frequent in ancient Near Eastern lore. Gilgamesh manages after harrowing adventures to get hold of the flower of immortality in the deep seas, only to lose it to the snake after having fallen asleep at the shore. In an analogic manner, Shahrayar and all the grievers are offered bliss and eternal youth, but lose it in their human curiosity.

In a highly symbolic episode, Shahrayar opens up the "rock in the form of an uneven dome."[44] An entrance is revealed and Shahrayar enters an illuminated palace studded with precious stones and perfumed with sweet frangrances. He plunges in the garden's pond and emerges as a young man. There, a girl informs him that he is the awaited bridegroom for their queen. The city of this queen is fabulously clean and splendid, and its inhabitants are all women. In this feminist utopia—which stands in stark contrast to the patriarchial world depicted in the framed stories—time does not leave its imprints in the form of ageing and dying. Shahrayar celebrates his marriage to the queen and lives happily with her, oblivious to the passage of time. In the royal palace all is open and accessible to Shahrayar, except for one door which should not be opened. Shahrayar is intrigued by it and says to himself, "Everything is clear except for this door."[45] As he turns the key and the door opens, he finds himself thrown out, and once again old and decrepit. He tries to open up the rock anew—with the rest of the Grievers—to no avail.

What does this grandiose vision signify? It points to Shahrayar, now an Everyman figure seeking wisdom, banished from blissful timelessness and condemned to continue searching for a lost paradise. The rock reminds him of its possibility, but denies him its attainment. Mystic joys and the sight of eternal truth are necessarily momentary, as the story suggests. Human nature brings the contemplator back to the "abode of torment," as the Grievers call their city and their state.[46] It is fitting then that this novel of Mahfouz, while pointing to the Sufi way as a mode of salvation from infernal reality and mad actuality, recognizes the momentary nature of such delivery and the impossibility of human beings dwelling in such a state. The destination attracts, but the road is endless. The mad/sane Abdullah says at the very end of the novel:

> It is an indication of truth's jealousy that it has not made for anyone a path for it, and that it has not deprived anyone of the hope of attaining it, and it has left people running in the deserts of perplexity and drowning in the seas of doubt . . . . Thus there is no attaining it, and no avoiding it—it is inescapable.[47]

The ending of the frame story shows two distinct things: first, that desire for wisdom and for power are incompatible; this is why Shahrayar quits the throne when he decides to seek truth. The Arabic word in the text rendered as "truth" by the translator is *al-haqq*. This term denotes a variety of meanings; only one of them is truth. It stands for divine order and divine bliss, and it is one of the ninety-nine names of God. Furthermore, it indicates what is opposite of *batil* (vain), and encompasses what is real and permanent. It also stands for "right" and "duty." What Mahfouz allegorizes in the finale of his novel is that the desire for wisdom necessarily takes the seeker toward the path of divine bliss, but because human beings are human, they can only have a taste of the sublime—symbolized in a paradisical scene of everlasting youth—without ever retaining such a state.

In this double-layered allegory of Mahfouz, the text forks into two modes of signifying. In one, it depicts and criticizes postcolonial absurdities and proposes a happy—and somewhat humorous—ending. The neighborhood ends up being governed by a mending cobbler, with an infatuated lover for a secretary, and a wise fool for a chief of police. One cannot avoid interpreting the happy end: a solution composed of *mending* with love and unconventional reason. The solution suggested by the novelist is in diagnosing the ill and sympathetically healing it: this is done by replacing the ruling clans with a triumvirate of alternative types drawn from simple, honest folks. This is clearly neither a political program nor an ideological manifesto; it is a projection of the vague but ever-present political sense common among the people in the *hara,* the popular neighborhood.

On the other level, the novelist moves to issues that can be subsumed under the rubric of political theory, namely the nature of kingship and its relationship to the spiritual sphere. Judging by the logic of the novel, worldly power and unworldly power cannot be reconciled. The spiritual sheikh keeps his distance from the sultan. It is his disciple, Shahrazad, who mediates between his principles and bloody power. She stands allegorically for the taming power of creative words. The true nature of the sultan, however, continues to be feared. But once he is transformed into a seeker of truth and salvation, he quits his throne. Shahrayar, having put his kingdom in order, does not stay to enjoy it, but leaves—inspired by Sindbad, the roaming Sufi, and his master Sheikh Balkhi, the fixed Sufi. He discovers through his own tragic story that Truth is not something you can have and possess once and for all.

Mahfouz's novel then takes a privileged theme in *The Arabian Nights,* that of "healing," and explores its application in the contemporary world. He starts his fiction where Shahrazad stops, but does not end it where she started. He uses an ending that conjures mythological and sacred accounts of the human condition. Mahfouz, using the infamous motif of the forbidden door in Shahrazad's discourse, evokes both Gilgamesh and Adam in the character of Shahrayar. His forked strategy of alluding to the real and specific on one hand, and to the epical and sacred on the other, makes of his novel a hybrid and complex form.

13

NOMADIC TEXT

The *Arabian Nights* has moved with ease and confidence from one cultural context to another, and has managed to transplant itself into different epochs. In his study of the influence of *The Arabian Nights* on European and American literatures, Robert Irwin suggests humorously—but correctly—in a chapter entitled *"Children of the Nights"* that "it might have been an easier, shorter chapter if [he] had discussed those writers who were not influenced by the *Nights*."[1] So pervasive has been the presence of *The Arabian Nights* in Western imaginations over the last three centuries that it is difficult to find writers who have escaped its fascination and abstained from alluding to it. This includes such writers and literati as Voltaire and Proust, Wordsworth and Joyce, Poe and Whitman.[2] How can one work be shared and internalized by so many writers who belong to different and often hostile schools and orientations?

Even more striking are the critical debates which have used *The Arabian Nights* as a text of reference—if not a battleground—to further their position.[3] This marvelous work also seems to cut across epochs and cultures: ancient Indians, medieval Persians and Arabs, Europeans during the Renaissance and the Age of Enlightenment, as well as people of the New World—both in its southern and northern hemispheres—have dwelt on this work. It is indeed a text for all times and places. How does this text manage to travel so well and not wither in alien climates and distant regions?

It is remarkable that a text which is neither sacred nor canonical can overpower and interpenetrate so many cultural and literary systems. No doubt, the very fact of its fluidity and tolerence for textual mutations and variations has strengthened its ability to migrate. Added to this, its segmentary character based on autonomous narrative blocks and detachable enframed and framing stories, make it easier to de-link the parts and recycle the narratives, or specific blocks in them, for an infinite number of new ends. There is no need to bind oneself to the whole chain, since one can choose the stories one fancies without having to deal with the rest. There is thus a double flexibility in the text of *The Arabian Nights:* stylistically, it offers an unfixed discourse and structurally it offers loose (but by no means absent) links of articulation. It can, in other words, be easily deconstructed and reconstructed, rendering itself an example of a recyclable artifact.

The variety of themes and motifs in *The Arabian Nights* offers essentially an encyclopedia of narrative tales and genres. This allows for the coexistence of a variety of narratives: short and long, elaborate and simple, fables and epics, sacred and pornographic, childish and philosophical. *The Arabian Nights* also combines many narrative techniques—from boxing and embedding, perspectivism and self-reflexivity, juxtaposition of poetry and prose, tragic and comic plotting—thus allowing any sensibility to find an echo in one or more of the heterogeneous samples. The unity of the whole is at a deep level, permitting diversity on the surface level.

It is, then, the richness and variety of the text with the possibilities of excision and refashioning inherent in it that explains its continuous appeal and influence. But that is not all, for collections of stories abound and none really occupy the privileged position of *The Arabian Nights* in the world's imagination. The reason for this, I believe, lies in the nature of the frame story which justifies the telling and transforms the framework from a contrived fictional gadget or a narrative machine to an engendering matrix. The frame story joins narration and creativity with their raison d'être; it turns narration itself upon itself. It is a self-reflexive text, and in that sense it appeals not only to those who enjoy a good narrative, but also to those who like to understand the phenomenon of narration. Unlike other collections that may have moral, religious, or social ends, *The Arabian Nights'* end is contemplating its own activity. It is somewhat like an *ars poetica*, a poem about writing poetry, or a play about the performing of a play. Such works will always capture the interest of those who wonder about the literary process itself, the nature of art and fiction, and indeed the identities and inversions of human activity in its myriad forms.

The thematic thrust of the frame story, which offers a myth of myths, is based on deploying fundamental drives or instincts—those of life and death, of integration and disintegration—about which not enough can ever be said. The text seems to perceive that it is embarking on a never-ending path, and thus projects an infinite discourse—a narration that goes on and on. This ongoing narrative impulse has proved to be contagious: not only do its readers want to reread it, but they also want to rewrite it. It has, if one may borrow from Eco his term *opera aperta,* "open structure." It is not only a work that offers a hope, it is also a work that invites participation in the form of rewriting, recompiling, or reinterpreting. The ending is not a real closure, but more of bringing down of a curtain on a stage to stop the performance for the night, while promising more performances and sequels.

The nomadic character of *The Arabian Nights* stems from an intersection of several factors: (1) the variety of the enframed genres with an overall framing unity and a matricial base; (2) the work revolves around elemental forces in human existence and thus speaks to everyone, everywhere; (3) the work addresses itself to the problematic of its very being—narration—constituting what amounts to the creation of a myth of the origin of verbal creativity and its healing powers; and (4) the unlimited options afforded by the stylistic fluidity and structural flexibility of the work.

But above and beyond these factors, what makes *The Arabian Nights* such a widely and diversely intersting text is its "otherness." Its beauty is unconventional; it is darkly beautiful, for it articulates the beauty of what is suppressed and oppressed. It uncovers unspeakable desires and marginalized types. Women, slaves, and the riffraff are central. It is not only that Shahrazad narrates her stories at night that makes the poetics of the work nocturnal—it is also because she adopts a nocturnal rhetoric and a Dionysian poetics. All the chaotic, anarchic, and subaltern drives constitute the "otherness" that is aired freely in the text. Inasmuch as civilizations everywhere are based on repression, the need to acknowledge what is repressed is essential and a relief. When reading *The Arabian Nights,* we feel that we are getting even with canonical values and their tyranny. Even though *The Arabian Nights* constitutes no longer a taboo, it remains for the West, and possibly for the world at large, an alien cultural product with an-other poetics. In Arab culture, it is identified with the rabble and can never aspire to canonization, no matter how influential it has become with the literary elite. At the deepest level, it is precisely this "otherness"— aesthetic and cultural—that makes the work so continuously appealing. A text that evokes the distanced and the buried makes one feel a sense of restoration in internalizing it.

Many cultures, needless to say, have contributed to *The Arabian Nights* as we know it, but it remains associated with the Arabs who have preserved it. Is there something in early Arab aesthetics and culture that touched a certain chord when first listening to the narratives of *The Arabian Nights?* It is difficult to answer such questions, but we can speculate as to why the Arabs held on to this work despite the fact that it went against the grain— at least against the canons of the literary establishment.

I would venture to explain the persistence and growth of this collection of tales in Arab culture as a result of the fact that it complements and dovetails with the *qasida,* the classical Arab ode. Both types are made to move easily in a nomadic life style. The Bedouins in their moves from one place to another had developed art forms that suited their nomadism and migrations. Dramatic performances need a fixed stage and an elaborate theatrical institution, which nomads could not afford given their way of life. This does not mean that there was no drama, but it means that dramatic art was probably subsumed in ritual drama and holy sacrifice. Narrative and poetry, on the other hand, need one *rawi* to recite the text, and this recitor needs an exceptional memory in order to narrate and declaim. Even though writing was well-known in pre-Islamic Arabia, the Bedouin life style, ever on the move, imposed an economy of tools and reduced what was to be carried around to the minimum. Mnemonic aids were a necessity in this cultural ambiance, and Arabic poetry developed its own structural and rhythmic devices that would ensure the memorization of a text. Monorhyme prosody and limited meters helped pack up Arabic lyricism from one place to another, in specifically defined verbal containers, so to speak. A parallel device that helped preserve prose narratives used an opposite, albeit complementary, strategy. It made use of expandable containers that functioned like verbal accordions. In *The Arabian Nights,* the complex narrative structure allows for the maximum capacities of enfolding, while permitting and even encouraging stylistic liberty and license. In the *qasida* the complex poetic meters control the stream of words and subordinate them to the straightjackets of prosody. Both strategies tap and channel verbal creativity, but in classical Arabic poetry the formulation affects the very order of signifiers, while the unacanonical formulation of *The Arabian Nights* affects the order of signifieds. Textual nomadism is the result of an entrenched oral culture and the lack of affixing institutions. Although the Arabs had their oasis towns in Arabia before Islam where writing was known and used, a culture of writing was not yet in evidence— with all that it implies in changes of thought and knowledge. After the advent of Islam and the rise of powerful and settled caliphates in Syria, Iraq, Spain, etc., one would not expect a poetics built on orality to persist, yet it did—alongside a culture based on the book and *écriture.* The poetics of the nomads exemplified in the *qasida* remained overpowering, even though a more written poetics was developing in what came to be called *adab,* with its new prose rhythms and elaborate sentence structures. With writing, texts developed in the medieval Arab world that covered philosophical treatises and refined narratives, while some works—like *The Arabian Nights*—though written down by narrators, were never part of the literary canon and thus continued to carry the imprint of free oral diversifications. But unlike the oral poetics of the *qasida, The Arabian Nights* was neither glorified nor recognized as literature. If the poetics of the *qasida* represented the Apollonian streak—the poetics of broad daylight—that of *The Arabian Nights* represented the Dionysian streak, to borrow the Nietzschean opposition, a poetics of the dark and of secret nights. The poetics of *The Arabian Nights* is determinedly nocturnal: it deals with nocturnal narrations and stands for a tenebrous aesthetics. Its poetics is nocturnal, literally and metaphorically.

NOTES

Chapter One

1. Nabia Abbott, "A Ninth-Century Fragment of the 'Thousand Nights': New Light on the Early History of the *Arabian Nights,*" *Journal of Near Eastern Studies* 8 (July 1949): 123–33.
2. As quoted by E. Littman in *Encyclopedia of Islam,* new edition, s.v. "Alf Layla wa Layla."
3. Ibid.
4. Suhayr al-Qalamawi, *Alf layla wa layla* (Cairo, Dar al-Ma'arif, 1966), 27.
5. Muhsin Mahdi, *Kitab alf layla wa layla* (Leiden: E. J. Brill, 1984); translated into English by Husain Haddawy, *The Arabian Nights* (New York: W.W. Norton, 1990). For a discussion of this edition and its translation see the reviews of Ferial J. Ghazoul in *International Journal of Middle East Studies* 19, no. 2 (1987): 246–48, and Charles Butterworth in *Interpretation* 21, no. 1 (Fall 1993): 59–66, respectively.
6. Muhsin Mahdi, "Mazahir al-riwaya wa-l-mushafaha fi usul 'alf layla wa layla,'" *Revue de l'Institut des Manuscrits Arabes* 20 (May 1974): 125–44.
7. Jan Vansina, *Oral Tradition: A Study in Historical Methodology,* trans. H. M. Wright (London: Routledge and Kegan Paul, 1965), 121–29.
8. For an account of translations, see M. Gerhardt, *The Art of Story-Telling, A Literary Study at the Thousand and One Nights,* (Leiden: E. J. Brill, 1963), 65–113; and more recently Robert Irwin, *The Arabian Nights: A Companion* (London: Allen Lane/Penguin, 1994), 9–41.
9. Muhsin Mahdi, in his introduction to his edition of *Kitab alf layla wa layla,* provides diagrams of the earliest known source which he edits, and postulates a proto-text, an urtext, albeit the impossibility of its reconstruction. For an exhaustive discussion of Mahdi's criticism, see Irwin, *The Arabian Nights: A Companion,* 54–61.

10. Claude Lévi-Strauss, "La geste d'Asdiwal," *Annuaire* 1958–1959, Section des Sciences Religieuses (Paris: Ecole Pratique des Hautes Etudes): 2–43.

11. A. Salhani, ed., *Alf layla wa layla,* 5 vols. (Beirut: The Catholic Press, 1914), 1–2. My translation.

12. Antoine Galland, *Les mille et une nuits* (Paris: Morizot, n.d.), 4.

13. M. Soifer and I. Shapiro, eds., *Golden Tales from the Arabian Nights* (New York: Simon and Schuster, 1957), 9.

14. I have used the Lane translation, which is based on the Cairo–Bulaq edition. I have provided in square brackets that which he has omitted from the original. E. W. Lane, trans., *The Thousand and One Nights,* 3 vols. (London, Chatto and Windus, 1912), I:5.

15. Haddawy, *The Arabian Nights,* 5.

16. *The Arabian Nights* is a narrative in which a sequence of fictional events produces other narratives. There is, therefore, a basic story which both embraces and generates other stories. The productive narrative construction is referred to as the frame story and the produced narratives are the enframed stories. The comparative studies later in this book rely on works that have been affiliated to *The Arabian Nights'* frame story or/and the enframed stories.

17. Michael Riffaterre, "L'explication des faits littéraires," in *L'enseignement de la littérature,* eds. S. Doubrovsky and T. Todorov (Paris: Plon, 1971), 333.

18. Abd al-Rahman al-Safati al-Sharqawi, ed., *Kitab alf layla wa layla,* 2 vols. (Cairo: Matba'at Bulaq, 1835).

19. Gerhardt, *The Art of Story-Telling,* 4.

20. Lane's style is closer to the original Cairo–Bulaq edition (Cairo I), but Burton's is more accurate in following the events.

21. Edward W. Said links the idea of textuality to preservation, that is, persistence in time and multiplication in space, in "The Text as Practice and as Idea," *Modern Language Notes* 88 (December 1973): 1071–1102.

22. Karl Marx, *A Contribution to the Critique of Political Economy,* ed. M. Dobb (New York: International Publishers, 1970), 217.

23. Claude Lévi-Strauss, "Interview," *Diacritics* I (Fall 1971): 48.

24. Jean Piaget, "How Children Form Mathematical Concepts," *Scientific American* (November, 1953), reprint (San Fransisco: W. H. Freeman and Co., 1953).

25. This is all the more astonishing when one considers the excellent work on the stylistics of Turkish folk literature, especially the work of Basgöz and Boratov.

26. Lévi-Strauss, "La geste d'Asdiwal."
27. Edward W. Said, *Joseph Conrad and the Fiction of Autobiography* (Cambridge: Harvard University Press, 1966).
28. Michael Riffaterre handles this in more than one place. See, for example, the following articles which are devoted to the problematic: "Le poème comme représentation," *Poétique* 4 (1970): 401–18; "Système d'un genre déscriptif," *Poétique* 9 (1972): 15–30; and "The Self-Sufficient Text," *Diacritics* III: 3 (Fall 1973): 39–45.
29. Gustave von Grünebaum, "Idéologie musulmane et esthétique arabe." *Studia Islamica* 3 (1955): 18. Contrast this biased view with those who attempted to explain Arab formalism as a viable system: A. Hamori, *On the Art of Medieval Arabic Literature* (Princeton: Princeton University Press, 1974); J. Stetkevych, "The Arabic Lyrical Phenomenon in Context," *Journal of Arabic Literature* 6 (1975): 57–77; Pierre Cachia, "The Conflicts of East and West in Contemporary Egyptian Taste," *Glasgow University Oriental Society Trans.* 14 (1950–1952): 26–35.
30. Von Grünebaum concludes, "Islamic civilization is thoroughly sycretistic, and it proves its vitality by coating each and every borrowing with its own inimitable patina," *Medieval Islam* (Chicago: University of Chicago Press, 1969), 319. Compare this view of "coating" to that of *bricolage,* as developed by Lévi-Strauss and adopted by Jacques Berque, as a "système de remplois," which Berque associated with a Tunisian mosque, a sample of Arab–Islamic culture: "Mais toute culture n'est-elle pas, comme la mosquée de Kairouan, faite de pièces et de morceaux empruntes loin d'alentour, selon les strates chronologiques ou les distances géographiques ou sociales les plus diverses?" *L'Orient second* (Paris, Gallimard, 1970), 35.
31. More recently, the debt of classical civilization to the Asians and Africans has been argued. See, for example, Martin Bernal, *Black Athena* (New Brunswick: Rutgers University Press, 1987).
32. Von Grünebaum, *Medieval Islam,* 302–3.
33. W. K. Simpson, ed., *The Literature of Ancient Egypt: An Anthology of Stories, Instructions and Poetry* (New Haven: Yale University Press, 1972).
34. *Encyclopedia of Islam,* new edition, s.v. "Hamasa," by Charles Pellat.
35. Coincidentally or not, Charles Pellat is a specialist on al-Jahiz. He is the author of *Le milieu basrien et la formation de Gahiz* (Paris: Adrien-Maisonneuve, 1953).
36. Recently some works have dealt with the aesthetic aspect of one or

more stories of *The Arabian Nights*. See for example, André Miquel, *Un conte des mille et une nuits: Ajib et Gharib* (Paris: Flammarion, 1977); Jamel Eddine Bencheikh, *Les mille et une nuits ou la parole prisonnière* (Paris: Gallimard, 1988); and Sandra Naddaff, *Arabesque* (Evanston: Northwestern University Press, 1991).

Chapter Two

1. Vladimir Propp, *The Morphology of the Folktale,* second edition, ed. L. A. Wagner (Austin and London: University of Texas Press, 1968).
2. Tzvetan Todorov, "The Two Principles of Narrative," *Diacritics* I: 1 (Fall 1971): 37–44.
3. A narrative block is a textual unit. It constitutes a segment of the story that can (potentially) make narrative sense autonomously.
4. The number of rings varies in the different manuscripts/editions of *The Arabian Nights*. In Mahdi's edition, there are ninety-eight. But the exact number of rings in itself and in this specific context is not important. What is significant is the indication of an enormous quantity (be it ninety-eight or five hundred and seventy) of lovers.
5. Lane, *The Thousand and One Nights,* I:10.
6. Søren Kierkegaard, *Repetition: An Essay in Experimental Psychology,* trans. W. Lowrie (Princeton: Princeton University Press, 1946), 152.
7. Lane, *The Thousand and One Nights,* I:4. Emphasis mine.
8. At the end of *The Thousand and One Nights,* when the happy ending is announced and Shahrayar pardons Shahrazad, the color af the night is said to have been "whiter than the face of the day." Lane, III:672.
9. Ibid., I:10.

Chapter Three

1. Riffaterre expounds the working of the matrix in these articles: "Modèles de la phrase littéraire," in *Problèmes de l'analyse textualle,* ed. Pierre Léon et al. (Paris: Didier, 1971), 133–48; "Paragram and Significance," *Semiotext(e)* I (Fall 1974): 72–87; and "Semantic Overdetermination in Poetry," *Poetics and Theory of Literature* 2 (1977): 1–19.
2. Lane, *The Thousand and One Nights,* I:5, 13. The Cairo–Bulaq edition uses this phraseology (I:3); other editions may not use the same wording but the implication is that of a "wound." In Mahdi's edition, Shahzaman refers to his grief (rather than wound), but when his brother hears the story, he "became very angry and almost dripping blood,"

as the Arabic text tells us ("ghadiba ghadaban shadidan hatta kada an yataqatara daman" (61). The blood here is related to wounding by association, though the term "wound" is absent. Derrida has taught us in his analysis of Plato's *Phaedrus* that a term may function in the text without being present; by sheer insinuation. See Jacques Derrida, *La dissémination* (Paris: Seuil, 1972), 69–197.

3. "Wa ana uhadithuki hadithan yakanu fihi al-khalas," Sharqawi, ed. *Alf layla wa layla*, I:6.

4. Michel Foucault, ""Nietzsche, Freud, Marx," *Nietzsche* (Paris: Les Editions de Minuit 1967), 183.

5. Edward W. Said, *Beginnings: Intention and Method* (New York: Basic Books Inc., 1975), 306.

6. See, for example, Abu al-Hasan al-Mas'udi, *Muruj al-dhahab wa ma'adin al-jawhar,* ed. Charles Pellat (Beirut: Manshurat al-Jami'a al-Lubnaniyya, 1966).

7. Mamluk Egypt for a number of reasons was the intellectual environment in which many of these works were written, including those by al-Ibshihi (1388–1446), al-Nuwayri (1279–1332), Ibn Fadl-Allah al-'Umari (1301–48), and al-Qalqashandi (d. 1418). See André Miquel, *La littérature arabe* (Paris: Presses Universitaires de France, 1969), 87–88.

8. Abu Zayd al-Hilali, who was black by complexion, was called Sa'ad. The black character in the epic of Sayf bin dhi Yazan is called Sa'dun. The patron saint *(wali)* of blacks in Tunisia is called Sidi Sa'ad.

9. Lane, *The Thousand and One Nights,* I:4.

10. Ibid., I:10.

11. Ibid., III:671.

12. Stéphane Mallarmé, *Oeuvres complètes,* (Paris: Gallimard, 1945), 1488.

13. *Encyclopedia of Islam,* s.v., "Sirat 'Antar," by B. Heller.

14. Ibn Khaldun, *The Muqaddima: An Introduction to History,* trans. Franz Rosenthal (Princeton: Princeton University Press, 1967), vol. I:3–4.

15. Jabir ibn Hayyan, *Essai sur l'histoire des idées scientifiques dans l'Islam,* ed. P. Kraus (Cairo: Librairie al-Khangi, 1935), 9.

16. Abu Hilal al-'Askari, *Kitab al-sina'atayn: al-kitaba wa-l-shi'r,* ed. 'Ali Bajawi and Muhammad Ibrahim (Cairo: 'Isa al-Babi, 1971), 7.

17. Lane, *The Thousand and One Nights,* I:1–2.

18. See Jacques Durand, "Rhétorique du nombre," in *Communications* 16 (1970), 125–32.

19. Wallace Stevens, *The Palm at the End of the Mind,* ed. Holly Stevens (New York: Vintage Books, 1972), 20.

20. The number of grains of wheat which Sissa demanded were 2^{64-1} or 18, 446, 744, 073, 709, 551, 615. See E. Kasner and J. Newman, *Mathematics and the Imagination* (New York: Simon and Schuster, 1967), 173.

21. See Abbott, "A Ninth–Century Fragment," 131.

22. Cairo, Dar al-Kutub, Z 13523, *Alf layla wa layla*, 4 vols.

23. Mahmoud Tarchouna, ed., *Ma'at layla wa layla* (Tunis: Al-Dar al-'Arabiyya li-l-Kitab, 1979), 5–13.

24. Manuscript Z 13523, Dar al-Kutub, Cairo. My translation.

25. Joseph-Arthur de Gobineau, *Trois ans en Asie: de 1855 a 1858*, 2 vols. (Paris: Editions Bernard Grasset, 1922), II:68–105.

26. Nur Ali-Shah Elahi, *L'Esotérisme kurde*, trans. Mohammed Makri (Paris: Editions Albin Michel, 1966), 138, 174.

27. Jabir Ibn Hayyan, *Essai sur l'histoire des idées scientifiques dans l'Islam*, 75, and *Rasa'il Ikhwan al-Safa' wa khullan al-wafa'*, 4 vols. (Beirut: Dar Beirut and Dar Sadir, 1957), I:109.

28. Henri Corbin, *Histoire de la philosophie islamique* (Paris: Gallimard, 1964), 20.

Chapter Four

1. On the question of genres in *The Arabian Nights*, see Gerhardt, *The Art of Story-Telling*, 119–374, and more recently Peter Heath, "Romance as Genre in The Thousand and One Nights," *Journal of Arabic Literature* XVIII:1–21; XIX:1–26.

2. This story covers the following nights in the Cairo–Bulaq edition: 44–145, I:139–301.

3. On the question of *dédoublement*, see Derrida's interpretation of Mallarmé's "Mimique" in *La dissémination*, 199–317.

4. See Edward Said in his "Introduction" to Halim Barakat, *Days of Dust*, trans. Trevor le Gassick (Wilamette, Ill.: Medina University Press International, 1974), ix–xxxiv.

5. Lucienne Rochon, *Lautréamont et le style homérique* (Paris: Archives des Lettres Modernes, 1971).

6. See Hamori's study of a "modern" Abbasid poet: Andras Hamori, "Examples of Convention in the Poetry of Abu Nuwas," in *Studia Islamica* 30 (1969): 5–26.

7. Genette uses the term of "macro-structure narrative" and "micro-structure stylistique" to depict the two levels of narration and representation. See Gérard Genette, *Figures III* (Paris: Editions du Seuil, 1972), 59.

8. *Encyclopedia of Islam*, s.v. "Sira," by G. Levi Della Vida.

9. A. J. Arberry, trans., *The Koran Interpreted*, 2 vols. (New York: The Macmillan Company, 1970), I:340.

10. G. Levi Della Vida, "Sira."

11. Ibid.

12. Ihsan 'Abbas, *Fann al-sira* (Beirut: Dar al-Thaqafa, 1956), 17.

13. Abu Ishaq al-Tha'albi, *Qisas al-anbiya'* (Beirut: al-Maktaba al-Thaqafiyya, n.d.). My translation.

14. 'Abbas, *Fann al-sira*, 19.

15. Ibid., 25.

16. Edward W. Lane, *The Manners and Customs of the Modern Egyptians* (London: Everyman's Library, 1963), 397.

17. Rene Wellek and Austin Warren, *Theory of Literature* (New York: Harcourt, Brace & World, 1956), 231.

18. Richard F. Burton, trans., *The Book of the Thousand Nights and a Night*, 16 vols. (London: Burton Club, n.d. [1985–1988 reprint]), III:114.

19. Aristotle wrote: "Recognition is most beautiful when it arises at the same time as reversal," *Poetics*, trans. K. Telford (Chicago: Henry Regnery Company, 1970), 20.

20. Tomashevsky uses the terms "free" and "bound" in connection with motifs: "The motifs which cannot be omitted are bound motifs; those which may be omitted without disturbing the whole causal-chronological course of events are free motifs." See Boris Tomashevsky, "Thematics," *Russian Formalist Criticism: Four Essays*, trans. L. Lemon and M. Reis (Lincoln: University of Nebraska Press, 1965), 68.

21. Burton, *The Book of the Thousand Nights and a Night*, II:78.

22. Lane, *The Thousand and One Nights*, I:10.

23. Burton, *The Book of the Thousand Nights and a Night*, II:91. This is somewhat different from the Cairo–Bulaq version, but it gives the same effect as a number of scenes scattered in the Cairo–Bulaq edition which it would be very difficult to render coherently without numerous and lengthy quotations.

24. Similarly, Riffaterre has shown how the symbolist and surrealist styles, usually considered as the triumph of private associations over textual coherence, are in fact generated through rigorous and orderly textual network. In the same vein, Foucault showed the implacable order of a phantasmagoric work of Flaubert. See Michael Riffaterre, "Dynamisme des mots: les poèmes en prose de Julien Gracq," *L'Herne*

20 (1972): 152–64; and "La métaphore filée dans la poésie surréaliste,"
Langue Française 3 (September 1969): 46–60; and Michel Foucault,
"Introduction," in Gustave Flaubert, *La tentation de Saint Antoine*
(Paris: Editions Gallimard, 1971), 7–33.

25. Burton, *The Book of the Thousand Nights and a Night,* II:77.
26. Gerhardt, *The Art of Story-Telling,* p. 117.
27. *Encyclopedia of Islam,* new edition, s.v. "Ash'ab," by Franz Rosenthal.
28. Vladimir Jankélévitch, *L'ironie* (Paris: Flammarion, 1964), 35.

Chapter Five

1. They cover the following nights in the Cairo–Bulaq edition: 146–53;
   I:301–20.
2. This story covers the following nights in the Cairo–Bulaq edition: 899–
   930; II:460–502.
3. Todorov uses the terms "figural" and "symbolic" organization when
   discussing riddles. The figural deals with the dialectical relationship
   enclosed within the riddle; the symbolic with its tropical nature. See
   Tzvetan Todorov, "L'analyse du discours: L'exemple des devinettes,"
   Journal de psychologie normale et pathologique 1–2 (January–June
   1973): 135–55.
4. *Princeton Encyclopedia of Poetry and Poetics,* 1965, s.v. "Fable in
   Verse," by A. L. Sells, 269.
5. Ibid.
6. For enumeration of these works see Musa Sulayman, *al-Adab al-qasassi
   'ind al-'Arab* (Beirut: Dar al-Kitab al-Lubnani, 1969), 28.
7. Lane, *The Book of the Thousand Nights and a Night,* I:10.
8. Ibid., I:13.
9. Uspensky insists on the "dependence of point of view on the subject of
   description": "the point of view is determined not only by the describing subject (the author) but by the described object (which may
   be a particular character or a particular situation)." See Boris Uspensky,
   *A Poetics of Composition: The Structure of the Artistic Text and Ty-
   pology of a Compositional Form,* trans. V. Zavarin and S. Wittig (Berkeley: University of Caifornia Press, 1973), 120.
10. Lane, *The Thousand and One Nights,* II:49.
11. Ibid., II:49.
12. Ibid., II:51.
13. Ibid., II:51.

14. Burton, *The Book of the Thousand Nights and a Night*, II:330–31.
15. Ibid., III:155.
16. Ibid., IX:38.
17. *Princeton Encyclopedia of Poetry and Poetics*, 1965, s.v. "Simile," by George Whalley, 767.
18. Burton, *The Book of the Thousand Nights and a Night*, IX:43.
19. Ibid., IX:46.
20. Ibid., IX:58.
21. Ibid., IX:47.
22. Ibid., IX:97–98.
23. The pheno-text is the text as experienced by the reader through its immediate features, which are invariably generated by a geno-text which constitutes the fundamental compositional characteristics of the text. See Oswald Ducrot and Tzvetan Todorov, *Dictionnaire encyclopédique des sciences du langage* (Paris: Seuil, 1972), 447.
24. Abu Hilal al-'Askari, *Kitab al-sina'atayn*, 249.
25. L. Cooper, trans., *The Rhetoric of Aristotle* (New York: D. Appleton and Co., 1932), 207.

Chapter Six

1. The story covers the following nights in the Cairo–Bulaq edition: 536–66; II:2–37.
2. Framing is a particular instance of embedding. In both cases, stories are inserted within other stories. Embedding indicates simply an inclusion of one narrative within another, while framing suggests a narrative producing other narratives.
3. Lane, *The Thousand and One Nights*, III:4.
4. Uspensky, who worked on the problem of representation in the verbal and visual spheres, uses the terms "direct" and "inverted" perspectives. See Uspensky, *A Poetics of Composition*.
5. Lane, *The Thousand and One Nights*, III:3.
6. Ibid., III:23.
7. Allen Dundes, "Structural Typology in North American Indian Folktales," in *The Study of Folklore*, ed. Allen Dundes (Englewood Cliffs: Prentice-Hall, Inc., 1965), 206–15.
8. Sylvia Pavel, "La prolifération narrative dans les 'Mille et Une Nuits,'" *Canadian Journal of Semiotic Research* 2 (Winter 1974): 21–40.
9. Tzvetan Todorov, *Grammaire du Décameron* (The Hague: Mouton, 1969), 82–83.

10. Ibid., 95.

11. 1/7 = 0.142857142857 . . . etc. Hence, the use of the number 7 for magical operations, especially in connection with luring and obsessing.

12. Ibn Tufayl, *Hayy ibn Yaqzan*, trans. L. E. Goodman (New York: Twayne Publishers, 1972).

13. H. E. Butler, trans., *The Institutio Oratoria of Quintilian*, 4 vols. (London: William Heinemann, 1922), III:339.

14. Abu Hilal al-'Asakri, *Kitab al-sina'atayn*, 378.

15. Lane, *The Thousand and One Nights*, III:16

16. Ibid., III:28.

17. Ibid., III:25.

18. *Encyclopedia of Islam*, s.v. "Gharib," by S. Bonebakker.

19. Lane, *The Thousand and One Nights*, III:11.

20. Ibid., III:21.

21. Ibid., III:20–21.

22. Conceit has been discussed mostly in the context of poetry, but a number of works in modern fiction can be classified as extended conceits, in particular those of Kafka and Beckett.

23. *Princeton Encyclopedia of Poetry and Poetics*, 1965, s.v. "Conceit," by Frank Warnke and Alex Preminger.

24. Lane, *The Thousand and One Nights*, III:43–44.

25. Allen Dundes, ed., *Every Man His Way: Readings in Cultural Anthropology* (Englewood Cliffs: Prentice-Hall, 1968), 21.

26. Lane, *The Thousand and One Nights*, III:54.

27. Gerhardt, *The Art of Story-Telling*, 236–63.

28. Vansina, who worked on the typology of oral tradition, wrote that the relationship between dependent free texts (and even between dependent fixed texts) cannot be established through textual analysis alone, but needs circumstantial evidence. See Vansina, *Oral Tradition: A Study in Historical Methodology*, 129.

29. Burton, *The Book of the Thousand Nights and a Night*, VI:30. This statement is repeated at the end of every night.

30. Ibid., VI:34.

31. Ibid.

32. Ibid., VI:35.

33. Bettelheim sees it as the struggle between the reality principle and the pleasure principle. See Bruno Bettelheim, *The Uses of Enchantment: Meaning and Importance of Fairy Tales* (New York: Vintage Books, 1977), 84.

34. Claude Lévi-Strauss, *Anthropologie structurale* (Paris: Librairie Plon, 1958), 183–203.

35. I. M. Lewis, *Ecstatic Religion: An Anthropological Study of Spirit Possession and Shamanism* (Harmondsworth: Penguin Books, 1971), 195.

36. *Hadra* is a Maghrebi seance involving possession, roughly comparable to the Egyptian *zar*.

37. "A savoir que la danseuse *n'est pas une femme qui danse* . . . mais une métaphore . . . et *qu'elle ne danse pas*, suggérant, par le prodige de racourcis ou d'élans, avec une écriture corporelle ce qu'il faudrait des paragraphes en prose dialoguée autant que descriptive, pour exprimer, dans la rédaction: poème dégagé de tout appareil du scribe." See Mallarmé, *Oeuvres complètes*, 304.

38. The essence of carnivalization is the transposition of diverse forms in a ritualistic performance, where the participants live a liberating experience. See Mikhail Bakhtin, *Problems of Dostoevsky's Poetics*, trans. Caryl Emerson (Minneapolis: University of Minnesota Press, 1984), 122–24.

39. Vladimir Propp, *Istoricheskie korni volshebnoj skazki* (Leningrad: Izdatel'stvo Leningradskogo Gosudarstvennego Universiteta, 1946).

40. I. Basgoz, "The Dream Motif in Turkish Folk Stories, and Shamanistic Initiation," *Asian Folklore Studies* 26 (1967): 1–18.

41. Hamori, *On the Art of Medieval Arabic Literature*, 3–77.

42. A. al-Bayyati, "al-Batal al-usturi wa-l-malhami," *Afaq 'Arabiyya* 7 (May 1976): 64–71.

43. Maurice Bouisson, *Le secret de Shéhérazade* (Paris: Flammarion, 1961).

44. Gerhardt provides a detailed differentiation of elements and layers in the story. Hamori corrects and complements her reading. See Gerhardt, *The Art of Story-Telling*, 195–235; and Hamori, *On the Art of Medieval Arabic Literature*, 145–63.

Chapter Seven

1. Victor Turner, the British anthropologist, coins the term "anti-structure" to describe situations where the habitual differences in status are obliterated, as in revolutions, pilgrimages, periods of religious fervor, etc. In a similar vein, I use "destructuring" to indicate not the lack of structure but the destruction of a given structure. It is by no means chaos, but the (temporary) crumbling down of distinctions. See Victor Turner, *The Ritual Process: Structure and Anti-Structure* (Chicago: Aldine, 1969).

2. These stories cover the following nights in the Cairo–Bulaq edition: 1–8; I:6–51.

3. Lane, *The Thousand and One Nights*, I:41–42.
4. Marcel Mauss, *The Gift: Forms and Functions of Exchange in Archaic Societies*, trans. Ian Cunnison (New York: The Norton Library, 1967).
5. Tzvetan Todorov, "Les hommes-récits," in *Poétique de la prose* (Paris: Seuil, 1971), 78–91.
6. For a hermeneutic reading of this story, see Hamori, *On the Art of Medieval Arabic Literature*, 164–80, and for a more recent analysis of it based on Mahdi's edition, see Sandra Naddaff, *Arabesque* (Evanston: Northwestern University Press, 1991).
7. Lane, *The Thousand and One Nights*, I:120.
8. Ibid., I:121.
9. Ibid.
10. Ibid., I:121–22.
11. Ibid., I:126–27.
12. Samuel Coleridge, "Biographia Literaria," in *Critical Theory Since Plato*, ed. Hazard Adams (New York: Harcourt Brace Jovanovich, 1971), 471.

Chapter Eight

1. "The use of the term 'cathexis' never escapes a certain ambiguity which analytic theory has nowhere managed to dispel." In J. Laplanche and J. B. Pontalis, *The Language of Psycho-Analysis*, trans. D. Nicholson-Smith (New York: W.W. Norton, 1973), 63.
2. J. G. Kennedy, "Nubian Zar Ceremonies as Psychotherapy," *Human Organization* 26 (Winter 1967): 186.
3. Ibid., 187.
4. Ibid.
5. H. Barclay, *Buurri al Lamaab: A Suburban Village in the Sudan* (Ithaca: Cornell University Press, 1964), 200. For a comparative psycho-anthropological study of the *zar*, see Fatima al-Masri, *al-Zar* (Cairo: Al-Hay'a al-Misriyya al-'Amma li-l-Kitab, 1975).

Chapter Nine

1. Giambattista Vico, *The New Science*, trans. T. D. Bergin and M. H. Fisch (Ithaca: Cornell University Press, 1970), 85–96.
2. A. Berriedale Keith, *A History of Sanskrit Literature* (London: Oxford University Press, 1920), 361.

3. Gerhardt, *The Art of Story-Telling*, 9.
4. *The Panchatantra*, trans. Arthur W. Ryder (Chicago: The University of Chicago Press, 1925), 15. For another translation, see Franklin Edgarton, trans., *The Panchatantra* (London: George Allen and Unwin, 1965); for the cultural background of *The Panchatantra*, see Apurba Chandra Barthakuria, *India in the Age of the Panchatantra* (Calcutta: Punthi-Pustak, 1992); and for variants of the work, see Varadraj Huilgol, *The Panchatantra of Vasughaga: A Critical Study* (Madras: New Era Publications, 1987).
5. Sharqawi, ed., *Alf layla wa layla*, I:6.
6. Ryder, trans. *The Panchatantra*, 41–42.
7. Ibid., 42.
8. Sharqawi, *Alf layla wa layla*, I:234–55.
9. Ibid., I:139–301.
10. Ryder, trans., *The Panchatantra*, 174–82.
11. Ibid., 454–61.
12. Ibid., 49–54.
13. Ibid., 62–71.
14. Ibid., 412–14.
15. Sharqawi, ed., *Alf layla wa layla*, I:10–24.
16. H. Zotenberg, *Histoire d'Ala al-Din ou la lampe merveilleuse* (Paris: Imprimerie National, 1888).
17. Sharqawi, ed., *Alf layla wa layla*, I:2–4.
18. Ibid., I:531–33.
19. Ibid., I:533–34.
20. Ibid., I:234–55.
21. Ibid., I:4–6; II:619.
22. Ryder, trans., "Introduction," *The Panchatantra*, 5.
23. As drawn by C. S. Lewis, *The Allegory of Love: A Study in Medieval Tradition* (New York: Oxford University Press, 1958).
24. Sharqawi, ed., *Alf layla wa layla*, I:36–41.
25. Michael Riffaterre, "La métaphore filée dans la poésie surréaliste," *Langue Française* 3 (September 1969): 46.
26. Ryder, trans., *The Panchatantra*, 22.
27. Claude Lévi-Strauss, *Totemism*, trans. Rodney Needham (Boston: Beacon Press, 1963), 16.
28. Sharqawi, ed., *Alf layla wa layla*, I:28–29.
29. Ryder, trans., *The Panchatantra*, 25.
30. Ibid., 41–42.
31. Ibid., 81–88.

32. Sharqawi, ed., *Alf layla wa layla,* II:86–105.

33. On dominance in literary context, see Roman Jakobson, "The Dominant," in Ladislav Matejka and Krystyna Pomorska, eds., *Readings in Russian Poetics* (Ann Arbor: University of Michigan Press, 1978), 82–87.

34. Ryder, trans., *The Panchatantra,* 274–76.

35. Ibid., 273.

36. Ibid., 276.

37. Ibid., 274.

38. Sharqawi, ed., *Alf layla wa layla,* I:274.

39. Ibid., I:4.

Chapter Ten

1. The story in Arabic is found in only one published version of *The Arabian Nights,* the edition known as Breslau, after the place of publication, of which the first eight volumes were edited by M. Habicht (1825–38) and the last four by F. Fleischer (1842–43). The story is on pages 133–89 of volume IV (published in 1828). It is one of the stories of the Harun cycle. Antoine Galland (1646–1715) gives a French translation of the story without leaving a manuscript original. Galland's "Histoire du dormeur éveillé" does not correspond completely to the Arabic text of the Breslau edition. The latter is generally preferred for critical studies and is used in this chapter. References to it in the chapter use the name of the editor, Habicht, for the sake of convenient identification.

2. There are a number of translations of this story in European languages. All quotations in this article are from Richard Burton's translation in *Supplemental Nights* (London: Burton Club, n.d.[1886]), I:1–29.

3. In *The Taming of a Shrew,* an anonymous play and analogous to Shakespeare's *The Taming of the Shrew,* Sly reappears at the end. For discussion of both plays, see G. I. Duthie, *"The Taming of a Shrew and The Taming of the Shrew,"* in *The Review of English Studies* XIX:76 (October 1943): 337–56; Thelma Nelson Greenfield, "The Transformation of Christopher Sly," *Philological Quarterly* XXXIII:1 (January 1954): 34–42.

4. Although the authoritative text of *The Taming of the Shrew* is that of the First Folio (1623), there is considerable debate about the earliest version of it. The question is somewhat complicated by the existence of

The Taming of a Shrew, first published in 1594. The debate, of course, does not change the fact that *The Taming of the Shrew* is still one century earlier than the official appearance of *The Arabian Nights* in Europe.

5. On Arabic influence on pre-Shakespearean England, see Dorothee Metlitzki, *The Matter of Araby in Medieval England* (New Haven: Yale University Press, 1977) and Maria Rosa Menocal, *The Arabic Role in Medieval Literary Theory* (Philadelphia: University of Pennsylvania Press, 1987).

6. For the importance of the oral tradition in *The Taming of the Shrew,* see S. L. Bethel, *Shakespeare and the Popular Dramatic Tradition* (London: Staples Press, 1944); E. M. W. Tillyard, "The Fairy-Tale Element in *The Taming of the Shrew,*" in Edward Bloom, ed., *Shakespeare 1564–1964* (Providence: Brown University Press, 1964), 110–14; Jan Harold Brunvand, "The Folktale Origin of *The Taming of the Shrew,*" *Shakespeare Quarterly* XVII:4 (Autumn 1966): 345–59; W. B. Thorne, "Folk Elements in *The Taming of the Shrew,*" *Queen's Quarterly* LXXV:3 (Autumn 1968), 482–96.

7. W. A. Clouston, "Variants and Analogues of Some of the Tales in Volumes XI and XII," (appendix) in Richard F. Burton, trans., *Supplemental Nights,* II:209.

8. Geoffrey Bullough, ed., *Narrative and Dramatic Sources of Shakespeare* (New York: Columbia University Press, 1966), I:58–59.

9. See also Richard Hosley, "Source and Analogues of *The Taming of the Shrew,*" *The Huntington Library Quarterly* XXVII:3 (May 1964): 289–308; Oscar James Campbell, ed., *The Reader' s Encyclopedia of Shakespeare* (New York: Thomas Crowell Company, 1966), 844; Kenneth Muir, *The Sources of Shakespeare's Plays* (London: Methuen, 1977), 19.

10. The following studies address the question of unity of *The Taming of the Shrew* from different perspectives, touching on the relationship of the induction to the inner play: Cecil C. Ceronsy, "'Supposes' as the Unifying Theme in *The Taming of the Shrew,*" *Shakespeare Quarterly* XIV:1 (Winter 1963): 15–30; Norman Sanders, "Themes and Imagery in *The Taming of the Shrew,*" in S. K. Heninger et al., eds. *Renaissance Papers 1963* (Japan: Charles Tuttle, 1964), 63–72; Sears Jayne, "The Dreaming of *The Shrew,*" *Shakespeare Quarterly* XVII:1 (Winter 1966): 41–56; Richard Henze, "Role Playing in *The Taming of the Shrew,*" *Southern Humanities Review* IV:3 (Summer 1970): 231–40; François Delphy, "Emboîtement, déboîtement et mise en boîte

dans *La mégère apprivoisée," Les Langues Modernes* LXXI:3 (1977): 249–55; Charles R. Forker, "Immediacy and Remoteness in *The Taming of the Shrew* and *The Winter's Tale*," in C. M. Kay and H. E. Jacobs. eds., *Shakespeare's Romances Reconsidered* (Lincoln: University of Nebraska Press, 1978), 135–48.

11. Burton, *Supplemental Nights,* I:7 [Habicht, IV:145]
12. Ibid., I:7–8 [Habicht, IV:145–46].
13. For discussion of the theme of disillusionment in "The Sleeper Awakened" and in comparative context, see Gerhardt, *The Art of Storytelling,* 443–50.
14. William Shakespeare, *The Taming of the Shrew* (Harmondsworth: Penguin, 1968), Induction 1:3–5.
15. Ibid., Induction 1:32–39.
16. Ibid., Induction 2:12–15.
17. Ibid., Induction 2:16–19.
18. Ibid., Induction 2:67–70.
19. Burton, *Supplemental Nights,* I:2 [Habicht, IV:135].
20. Shakespeare, *The Taming of the Shrew,* Induction 2:48–59.
21. For further discussions of this point, see Kenneth Muir, "Much ado about the Shrew," *Trivium* VII (May 1972): 1–4; Marianne L. Novy, "Patriarchy and Play in *The Taming of the Shrew*," *English Literary Renaissance* IX:2 (Spring 1979): 264–80.

Chapter Eleven

1. Jorge Luis Borges, *Seven Nights,* trans. Eliot Weinberger (New York: New Directions, 1980), 42.
2. John Barth, "Interview," *Wisconsin Studies in Contemporary Literature* VI:1 (Winter–Spring 1965): 6.
3. Tzvetan Todorov, "Les hommes-récits."
4. Michel Foucault, "Qu'est-ce qu'un auteur?" *Bulletin de la Sociéte Française de Philosophie* XIII:3 (July–September 1969): 78. See the English translation, "What Is an Author?" in Josue Harari, ed., *Textual Strategies* (Ithaca: Cornell University Press, 1979), 142.
5. Jacques Lacan, *Ecrits I* (Paris: Seuil, 1966), 51.
6. Borges, *Seven Nights,* 46.
7. Ibid., 54.
8. Barth, "Interview," 4.
9. John Barth, "The Literature of Exhaustion," *The Atlantic* 220: 2 (August, 1967): 31.

10. Ibid.

11. See, among others, John Stark, *The Literature of Exhaustion. Borges, Nabokov and Barth* (Durham: Duke University Press, 1974).

12. Stephen Peithman, ed., *The Annotated Tales of Edgar Allan Poe* (New York: Doubleday, 1981), 464–77.

13. Arthur Holmberg, "Carlos Fuentes: A Play on Memory and Myths," *International Herald Tribune*, June 28, 1982.

14. N. T. di Giovanni et al., eds., *Borges on Writing* (New York: Dutton, 1973), 114.

15. Jorge Luis Borges, *The Aleph and Other Stories 1933–1969*, ed. and trans. N. T. di Giovanni (New York: Dutton, 1970), 87–90.

16. John Barth, *Chimera* (Greenwich: Fawcett, 1973), 9–64.

17. David Morrell, *John Barth* (University Park: Pennsylvania State University Press, 1976), 147.

18. Borges, *Seven Nights,* 50.

19. di Giovanni, *Borges,* 104.

20. di Giovanni, *Borges,* 109–10; on the impact of *The Arabian Nights* on Borges, see Muhammad Abu al-'Ata, "Alf layla hilm Borges," and Ibtihal Yunis, "Athr al-turath al-sharqi wa alf layla wa layla fi ru'yat al-'alam 'ind Borges," *Fusul* XIII:2 (Summer 1994): 338–47 and 348–74, respectively.

21. Borges, *The Aleph,* 271.

22. Ibid., 115–25; see also Borges' note to this story, 273–74.

23. Ibid., 90.

24. Barth, *Chimera,* 64.

25. Ibid., 13.

26. Jorge Luis Borges, "Averröes' Search," in *Labyrinths*, trans. Donald Yates and James Irby (New York: New Directions Books, 1964), 148–55.

27. Morrell, *John Barth,* 157.

28. Borges, *The Aleph,* 89.

29. Shreds of John Barth's life are often found in his fictional work, from his earliest novel *The Floating Opera* (1967) to his most recent *Once Upon a Time* (1994).

30. Barth, *Chimera,* 20.

31. Ibid., 64.

32. Ibid., p. 35.

33. On the sense of the real, see Roland Barthes, "L'effet de réel" and Michael Riffaterre, "L'illusion référentielle" in Gérard Genette and Tzvetan Todorov, eds., *Littérature et réalité* (Paris: Seuil, 1982), 81–90 and 91–118, respectively.

34. See Yusuf Dishi, "Isti'arat alf layla wa layla," *Fusul* XIII:2 (Summer 1994): 323–37.
35. Mark Edmundson, "The End of the Road," *The New Republic* (April 22, 1991): 44.
36. Ibid., 44–45.
37. Steve M. Bell, "Southern Boom," *American Book Review* XIV (February/March 1993): 25.
38. Robert Towers, "Tripping the Not-So-Light Fantastic," *The New York Review of Books* (April 25, 1991): 46.
39. John Barth, *The Last Voyage of Somebody the Sailor* (Boston: Little, Brown and Company, 1991), 56.
40. Ibid., 111.
41. Ibid., 54.
42. Ibid., 133.

Chapter Twelve

1. For the complete texts of the prosecution and defense arguments, see *Fusul* XII:4 (Winter 1994): 271–93.
2. See on the involvement of Taha Hussein and Tawfiq al-Hakim with *The Arabian Nights* within the sociological context of Egypt: Shukry 'Ayyad, "Shahrazad bayn Taha Husayn wa-l-Hakim," *Fusul* XIII:2 (Summer 1994): 9–19.
3. Taha Hussein, "Introduction," in Suhayr al-Qalamawi, *Alf layla wa layla* (Cairo: Dar al-Ma'arif, 1966), 7–9.
4. As selective examples, one can cite in drama: Tawfiq al-Hakim and Alfred Farag; in fiction: 'Izz al-Din Madani and Badr al-Dib. See also the novel by the Syrian writer Rafik Schami, *Damascus Nights,* translated from the German by Philip Boehm (New York: Scribner, 1993).
5. For a study of *The Arabian Nights* in contemporary Arabic poetry, see 'Abdul-Rahman Bseiso, "Aqni'at alf layla fi-l-shi'r al-hadith," *Fusul* XIII:2 (Summer 1994): 111–45.
6. See on rhetorical strategies of the oppressed in medieval Arab culture, Gaber Asfour, "Balaghat al-maqmu'in," *Alif: Journal of Comparative Poetics* 12 (1992): 6–49.
7. See for example, Muhsin Mahdi, "Remarks on the *1001 Nights,*" *Interpretation* III:2/3 (Winter 1973): 157–68; also Ahmad Muhammad al-Shahhadh, *al-Malamih al-siyasiyya fi hikayat alf layla wa layla* (Baghdad: Wizarat al-I'lam, 1977).

8. Taha Hussein, *Ahlam Shahrazad* (Cairo: Dar al-Ma'arif, 1958), 117; Taha Hussein, *The Dreams of Scheherazade*, trans. Magdi Wahba (Cairo: General Egyptian Book Organization, 1974), 87. All quotations refer to these editions, with the pages from the English translation given first, followed by the pages from the Arabic original in brackets.

9. Ibid., 97–98 [130].

10. Ibid., 106 [141].

11. Naguib Mahfouz, *Layali alflayla* (Cairo: Maktabat Misr, 1982); Naguib Mahfouz, *Arabian Nights and Days*, trans. Denys Johnson-Davies (Cairo: The American University in Cairo Press, 1995). All quotations refer to these editions, with the pages from the English translation given first, followed by the pages from the Arabic original in brackets.

12. Naguib Mahfouz, "Alf layla ahatat bi-l-hadara al-sharqiyya [Interview]," *Fusul* XIII:2 (Summer 1994): 380. My translation.

13. Naguib Mahfouz, *Khammarat al-qitt al-aswad* (Cairo: Maktabat Misr, 1969), 259–75; *God's World: An Anthology of Short Stories*, trans. Akef Abadir and Roger Allen (Minneapolis: Bibliotheca Islamica, 1973), 63–74.

14. Mahfouz, *Arabian Nights and Days*, 32 [42].

15. Ibid., 25 [34].

16. Sonallah Ibrahim's novel *Dhat* (Cairo: Dar al-Mustaqbal al-'Arabi, 1992) appeared in French translation by Richard Jacquemond, *Les années de Zeht* (Arles: Actes Sud, 1993). See a study of the novel in Samia Mehrez, *Egyptian Writers Between History and Fiction* (Cairo: The American University in Cairo Press, 1994), 119–45.

17. Mahfouz, *Arabian Nights and Days*, 64 [84].

18. For example, one character in Mahfouz's novel says that "the sultan is still a bloodthirsty ruler despite his unexpected change of heart," (36 [48]) and Shahrazad says that "there is no trusting the blood-shedder," (99 [130]).

19. Mahfouz, *Arabian Nights and Days*, 8 [12].

20. Ibid., 171 [222].

21. For the correspondence of (most of) the tales in Mahfouz's novel to their analogues in *The Arabian Nights*, see Nabila Ibrahim, *Fann al-qass* (Cairo: Maktabat Gharib, n.d.), 114–37; for the relationship of the Mahfouzian corpus to Arabic classical heritage, see the following papers presented at the International Symposium on "Naguib Mahfouz and the Arabic Novel," Cairo University, March 17–20, 1990: Valeria

Kirpitchenko, "Ibda' Najib Mahfuz wa-l-turath al-'arabi" and Ibrahim al-Sa'afin, "Nagib Mahfuz: jadal al-ana wa-l-turath." See also Rasheed El-Enany, *Naguib Mahfouz: The Pursuit of Meaning* (London: Routledge, 1993), 159–68, and by the same author, *Najib Mahfuz: Qira'a ma bayn al-sutur* (Beirut: Dar al-Tali'a, 1995), 80–100.

22. Yahya al-Rakhawy, an Egyptian psychiatrist and critic, sees this last chapter of Mahfouz's novel as a contrived sequel and explains its presence by the author's fear of what he has revealed about human nature. Thus the author inserts a belated epilogue with a glimmer of hope. See Yahya al-Rakhawy, *Qira'at fi Najib Mahfuz* (Cairo: Al-Hay'a al-'Amma li l-Kitab, 1992), 51–85.

23. Italo Calvino, *Invisible Cities,* trans. William Weaver (New York: Harcourt Brace Jovanovich, Inc., 1974), 165.

24. Mahfouz, *Arabian Nights and Days*, 129 [168].

25. Ibid., 144 [187].

26. On the correspondence between medieval theories of love and *The Arabian Nights* tales, see Andras Hamori, "Notes on Two Love Stories from the *Thousand and One Nights,*" *Studia Islamica* XLIII (1976): 65–80.

27. Mahfouz, *Arabian Nights and Days*, 104 [136].

28. Ibid., 99 [130].

29. Ibid., 7 [11].

30. Ibid., 131 [170].

31. Sabry Hafez, "Jadaliyat al-binya al-sardiyya al-murakkaba fi layali Shahrazad wa Najib Mahfuz," *Fusul* XIII:2 (Summer 1994): 20–97.

32. Mahfouz, *Arabian Nights and Days*, 207 [267].

33. Ibid., 209 [270].

34. Ibid., 211 [272].

35. Ibid., 211–12 [273–74].

36. Ibid., 212–13 [274].

37. Ibid., 213–14 [275].

38. Ibid., 214–15 [276–77].

39. Ibid., 215 [277].

40. Ibid., 217 [279].

41. Ibid., 218 [281].

42. Ibid., 219 [282–83].

43. Ibid., 161 [208].

44. Ibid., 223 [285].

45. Ibid., 227 [291].

46. Ibid., 223 [286]. For more on the mystic element in the work of Mahfouz, see Hamdi Sakkut, "Naguib Mahfouz and the Sufi Way" in *The View*

from Within: Writers and Critics on Contemporary Arabic Literaure,
ed. Ferial J. Ghazoul and Barbara Harlow (Cairo: The American University in Cairo Press, 1994), 90–98.
47. Mahfouz, *Arabian Nights and Days,* 228 [293].

Chapter Thirteen

1. Irwin, *The Arabian Nights: A Companion,* 290–91.
2. On the presence of *The Arabian Nights* in literature and culture, see Hiam Aboul-Hussein and Charles Pellat, *Cheherazade: Personnage littéraire* (Alger: SNED, 1981), and Peter Caracciolo, ed., *The Arabian Nights in English Literature* (London: Macmillan, 1988).
3. See on the role of *The Arabian Nights* in shaping nineteenth-century criticism in England: Muhsin Jassim Ali, *Scheherazade in England* (Washington, D.C.: Three Continents Press, 1981).

BIBLIOGRAPHY

'Abbas, Ihsan. *Fann al-sira*. Beirut: Dar al-Thaqafa, 1956.

Abbott, Nabia. "A Ninth-Century Fragment of the 'Thousand Nights.' New Light on the Early History of the *Arabian Nights*." In *Journal of Near Eastern Studies* (July 1949): 129–64.

Aboul-Hussein, Hiam and Charles Pellat. *Cheherazade: Personnage littéraire*. Alger: SNED, 1981.

Abu al-'Ata, Muhammad. "Alf layla hilm Borges." In *Fusul* XIII:2 (Summer 1994): 338–47.

Ali, Muhsin Jassim. *Scheherazade in England*. Washington, D.C.: Three Continents Press, 1981.

Arberry, A. J., trans. *The Koran Interpreted*. New York: The Macmillan Company, 1970.

Aristotle. *Poetics*. Translated by K. Telford. Chicago: Henry Regnery Company, 1970.

Asfour, Gaber. "Balaghat al-maqmu'in." In *Alif: Journal of Comparative Poetics* 12 (1992): 6–49.

al-'Askari, Abu Hilal. *Kitab al-sina'atayn: al-kitaba wa-l-shi'r*. Edited by Ali Bajawi and Muhammad Ibrahim. Cairo: Issa al-Babi, 1971.

'Ayyad, Shukry. "Shahrazad bayn Taha Husayn wa-l-Hakim." In *Fusul* XIII:2 (Summer 1994): 9–19.

Bakhtin, M. *Problems of Dostoevsky's Poetics*. Translated by Caryl Emerson. Minneapolis: University of Minnesota Press, 1984.

Barclay, H. *Buurri al Lamaab: A Suburban Village in the Sudan*. Ithaca: Cornell University Press, 1964.

Barth, John. "Interview." In *Wisconsin Studies in Contemporary Literature* VI:1 (Winter–Spring 1965).

———. "The Literature of Exhaustion." In *The Atlantic* 220: 2 (August, 1967): 29–34.

———. *Chimera*. Greenwich: Fawcett, 1973.

———. *The Last Voyage of Somebody the Sailor*. Boston: Little, Brown and Company, 1991.

Barthakuria, Apurba Chandra. *India in the Age of the Panchatantra*. Calcutta: Punthi-Pustak, 1992.

Barthes, Roland. "L'effet de réel." In *Littérature et réalité.* 81–90. Edited by Gérard Genette and Tzvetan Todorov. Paris: Seuil, 1982.

Basgöz, I. "The Dream Motif in Turkish Folk Stories and Shamanistic Initiation." In *Asian Folklore Studies* 26 (1967):1–18

al-Bayyati, 'Adil. "al-Batal al-isturi wa-l-malhami." In *Afaq 'Arabiyya* 7 (May 1976): 64–71.

Bell, Steve M. "Southern Boom." In *American Book Review* XIV (February/March 1993).

Bencheikh, Jamel Eddine. *Les mille et une nuits ou la parole prisonnière.* Paris: Gallimard, 1988.

Bernal, Martin. *Black Athena.* New Brunswick: Rutgers University Press, 1987.

Berque, Jacques. *L'Orient second.* Paris: Gallimard, 1970.

Bethel, S. L. *Shakespeare and the Popular Dramatic Tradition.* London: Staples Press. 1944.

Bettelheim, Bruno. *The Uses of Enchantment: The Meaning and Importance of Fairy Tales.* New York: Vintage Books, 1977.

Borges, Jorge Luis. "Averroës' Search." In *Labyrinths.* 148–55. Translated by Donald Yates and James Irby. New York: New Directions Books, 1964.

———. *Seven Nights.* Translated by Eliot Weinberger. New York: New Directions, 1980.

———. *The Aleph and Other Stories 1933–1969.* Translated and edited by N. T. di Giovanni. New York: Dutton, 1970.

Bouisson, Maurice. *Le secret de Shéhérazade.* Paris: Flammarion, 1961.

Brunvand, Jan Harold. "The Folktale Origin of *The Taming of the Shrew.*" In *Shakespeare Quarterly* XVII:4 (Autumn 1966): 482–96.

Bseiso, 'Abd al-Rahman. "Aqni'at alf layla fi-l-shi'r al-hadith." In *Fusul* XIII:2 (Summer 1994): 111–45.

Bullough, Geoffrey, ed. *Narrative and Dramatic Sources of Shakespeare.* New York: Columbia University Press, 1966.

Burton, R. F., trans. *The Book of the Thousand Nights and a Night.* 10 vols. London: The Burton Club, n.d. [1886].

———., trans. *Supplemental Nights.* 6 vols. London: Burton Club, n.d.[1886].

Butler, H. E., trans. *The Institutio Oratoria of Quintilian.* 4 vols. London: William Heinemann, 1920–1923.

Butterworth, Charles. Review of Muhsin Mahdi, *Kitab alf layla wa layla.* In *Interpretation* 21, no. 1 (Fall 1993): 59–66.

Cachia, P. J. E. "The Conflict of East and West in Contemporary Egyptian Literary Taste (with special reference to Taha Husayn)." In *Glasgow University Oriental Society Trans.* 14 (1950–1952): 26–35.

Cairo. Dar al-Kutub. Z 13523. *Alf layla wa layla*. 4 vols.

Calvino, Italo. *Invisible Cities*. Translated by William Weaver. New York: Harcourt Brace Jovanovich, 1974.

Campbell, Oscar James, ed. *The Reader's Encyclopedia of Shakespeare*. New York: Thomas Crowell Company, 1966.

Caracciolo, Peter, ed., *The Arabian Nights in English Literature*. London: Macmillan, 1988.

"Carlos Fuentes: A Play on Memory and Myths." In *International Herald Tribune* (June 28, 1982).

Ceronsy, Cecil C. "'Supposes' as the Unifying Theme in *The Taming of the Shrew.*" In *Shakespeare Quarterly* XIV:1 (Winter 1963): 15–30.

Clouston, W. A. "Variants and Analogues of Some of the Tales in Volumes XI and XII." Appendix to *Supplemental Nights*. Translated by Richard F. Burton. London: Burton Club, n.d.[1886].

Coleridge, S. T. "Biographia Literaria." In *Critical Theory Since Plato*, ed. H. Adams, 459–74. New York: Harcourt Brace Jovanovich, Inc., 1971.

Cooper, L., trans. *The Rhetoric of Aristotle*. New York: D. Appleton and Co., 1932.

Corbin, H. *Histoire de la philosophie islamique*. Paris: Gallimard, 1964.

Delphy, François. "Emboîtement, déboîtement et mise en boîte dans *La mégère apprivoisée.*" In *Les Langues Modernes* LXXI:3 (1977): 249–55.

di Giovanni, N. T. et al., eds. *Borges on Writing*. New York: Dutton, 1973.

Derrida, Jacques. *La dissémination*. Paris: Seuil, 1972.

Dishi, Yusuf. "Isti'arat alf layla wa layla." In *Fusul* XIII:2 (Summer 1994): 323–37.

Dundes, A., ed. *Every Man His Way: Readings in Cultural Anthropology*. Englewood Cliffs: Prentice-Hall, 1968.

————., ed. "Structural Typology in North American Indian Folk Tales." In *The Study of Folklore*. Englewood Cliffs: Prentice-Hall, 1965.

Durand, Jacques. "Rhetorique du nombre." In *Communications* 16 (1970): 125–32.

Duthie, G. I. *"The Taming of a Shrew* and *The Taming of the Shrew.*" In *The Review of English Studies* XIX:76 (October 1943): 337–56.

Edmundson, Mark. "The End of the Road." In *The New Republic* (April 22, 1991).

————. *Najib Mahfuz: Qira'a ma bayn al-sutur*. Beirut: Dar al-Tali'a, 1995.

Elahi, Nur Ali-Shah. *L'Esotérisme kurde*. Translated by Mohammed Mokri. Paris: Editions Albin Michel, 1966.

El-Enany, Rasheed. *Naguib Mahfouz: The Pursuit of Meaning.* London: Routledge, 1993.

Encyclopedia of Islam. New Edition. S. v. "Alf Layla wa Layla," by E. Littman.

———. S. v. "Hamasa (Arabic Literature)," by. C. Pellat

———. S.v. "Ash'ab," by F. S. A. Rosenthal.

———. S.v. "Gharib," by S. A. Bonebakker.

———. Old Edition. S.v. "Sira" by G. Levi Della Vida.

———. Old edition. S. v. "Sirat Antar," by B. Heller.

Forker, Charles R. "Immediacy and Remoteness in *The Taming of the Shrew* and *The Winter's Tale.*" In *Shakespeare's Romances Reconsidered.* 135–48. Edited by C. M. Kay and H. E. Jacobs. Lincoln: University of Nebraska Press, 1978.

Foucault, Michel. "Nietzsche, Freud, Marx." In *Nietzche,* 183–92. Paris: Les Editions de Minuit. 1987.

———. "Qu'est-ce qu'un auteur?" In *Bulletin de la Sociéte Française de Philosophie* XIII:3 (July–September 1969). "What Is an Author?" In *Textual Strategies.* Edited by Josue Harari. Ithaca: Cornell University Press, 1979.

———. "Introduction." In Gustave Flaubert, *La tentation de Saint Antoine.* 7–33. Paris: Editions Gallimard, 1971.

Galland, A., trans. *Les mille et une nuits.* Paris: Morizot, n. d.

Gennette. G. *Figures III.* Paris: Editions du Seuil, 1972.

Gerhardt, M. *The Art of Story-Telling: A Literary Study of the Thousand and One Nights.* Leiden: E. J. Brill, 1963.

Ghazoul, Ferial J. Review of Muhsin Mahdi, *Kitab alf layla wa layla.* In *International Journal of Middle East Studies* 19, no. 2 (1987): 246–48.

Ghazoul, Ferial J. and Barbara Harlow, eds. *The View from Within: Writers and Critics on Contemporary Arabic Literaure.* Cairo: The American University in Cairo Press, 1994.

Gobineau, A. de. *Trois ans en Asie (de 1855 a 1858).* 2 vols. Paris: Editions Bernard Grasset, 1922.

Goodman, L. E., trans. *Ibn Tufayl's Hayy ibn Yaqzan: A Philosophical Tale.* New York: Twayne Publishers, 1972.

Greenfield, Thelma Nelson. "The Transformation of Christopher Sly." In *Philological Quarterly* XXXIII:1 (January 1954): 34–42.

Grünebaum, G. E. von. "Idéologie musulmane et esthétique arabe." In *Studia Islamica* 3 (1955): 5–23.

———. *Medieval Islam.* 2nd edition. Chicago: University of Chicago Press, 1969.

Habicht, M. and F. Fleischer, eds. *The Arabian Nights.* Breslau. 1825–43.

Haddawy, Husain, trans. *The Arabian Nights.* New York: W.W. Norton, 1990.

Hafez, Sabry. "Jadaliyat al-binya al-sardiyya al-murakkaba fi layali Shahrazad wa Najib Mahfuz." In *Fusul* XIII:2 (Summer 1994): 20–70.

Hamori, A. "Examples of Convention in the Poetry of Abu Nuwas." In *Studia Islamica* 30 (1969): 5–26.

———. *On the Art of Medieval Arabic Literature.* Princeton: Princeton University Press, 1974.

———. "Notes on Two Love Stories from the *Thousand and One Nights.*" In *Studia Islamica* XLIII (1976): 65–80.

Henze, Richard. "Role Playing in *The Taming of the Shrew.*" In *Southern Humanities Review* IV:3 (Summer 1970): 231–40.

Holmberg, Arthur. "Carlos Fuentes: A Play on Memory and Myths." In *International Herald Tribune* (June 28, 1982).

Hosley, Richard. "Source and Analogues of *The Taming of the Shrew.*" In *The Huntington Library Quarterly* XXVII:3 (May 1964): 289–308.

Huilgol, Varadraj. *The Panchatantra of Vasughaga: A Critical Study.* Madras: New Era Publications, 1987.

Hussein, Taha. "Introduction." In Suhayr al-Qalamawi, *Alf layla wa layla.* 7–9. Cairo: Dar al-Ma'arif, 1966.

———. *Ahlam Shahrazad.* Cairo: Dar al-Ma'arif, 1958.

———. *The Dreams of Scheherazade.* Translated by Magdi Wahba. Cairo: General Egyptian Book Organization, 1974.

Ibn Khaldun, Abd al-Rahman. *The Muqaddima: An Introduction to History.* Translated by F. Rosenthal. 3 vols. Princeton: Princeton University Press, 1967.

Ibn Tufayl. *Hayy ibn Yaqzan.* Trans. L. E. Goodman. New York: Twayne Publishers, 1972.

Ibrahim, Nabila. *Fann al-qass.* Cairo: Maktabat Gharib, n.d.

Ibrahim, Sonallah. *Dhat.* Cairo: Dar al-Mustaqbal al-'Arabi, 1992.

———. *Les années de Zeth.* Translated by Richard Jacquemond. Arles: Actes Sud, 1993.

Irwin, Robert. *The Arabian Nights: A Companion.* London: Allen Lane/ Penguin, 1994.

Jakobson, Roman. "The Dominant." In *Readings in Russian Poetics.* Edited by Ladislav Matejka and Krystyna Pomorska. 82–87. Ann Arbor: University of Michigan Press, 1978.

Jankélévitch, V. *L'ironie.* Paris: Flammarion, 1964.

Jayne, Sears. "The Dreaming of *The Shrew.*" In *Shakespeare Quarterly* XVII:1 (Winter 1966): 41–56.

Kasner, E., and J. Newman. *Mathematics and the Imagination*. New York: Simon and Schuster, 1967.

Kay, C. M. and H. E. Jacobs. eds. *Shakespeare's Romances Reconsidered*. Lincoln: University of Nebraska Press, 1978.

Keith, Berriedale A. *A History of Sanskrit Literature*. London: Oxford University Press, 1920.

Kennedy, J. G. "Nubian Zar Ceremonies as Psychotherapy." In *Human Organization* 26 (Winter 1967): 185–94.

Kierkegaard, S. *Repetition: An Essay in Experimental Psychology*. Translated by W. Lowrie. Princeton: Princeton University Press, 1946.

Kirpitchenko, Valeria. "Ibda' Najib Mahfuz wa-l-turath al-'arabi." Presented at the International Symposium on "Naguib Mahfouz and the Arabic Novel." Cairo University, March 17–20, 1990.

Kitab alf layla wa layla. Ed. 'Abd al-Rahman al-Safati al-Sharqawi. 2 vols. Cairo: Matba'at Bulaq, 1835.

Kraus, P., ed. *Jabir ibn Hayyan: Essai sur l'historie des idees scientifiques dans l'Islam*. Cairo: Librairie el-Khangi, 1935.

Lacan, Jacques. *Ecrits I*. Paris: Seuil, 1966.

Lane, E. W. *The Manners and Customs of the Modern Egyptians*. London: Everyman's Library, 1963.

————., trans. *The Thousand and One Nights*. 3 vols. London: Chatto and Windos, 1912.

Laplanche, J., and J.-B. Pontalis. *The Language of Psychoanalysis*. Translated by D. Nicholson-Smith. New York: W. W. Norton and Co., Inc., 1973.

Lévi-Strauss, C. "Interview." In *Diacritics* I (Fall 1971): 44–50.

————. "La geste d'Asdiwal." In *Annuaire* 1958–1959. Paris: Ecole Pratique des Hautes Etudes, Section des Sciences Religieuses.

————. *Anthropologie structurale*. Paris: Librairie Plon, 1958.

————. *Totemism*. Translated by Rodney Needham. Boston: Beacon Press, 1963.

Lewis, C. S. *The Allegory of Love: A Study in Medieval Tradition*. New York: Oxford University Press, 1958.

Lewis, I. M. *Ecstatic Religion: An Anthropological Study of Spirit Possession and Shamanism*. Harmondsworth: Penguin Books, 1971.

Mahdi, Muhsin. "Mazahir al-riwaya wa-l-mushafaha fi usul alf layla wa layla." In *Revue de l'Institut des Manuscrits Arabes* 20 (May 1974): 125–44.

————. "Remarks on the *1001 Nights*." In *Interpretation* III:2/3 (Winter 1973): 157–68.

————, ed. *Kitab alf layla wa layla*. Leiden: E. J. Brill, 1984.

Mahfouz, Naguib. "Alf layla ahatat bi-l-hadara al-sharqiyya [Interview]." In *Fusul* XIII:2 (Summer 1994): 377–85.

———. *Arabian Nights and Days.* Translated by Denys Johnson-Davies. Cairo: The American University in Cairo Press, 1995.

———. *Khammarat al-qitt al-aswad.* Cairo: Maktabat Misr, 1969.

———. "Sharazad." In *God's World: An Anthology of Short Stories.* 63–74. Translated by Akef Abadir and Roger Allen. Minneapolis: Bibliotheca Islamica, 1973.

———. *Layali alf layla.* Cairo: Maktabat Misr, 1982.

Mallarmé, S. *Oeuvres complètes.* Pleiade edition. Paris: Gallimard, 1945.

Marx, K. *A Contribution to the Critique of Political Economy.* Edited by M. Dobb. New York: International Publishers, 1970.

al-Mas'udi, Abu al-Hasan. *Muruj al-dhahab wa ma'adin al-jawhar.* Edited by C. Pellat. Beirut: Manshurat al-Jami'a al-Lubnaniyya, 1966.

Mauss, M. *The Gift: Forms and Functions of Exchange in Archaic Societies.* Translated by I. Cunnison. New York: The Norton Library, 1967.

Mehrez, Samia. *Egyptian Writers Between History and Fiction.* Cairo: The American University in Cairo Press, 1994.

Menocal, Maria Rosa. *The Arabic Role in Medieval Literary Theory.* Philadelphia: University of Pennsylvania Press. 1987.

Mergen and his Friends. USSR: Progress Publishers, 1973.

Metlitzki, Dorothee. *The Matter of Araby in Medieval England.* New Haven: Yale University Press. 1977.

Miquel, André. *La littérature arabe.* Paris: Presses Universitaires de France, 1969.

———. *Un conte des mille et une nuits: Ajib et Gharib.* Paris: Flammarion, 1977.

Morrell, David. *John Barth.* University Park: Pennsylvania State University Press, 1976.

Muir, Kenneth. "Much ado about the Shrew." In *Trivium* VII (May 1972): 1–4.

———. *The Sources of Shakespeare's Plays.* London: Methuen, 1977.

Naddaff, Sandra. *Arabesque.* Evanston: Northwestern University Press, 1991.

Novy, Marianne L. "Patriarchy and Play in *The Taming of the Shrew.*" In *English Literary Renaissance* IX:2 (Spring 1979): 264–80.

The Panchatantra. Translated by Arthur W. Ryder. Chicago: The University of Chicago Press, 1925.

The Panchatantra. Translated by Franklin Edgarton. London: George Allen and Unwin, 1965.

Pavel, S. "La prolifération narrative dans les 'Mille et une nuits.'" In *Canadian Journal of Semiotic Research* 2 (Winter 1974): 21–40.

Peithman, Stephen, ed. *The Annotated Tales of Edgar Allan Poe.* New York: Doubleday, 1981.

Pellat, Charles. *Le milieu basrien et la formation de Gahiz.* Paris: Librairie Adrien-Maisonneuve, 1953.

Piaget, J. "How Children Form Mathematical Concepts." Reprinted from *Scientific American,* November 1953. San Francisco: W. H. Freeman and Co., 1953.

Princeton Encyclopedia of Poetry and Poetics. 1965 edition. S.v. "Simile," by George Whalley.

Princeton Encyclopedia of Poetry and Poetics. 1972 edition. S.v. "Conceit," by F. Warnke and A. Preminger.

———. S. v. "Fable in Verse," by A. L. Sells.

Propp, V. *Istoricheskie korni volshebnoj skazki.* Leningrad: Izdatel'stvo Leningradskogo Gosudarstvennogo Universiteta, 1946.

———. *The Morphology of the Folk Tale.* 2nd edition. Austin and London: University of Texas Press, 1975.

al-Qalamawi, S. *Alf layla wa layla.* Cairo: Dar al-Ma'arif, 1966.

Quintilian (Quintilianus, Marcus Fabius). *The Institutio of Quintilian.* Translated by H. E. Butler. 4 vols. London: William Heinemann, 1920–1923.

al-Rakhawy, Yahya. *Qira'at fi Najib Mahfuz.* Cairo: Al-Hay'a al-'Amma li-l-Kitab, 1992.

Rasa'il ikhwan al-safa' wa khullan al-wafa'. 4 vols. Beirut: Dar Beirut and Dar Sadir, 1957.

Riffaterre, M. "Dynamisme des mots: Les poèmes en prose de Julien Gracq." In *L'Herne* 20 (1972): 152–64.

———. "L'explication des faits littéraire." In *L'enseignement de la littérature,* edited by S. Doubrovsky and T. Todorov, 331–55, with discussion, 366–97. Paris: Plon, 1971.

———. "La métaphore filée dans la poésie surréaliste." In *Langue Française* 3 (September 1969): 46–60.

———. "Le poème comme représentation." In *Poétique* 4 (1970) :401–418.

———. "Modèles de la phrase littéraire." In *Problemes de l'analyse textuelle,* ed. Pierre Leon et al, 133–48. Paris: Didier, 1971.

———. "Semantic Overdetermination in Poetry." In *Poetics and Theory of Literature* 2 (1977): 1–19.

———. "Systeme d'un genre descriptif." In *Poétique* 9 (1972): 15–30.

———. "The Self-Sufficient Text." In *Diacritics* III: 3 (Fall 1973): 39–45.

————.''Paragram and Significance." In *Semiotext(e)* I (Fall 1974): 72–87.

————. "L'illusion référentielle." In *Littérature et réalité*. 91–118. Edited by Gérard Genette and Tzvetan Todorov. Paris: Seuil, 1982.

Rochon, L. *Lautréamont et le style homérique*. Paris: Archives des Lettres Modernes, 1971.

al-Sa'afin, Ibrahim. "Najib Mahfuz: jadal al-ana wa-l-turath." Presented at the International Symposium on "Naguib Mahfouz and the Arabic Novel." Cairo University, March 17–20, 1990.

Said, E. W. "The Text as Practice and as Idea." In *Modern Language Notes* 88 (December 1973): 1071–1102.

————. "Introduction." Barakat, H. I. *Days of Dust*. Translated by Trevor Le Gassick. ix–xxxiv. Wilmette, Ill.: Medina University Press International, 1974.

————. *Beginnings: Intention and Method*. New York: Basic Books, Inc., 1975.

————. *Joseph Conrad and the Fiction of Autobiography*. Cambridge: Harvard University Press, 1966.

Sakkut, Hamdi. "Naguib Mahfouz and the Sufi Way." In *The View from Within: Writers and Critics on Contemporary Arabic Literaure*. 90–98. Edited by Ferial J. Ghazoul and Barbara Harlow. Cairo: The American University in Cairo Press, 1994.

Salhani, A., ed. *Alf layla wa layla*. 5 Vols. Beirut: The Catholic Press, 1914.

Sanders, Norman. "Themes and Imagery in *The Taming of the Shrew.*" In *Renaissance Papers 1963*. Edited by S. K. Heninger et al. Japan: Charles Tuttle, 1964.

Schami, Rafik. *Damascus Nights*. Translated by Philip Boehm. New York: Scribner, 1993.

al-Shahhadh, Ahmad Muhammad. *Al-Malamih al-siyasiyya fi hikayat alf layla wa layla*. Baghdad: Wizarat al-I'lam, 1977.

Shakespeare, William. *The Taming of the Shrew*. Harmondsworth: Penguin, 1968.

al-Sharqawi, 'Abd al-Rahman al Safati, ed. *Kitab alf layla wa layla*. 2 vols. Cairo: Matba'at Bulaq, 1835.

Simpson, W., ed. *The Literature of Ancient Egypt: An Anthology of Stories, Instructions and Poetry*. New Haven: Yale University Pres 1972.

Soifer, M., and I. Shapiro, eds. *Golden Tales from the Arabian Nights*. New York: Simon and Schuster, 1957.

Stark, John. *The Literature of Exhaustion. Borges, Nabokov and Barth*. Durham: Duke University Press, 1974.

Stetkevych, J. "The Arabic Lyrical Phenomenon in Context." In *Journal of Arabic Literature* 6 (1975): 57–77.

Stevens, Wallace. *The Palm at the End of the Mind.* Edited by Holly Stevens. New York: Vintage Books, 1972.

Sulayman, M. *Al-Adab al-qasassi 'ind al-'arab.* Beirut: Dar al-Kitab al-Lubnani, 1969.

Tarchouna, Mahmoud, ed. *Ma'at layla wa layla.* Tunis: Al-Dar al-'Arabiyya li-l-Kitab, 1979.

Telford, K., trans. *Aristotle's Poetics.* Chicago: Henry Regnery Company, 1970.

Al-Tha'alibi, Abu Ishaq. *Qisas al-anbiyya'.* Beirut: al-Maktaba al-Thaqafiyya, n. d.

Thorne, W. B. "Folk Elements in *The Taming of the Shrew.*" In *Queen's Quarterly* LXXV: 3 (Autumn 1968): 482–96.

Tillyard, E. M. W. "The Fairy-Tale Element in *The Taming of the Shrew.*" In *Shakespeare 1564–1964,* 110–14. Edited by Edward Bloom. Providence: Brown University Press, 1964.

Todorov, T. "L'analyse du discours: L'exemple des devinettes." In *Journal de psychologie normale et pathologique* 1–2 (January–June 1973): 135–55.

———. *Grammaire du Décameron.* The Hague: Mouton. 1969.

———. "Les hommes récits." In *Poetique de la prose.* 78–91. Paris: Editions de Seuil, 1971.

———. "The Two Principles of Narrative." In *Diacritics* I: 1 (Fall 1971): 37–44.

——— and Oswald Ducrot. *Dictionnaire encyclopédique des sciences du langage.* Paris: Seuil, 1972.

Tomashevsky, B. "Thematics." In *Russian Formalist Criticism: Four Essays,* 61–95. Translated by L. Lemon and M. Reis. Lincoln: University of Nebraska Press, 1965.

Towers, Robert. "Tripping the Not-So-Light Fantastic." In *The New York Review of Books* (April 25, 1991).

Turner, V. *The Ritual Process: Structure and Anti-Structure.* Chicago: Aldine, 1969.

Uspensky, B. *A Poetics of Composition: The Structure of the Artistic Text and Typology of a Compositional Form.* Translated by V. Zavarin and S. Wittig. Berkeley: University of California Press, 1973.

Vansina, Jan. *Oral Tradition: A Study in Historical Methodology.* Translated by H. M. Wright. London: Routledge and Kegan Paul, 1965.

Vico, Giambattista. *The New Science.* Translated by T. D. Bergin and M. H. Fisch. Ithaca: Cornell University Press, 1970.

Wellek, Rene and Austin Warren. *Theory of Literature.* New York: Harcourt, Brace & World, 1956.

Yunis, Ibtihal. "Athr al-turath al-sharqi wa alf layla wa layla fi ru'yat al-'alam 'ind Borges." In *Fusul* XIII:2 (Summer 1994): 348–74.

Zotenberg, H. *Histoire d'Ala al-Din ou la lampe merveilleuse.* Paris: Imprimerie National, 1888.

INDEX

DATE DUE

OCT 0 0 2010			
APR 0 1 REC'D			
~~INTERLIBRARY LOAN~~	7-7-10	OK	